CW01647593

Hidden Treasures of Walt Disney World Resort Hotels

Histories, Mysteries & Theming

Jim Korkis

Theme Park Press
The Happiest Books on Earth
www.ThemeParkPress.com

© **2021 Jim Korkis**

No part of this publication may be reproduced, distributed, or transmitted in any form or by any means, including photocopying, recording, or other electronic or mechanical methods, without the prior written permission of the publisher, except for brief quotations embodied in critical reviews and certain other non-commercial uses permitted by copyright law.

Although every precaution has been taken to verify the accuracy of the information contained herein, no responsibility is assumed for any errors or omissions, and no liability is assumed for damages that may result from the use of this information.

Theme Park Press is not associated with the Walt Disney Company.

The views expressed in this book are those of the author and do not necessarily reflect the views of Theme Park Press.

Theme Park Press publishes its books in a variety of print and electronic formats. Some content that appears in one format may not appear in another.

Editor: Bob McLain
Layout: Artisanal Text
Cover: The thirty-story Cosmopolitan Hotel designed by Walt Disney for his Experimental Prototype Community of Tomorrow that would have been the first WDW resort hotel.

ISBN 978-1-68390-303-1
Printed in the United States of America

Theme Park Press | www.ThemeParkPress.com
Address queries to bob@themeparkpress.com

Dedicated to my friend and fellow Disney Historian Werner Weiss, a frequent traveler who over the years has shared with me more stories about different hotels where he stayed as well as insights into WDW resort hotels than I ever thought I wanted to know.

It made me more observant and critical of WDW resort hotels and for that I thank him with this dedication.

Contents

Introduction

This book is **NOT** a travel guide nor is it designed to help get discounts, pick the best room, select a good time of the year to book a vacation, review the restaurants, rate the swimming pools or anything else related to things that a good travel agent can help you accomplish.

There are plenty of travel guides and websites that can guide people in those matters as well as a plethora of travel consultants with more current information. This book is meant to be something different.

This book recounts some of the history and storytelling about the Walt Disney World Resort Hotels that is rarely if ever documented. In addition, this book is neither complete nor definitive but simply a compilation of some rarely known information about just some of the WDW resort hotels.

There are many, many more stories that need to be documented but this book is just a small sampling before some of this material gets lost as WDW constantly changes. A resort hotel traditionally meant a place where people could rest and reflect but Disney made its resort hotels a place of adventure that rivaled its theme parks in some cases.

I was hired by the Walt Disney World Travel Company one year to be the spokesman for their annual travel launch. Accompanied by a stage manager who made arrangements and set up the stage (that was flown to each location) in each convention room, I went to three different cities every week across the United States for ten weeks.

I gave a presentation with appropriate power point to hundreds of travel agents at each location about booking their clients for a WDW vacation in the coming year.

I told my friends that the schedule was so tight that I primarily just saw airports, the drive to and from the airport, hotels and convention rooms. Fortunately, in the limited remaining spare time I did get to spend a few hours of sightseeing in each city.

However, the majority of my time was spent in a wide variety of different hotel rooms and extolling to others about the many virtues of the resort hotels at Walt Disney World.

I also spent a day at the reservation call center in Orlando to get a sense of how people booked travel at WDW, the types of questions that were asked and the importance of up-selling within the limited time quota that was strictly monitored for each call.

The newest WDW resort to hype was Coronado Springs. Instead of discussing the story behind the resort, I had to concentrate on the different pricing levels of the rooms, the availability of the "largest ballroom in the southeastern United States" in the convention center and the various amenities.

To me and I guess a lot of others that was what a hotel was all about because after all one hotel was pretty much the same as any other hotel as I had personally discovered on my travels. The names and color schemes were different but basically they were all the same and offered exactly the same things.

It wasn't until a few months later when I became an instructor for the Disney Adult Discoveries department that did property tours for guests and business groups that I learned that a WDW resort hotel was more than just one of those many other hotels I had experienced.

On some of those tours, guests would be taken briefly to a handful of different resorts like the Wilderness Lodge and the instructor would point out some of the details and how they were chosen to support a consistent theme of the resort.

That exposure inspired me to do further research on WDW resort hotels that could be incorporated into new tours. In the process, I got to talk to Imagineers and cast members who opened the resorts.

Over the decades, so much of that information has been forgotten even by the cast members working at the resort. I felt it was important to document what material I had gathered over the years that made WDW resort hotels distinctly different in hopes of enhancing the experience for some Disney fans.

Be my guest as I share some stories you may never have heard.

Jim Korkis
Disney Historian
2021

Walt Disney World Resort Hotels

While some guests consider the WDW resorts just a location to rest briefly during their extended trips to the parks, others realize that the resorts themselves offer the same attention to detail and Disney magic as the theme parks. Most of these resorts have "hidden treasures" that are sometimes overlooked by guests.

In 1969, Walt's brother, Roy O. Disney addressed a group of developers in Orlando: "One thing I learned from the Disneyland project is to control the environment. Without that, we get blamed for things someone else does.

"Little hotels on the fringe of the park would jump their rates three times. I've seen it happen and I just can't take it because it reflects on us. If they don't run a good hotel operation for the Florida project, and those little honky-tonks come in there, we're blamed."

The Walt Disney Company never intended to get involved in operating hotels but in order to maintain the integrity of the overall project it had no other choice. After all, if the location was to be a vacation destination, there needed to be an option for guests to stay on property and that meant hotels. Even Walt Disney's original plans for the Florida property included a massive thirty-story internationally-themed hotel right in the middle of Epcot.

One of the significant differences between WDW and Disneyland was that guests would stay for multiple days so it was necessary to offer outstanding accommodations especially since Orlando only had roughly 5,800 hotel and motel rooms and many of those left much to be desired.

TIME magazine in its October 18, 1971 issue published roughly two weeks after the opening of Walt Disney World stated, "But it is the hotels, shops, beaches and other recreational facilities at Disney World that really set the new complex apart from Disneyland and its imitators.

"Disneymen call their creation a 'total destination resort' – not just a stopover, in other words, but a place to spend a weekend or a week. The prices at Disney World seem reasonable enough. Hotels range from $22 to $40 for a room large enough for a family of four.

"Package plans include one that offers three days and two nights at a hotel, three free days in the amusement area, free transport and $18 worth of sailing, riding or others sports – all for $61.50 per person ($25 per child)."

At one point, Imagineer Claude Coats created concept art for an attraction that would have been placed between The Contemporary Resort and the back of Tomorrowland and utilize the water of nearby Bay Lake.

According to Imagineer Tony Baxter, Claude Coats always loved dinosaurs and helped design the ones for the 1964 New York World's Fair and so guests would have been able by a twisting water ride to journey into the prehistoric past to confront life-sized dinosaurs.

The attraction was meant to connect the resort hotel directly with the park, a concept that came up several times during the design of WDW.

Roy O. Disney held discussions with executives of major hotel chains that had an interest on building hotels. Marriott and Western International (Westin Hotels & Resorts) were the front runners but Roy was troubled by the fact that all the chains wanted to operate them independently without Disney's direct control.

Eventually Hotel Plaza Boulevard was done under that arrangement where Disney leased the grounds to the chains and the chains built the hotels and provided the management teams to operate them.

Preview Boulevard was the name of the street off of State Route 535 that housed the Preview Center before WDW opened to give people an idea of what the vacation destination was.

Once the Center closed when WDW opened, the street was renamed Hotel Plaza Boulevard and became the home to what would later be called WDW Good Neighbor hotels in mid-1972 including Royal Plaza, Howard Johnson's TraveLodge and the Dutch Inn.

Over the decades these hotels would change ownership and name and new hotels would be built. A Walt Disney World Good Neighbor Hotel is required to meet certain criteria under Disney standards in order to ensure the highest standards of quality, comfort and service and must be updated regularly. Disney personally inspects to make sure these standards are maintained.

The rates are usually lower than the official WDW resort hotels. The Good Neighbor hotels have a special Disney concierge that can help guests purchase tickets, plan their park itinerary, and make reservations, as well as transportation to Disney property.

In 1991, Disney told travel agents that "seven individual hotels each operated by renowned hoteliers in the hospitality industry are conveniently located within walking distance of the Disney

Village Marketplace and Pleasure Island. They are a short ride from Typhoon Lagoon, Disney MGM Studios Theme Park, Epcot Center and Magic Kingdom.

"Buena Vista Palace, Grosvenor Resort, The Hilton, Hotel Royal Plaza, Howard Johnson Resort Hotel and Travelodge Hotel. Guests at all seven hotels enjoy exclusive benefits including complimentary use of Walt Disney World transportation to the parks, advance dinner reservations at restaurants through the Walt Disney World Resort including Epcot Center restaurants, preferred status in booking tee times at Disney's championship golf courses and other recreational activities, guaranteed admission to theme parks even on busiest days."

Finally, Roy decided to engage with United States Steel and its newly formed USS Realty Development Division for building the Contemporary and the Polynesian Village resorts. That company entered into a partnership with the Walt Disney Company to form Walt Disney Hotel Company, a totally separate and distinct subsidiary of Walt Disney Productions.

United States Steel Realty Development was introducing its then new "unitized modular" form of construction. It went into the partnership with Disney because it realized that the much anticipated Walt Disney World would be the premier showcase for what they considered an innovative building technique and would spark others to want to use its services.

The company was also allowed to participate in the design and development as well as the actual construction. The design work was primarily done by WED Enterprises (Imagineering) and Welton Becket and Associates of Santa Monica, California.

The Contemporary was to serve as the flagship resort for the vacation destination and also provide convention and banquet facilities.

The preview publicity for the resort hotels in 1971 stated, "Conceived by WED Enterprises, the Disney design and Imagineering firm, and Welton Becket & Associates, architects, each hotel will be a complete major attraction itself, with its own recreation activities, entertainment, dining facilities, and resort atmosphere.

"Additionally, guests in any hotel will be able to enjoy the facilities of all others during their stay in the Vacation Kingdom. The hotels are called 'theme resorts' because everything from interior décor to employees' costumes and dining rooms menus will carry out an overall theme. Unique swimming pools will meet the needs of every member of the family."

The goal was not to make the resorts just a location distinct from traditional hotels but offer an immersive experience just like the Magic Kingdom itself.

Basically, the concept was that the resorts would be "much like a small city in that it provides service to our guests twenty-four hours a day" according to the training guides for cast members.

Roy became unhappy with the work being done by his new business partner. Inspections revealed that workers were spending their time playing cards, taking naps and stealing material even though they were well aware of the approaching deadline. In addition, phantom employees had been created so that on payday, some people would pick up these additional checks and cash them.

Roy came up with a bond issue that raised enough funds for Disney to purchase U.S. Steel's interest in the project during construction and under the direction of Joe Fowler, Disney finished the work itself.

While Disney was known for its guest service, it had never operated a hotel. The Disneyland Hotel in Anaheim was owned and operated by Jack Wrather, a millionaire entrepreneur and television producer who was a friend of Walt Disney.

Wrather and his wife lived in Holmby Hills, like Walt Disney and his wife, and they became friends, especially since Wrather's television shows were also running on ABC, like Walt's weekly television series. That's why Walt turned to the millionaire to ask him to build a hotel at the exit of Disneyland so that guests could stay in quality lodging.

Walt didn't have the money to do so himself because all of his resources were invested in building Disneyland.

As Wrather recalled in an interview with the *Orange Country Register* newspaper in September 11, 1978:

"It was in 1954 when I got a call that Walt was putting in something very special out there in Anaheim and I was asked if I would be interested in building a hotel next to it. I had heard a little bit about the Disneyland plan but when they told me where it was being built, all I could exclaim was 'Anaheim! Oh, God! Anaheim!'

"Then I asked them why they didn't call Hilton or Sheraton since I wasn't in the hotel business. They said they had called them but Hilton or Sheraton never heard of Anaheim and weren't interested. If Walt hadn't sunk everything he had into the park at that time, he would have built the hotel himself. I was a kid in Long Beach and we used to come up to Knott's Berry Farm so I knew Anaheim well."

Wrather also knew, like Walt, that Anaheim was primed for major expansion. Walt was so desperate to have a hotel nearby for guests to stay that he gave Wrather a 99-year lease on the land across from the park that Disney had purchased (at a rate of $2,000 a year for the length of the lease, plus 2% of the gross on the rentals) and the exclusive rights to use the "Disney" name for the hotel and any future hotels that Wrather might build in Southern California (at a rate of

$25,000 per year) and Walt's assurance that he would not build a hotel in competition.

Walt was so grateful that while he was alive, he rejected all suggestions to renegotiate the contract or try to get ownership of the Disneyland Hotel. When the monorail was extended to the Disneyland Hotel, it was done so at only a nominal leasing fee for the hotel station for Wrather.

Under CEO Michael Eisner's leadership the Walt Disney Company purchased the Disneyland Hotel in 1988.

So when Roy decided that the Walt Disney Company would build and run the WDW resorts, it was necessary to find some way to train Disney cast members before the WDW resorts opened. Dick Milano, at that time the manager of Disneyland University, had a degree from a hotel management school.

Along with Van Arsdale France, the founder of Disney University, they created training programs that emphasized the Disney philosophy in dealing with guests mixed in with ideas from successful hotels to help train the staff of the Contemporary Resort and the Polynesian Village Resort.

In the October 15, 1972 issue of *Institutions* magazines (devoted to the hotel and food and beverage industries), Disney company management told the writer, "The hotels are running at close to 100% occupancy and turning down 1,000 reservation requests daily.

"The biggest difference between the pre-fabricated room at the two resorts other than theming is that bathrooms in the Contemporary have two sinks, a bath/shower combination and another shower. The Poly rooms have only one sink and a bath/shower, making the sleeping/living area slightly larger. Rooms in both hotels are furnished in similar manners

"Future hotels probably will not be this large, since most of top management agree that a hotel as large as the Contemporary is just not 'right' for Disney. It is too large to give guests the individual attention and service Disney people feel is necessary."

Room rates varied including the fact that originally there were going to be four different seasons with different rate schedules for each season. Of course, the size of the room and the view added to the cost. However, there were various discounts including AAA, Magic Kingdom Club, Cast Member and more. In general, a guest would expect to pay somewhere between $22 -- $44 a night.

Before Walt Disney World opened in October 1971, the Orlando area offered only a total of about 5,800 hotel and motel rooms. By June 1972, that total had jumped to around 10,000 rooms with another 7,000 more rooms under construction.

During that first year of WDW operation, hotels and motels were booked solid with tourists sometimes being diverted to Tampa and Daytona Beach for lodging (and an additional hour's drive back to Walt Disney World via hotel shuttle bus).

Financial challenges including the 1973 gas crisis prevented the Walt Disney Company from building more resorts for a decade because of the caution of then CEO Card Walker. Even though the existing Disney resorts were still filled to capacity, the opening of less expensive hotels along the border of WDW were cutting into the demand for more rooms.

However, with the commitment to build the Epcot Center theme park years later, it was clear that more hotels were a necessity to offer accommodations for the flood of guests expected to come. .

Partnering with the Tishman Corporation to build the Swan and Dolphin hotels helped minimize financial risk but CEO Michael Eisner wanted greater involvement and control. Eisner was appalled at the initial designs for two typical "refrigerator box" style hotels that would be placed near Hotel Plaza Boulevard.

"(While some in the Walt Disney Company advocated for that partnership), I was in another camp," said Imagineer Wing Chao to writer Ryan March . "One that believed we weren't simply growing our hotel business. We were growing our immersive entertainment business and nobody knew that business better than Disney."

Eisner fought to bring in architect Michael Graves to do the design even though he had never been involved previously in designing a hotel. Graves insisted on orchestrating both the interior and the exterior of the hotels.

When the two resorts opened, architectural critics dubbed it "archi-TORTURE" but Eisner was not dissuaded.

While planning for Euro Disneyland (now Disneyland Paris), Eisner heard that a small group of world famous architects known as the "Gang of Seven" were at a restaurant in Los Angeles having their traditional once-a-year dinner.

Eisner's mind starting racing and he told Art Levitt who he had just hired as his administrative assistant to go down there and bring them back to Burbank immediately.

Whatever Levitt said was convincing enough that the architects left in the middle of their meal and drove to the Disney Studios in Burbank and met with Eisner in a conference room. Eisner had ordered copious portions of Chinese takeout food so they could finish their dinner as Eisner explained what the Walt Disney Company planned to do just outside Paris.

Eisner's passion and vision engrossed the architects in the new project and brainstorming went on into the early hours. Eisner was now on a first name basis with the world's greatest architects and the results would soon be seen on WDW property.

Disney executive Dick Nunis said, "When we were building the hotels, we spent more for name architects. Michael said that someday if we have every famous architect represented here, people will come from all over to see their work."

Eisner's contention was that any building on Disney property no matter how minor or mundane had the potential to be entertaining, educational or enlightening.

In his biography, *Work In Progress,* Eisner writes, "I was ... exposed to art and architecture at an early age ... When I went to Disney I decided we ought to try and build great, innovative buildings rather than conventional, mediocre ones ..." Eisner decided that architecture is storytelling and Disney was a storytelling company.

Under his leadership, Eisner aggressively built dozens of new WDW resort hotels starting with the Grand Floridian Resort & Spa and the Caribbean Beach Resort.

Today, for a guest to stay one night in each of the WDW resort hotel rooms would take over seventy years. More than 700,000 square feet of ballroom, meeting and function space is available in five convention resorts throughout the Walt Disney World Resort.

As my friend and fellow Disney historian Werner Weiss wrote to me, "As we've talked about, there's a big difference between resorts that are fully themed (making you feel you're in another place and time), those that are more lightly themed (the moderates) those that are just decorated (the values), those that are products of their time, and those that are creative visions.

"I would call the Contemporary a creative vision (along with WDW Swan & Dolphin), but I would call Bay Lake Tower essentially a product of its time. I'm not sure where the Riviera fits into that structure (maybe lightly themed?).

"I would argue that a 'themed' room at Art of Animation is really a decorated room. You're not staying in the worlds that Ariel or Lightning McQueen inhabit. You're staying in a room (or suite) decorated with colors, characters, and art from popular movies.

"What's so amazing about the best Disney resorts is that they feel absolutely real even when there's nothing quite like them in the 'real world'. There's nothing quite like the Animal Kingdom Lodge in Africa, yet it transports you Africa.

"Each resort has its own history too. There is a lot of misinformation about their themes online. Even the Disney people who renovate them periodically with new decor sometimes fail to understand their themes."

The addition of new WDW resort hotels continue with Star Wars: Galactic Starcruiser that will offer a two-night immersive experience by 2022. Guests will board the *Halcyon* starcruiser to become part of their own Star Wars stories along with the ship's crew, fellow passengers and iconic Star Wars characters.

They will explore the bridge and engineering room, test their lightsaber skills, unwind in the onboard lounge and venture off the ship for an excursion to Batuu's Black Spire Outpost via their own exclusive entrance during time when the park is not open to park guests. The guests will have their own passenger cabin that can accommodate up to five people with a window "starport" into space. Rooms are designed with beds for adults and bunk beds for kids. The engineering room is designed as an interactive play area for kids.

Guests will be welcomed on the surface and ride a simulator style launch pod up to the ship. Once there, they will enter the atrium on the main deck of the Halcyon and get acclimated to the ship.

There will be activities and various role playing activities throughout the day. A guest might be asked to accept a mission from the Resistance and join in the action or be pressed into service to defend the ship from the forces of the First Order with lightsaber training available.

"It's unlike anything that exists today," said Bob Chapek, Chairman of Disney Parks and Resorts. "From the second you arrive, you will become a part of a *Star Wars* story! You'll immediately become a citizen of the galaxy and experience all that entails, including dressing up in the proper attire.

"Once you leave Earth, you will discover a starship alive with characters, stories, and adventures that unfold all around you. It is 100% immersive, and the story will touch every single minute of your day, and it will culminate in a unique journey for every person who visits."

The Walt Disney World Resorts

DELUXE

- The Contemporary (1971)
- Polynesian Village Resort (1971)
- Grand Floridian Resort & Spa (1988)
- Yacht Club (1990)
- Beach Club (1990)
- Wilderness Lodge (1994)
- Boardwalk Inn (1996)
- Animal Kingdom Lodge (2001)
- Star Wars: Galactic Starcruiser (2022)

MODERATE

- Caribbean Beach (1988)
- Port Orleans: French Quarter (1991)
- Port Orleans: Riverside (1992) formerly Dixie Landings
- Coronado Springs (1997)

VALUE

- All-Star Sports (1994)
- All-Star Music (1994)
- All-Star Movies (1999)
- Pop Century (2003)
- Art of Animation (2012)

OTHER

- Fort Wilderness Resort and Campground (1971)
- Golf Resort (1973)
- Disney Inn (1986)
- Shades of Green (1994)
- Walt Disney World Swan (1990) owned by the Tishman Hotel Corporation but operated by Starwood Hotels & Resorts Worldwilde under the Westin Hotels brand.
- Walt Disney World Dolphin (1990) owned by the Tishman Hotel Corporation but operated by Starwood Hotels & Resorts Worldwilde under the Sheraton Hotels brand.

DVC RESORTS

Disney Vacation Club (DVC) is a type of timeshare program that Disney describes as a "vacation ownership program" where members use an allotment of Vacation Points to schedule reservations at any DVC resort available. It all began in 1991.

In addition to the sites at Walt Disney World, DVC has locations at The Villas at Disney's Grand Californian Hotel & Spa (Anaheim, California), Disney's Hilton Head Island Resort (Hilton Head Island, South Carolina), Disney's Vero Beach Resort (Vero Beach, Florida) and Aulani Disney Vacation Club Villas (Ko Olina, Hawaii.)

In December 2004, Bob Iger who at the time was President and Chief Operating Officer of the Walt Disney Company told the cast at a town hall meeting at Disney's Coronado Springs Resort, "The Disney Vacation Club is a tremendous business. We have some DVC units off property, but by and large, if we're going to invest money in that direction, we're better off building more DVC units at the Walt Disney World Resort because our overall strategy here as a business is to extend stays and increase repeat visitation."

- Disney's Old Key West Resort (1991)
- Disney's Boardwalk Villas Resort (1996)
- Boulder Ridge Villas (Wilderness Lodge) (2000)
- Disney's Beach Club Villas (2002)
- Saratoga Springs Resort & Spa (2004)
- Animal Kingdom Lodge Villas (Jambo House and Kidani Village) (2007)
- Bay Lake Tower (Contemporary Resort) (2009)
- Grand Floridian Resort & Spa Villas (2013)
- Disney's Polynesian Villas & Bungalows (2015)
- Copper Creek Villas and Cabins (Wilderness Lodge) (2017)
- Disney's Riviera Resort (2019)
- Reflections: A Disney Lakeside Lodge (2022)

Hilton Inn South

May 1970

Walt Disney's father Elias married Flora Call on January 1, 1888, in Kismet, Florida, roughly fifty miles from the land on which Walt Disney World would eventually be built. He was twenty-eight years old and she was nineteen.

That same year, he took a job as the manager of the Hallifax Hotel in Daytona Beach. The hotel was very successful during the summer months when tourists who were visiting to frolic on the beach needed a place to stay.

However, once fall arrived, attendance dropped off significantly and Elias could not make a living especially with the birth of their first son Herbert. That hotel no longer exists although there is still a Hallifax Avenue where the Hallifax Hotel once stood.

Elias worked briefly as a mailman in Kissimmee and finally bought a small orange grove but a frost destroyed his entire crop and he was stricken with malaria.

The Disney family relocated to Chicago because Elias' younger brother, Robert had moved there in 1889 and built a hotel in anticipation of the upcoming Chicago World's Fair in 1893. It was named the World's Columbian Exposition, to commemorate Christopher Columbus' discovery of America 400 years earlier.

Elias hoped to find work as a carpenter building pavilions for the fair since construction would begin early in 1891. He did and was paid a dollar a day, seven days a week. After the fair opened, he found work as a building contractor thanks to that credit on his resume.

So both Walt's father and uncle were involved with running hotels before Walt was even born in 1901. However, the Walt Disney Company was involved in operating a hotel in Central Florida before Walt Disney World was built.

Orlando attorney Finley Hamilton dabbled in real estate. He paid attention when in 1965 Walt Disney announced he was building an amusement enterprise. He purchased ten acres of palmetto-covered scrub in April 1968 for $90,000. People thought he was crazy because it was quite literally in the middle of nowhere and only accessible by a dirt road.

"They called it 'Finley's Folly,' everyone, all my friends," Hamilton said. "They said it was in the boondocks."

Finley thought tourists heading to Walt Disney World would see his hotel, exit on Sand Lake Road and head north on his new paved road. He was right. When WDW opened, it was the only hotel between Orlando and Walt Disney World property.

"It turned out to be highly successful. I made a lucky guess. That's what it amounts to," said Hamilton who died in 2012 at the age of 89 from complications of pneumonia.

"He quite enjoyed swimming against the current," said his first wife Virginia "He was extremely intelligent and analytical. He also possessed tremendous foresight."

A 1949 graduate of Stetson Law School, Hamilton opened a law practice in Orlando but saw a brighter future in construction, land development and the hospitality industry. He served as president of the Young Democrats of Orange County and of the Florida Hotel and Motel Associations. In the early days of tourism, his properties offered more than 1,000 hotel rooms.

His second wife Susan recalled he had a collection of silly hats he wore for fun including one with a lobster on top. "He just had a flair about him," she said. "He was a little outrageous, but also the most generous, kindhearted man I've ever known."

Hamilton had previously opened a Hilton Inn on West Colonial Drive making him just the second franchisee of the prestigious Hilton chain. It was so successful that he earned enough to afford a Cadillac limousine and a chauffeur.

He called his new hotel The Hilton Inn South and it opened in 1968.

Three months later, Hamilton and his partner, Jack Zimmer, bought about 29 more acres for $10,000 an acre. They soon resold the land as hotel sites for up to $200,000 an acre. There were eleven hotels with 3,900 rooms along International Drive by 1973.

The two story, horseshoe shaped Hilton Inn South had 140 guest rooms and a covered pool as well as several meeting rooms.

Because it was so near Disney property, the Walt Disney Company offered to manage it for Hamilton for sixteen months until Walt Disney World opened so they could train their staff for the Contemporary and the Polynesian Village resorts specifically.

Hamilton and his partner paved the nearby dirt road. Hamilton wanted to call it "Hamilton Drive" but there was another street by that name in Orlando already so he had to settle for "International Drive".

"I came up with International Drive because it sounded big and important," said Hamilton.

Hamilton and his partner Jack Zimmer later sold plots they initially bought surrounding International Drive at $10,000 an acre for $100,000 to $200,000 an acre.

There was no overall plan for the property and they sold whatever size parcels buyers wanted to purchase which accounts for the chaotic nature of the area today.

When the Disney Company determined they would run the WDW resort hotels themselves, Disney executive John Curry was put in charge and he hired about a half dozen managers from Western Internationall who were originally going to run the Polynesian. Marriot would have originally handled the Contemporary.

Curry was personally hired by Walt Disney in August 1966 to oversee the hotel division.

Born in Yosemite National Park at Camp Baldy, which was one of a number of park properties his parents operated, Curry grew up helping run the operations after his father died at an early age.

The family's company was Amfac, the successor to the Fred Harvey Company. Disney met Curry in the 1960s at Yosemite, where Disney was scouting opportunities to build a Mineral King hotel and ski park.

Curry later left Orlando in 1972 for Hilton Head, South Carolina, and soon became president of his own condominium-development-consulting firm.

Harris Rosen who would later go on to become a huge hotel owner in Orlando was then working for Disney as an administrator of hotel planning. One of his responsibilities was to mock up full size models for the front desks of the Contemporary and Polynesian to trouble shoot any problems like the width of the counter.

Dan Darrow was brought in from the Sheraton as General Manager. Bill "Sully" Sullivan who had worked at Disneyland since 1955 and assistant managed the It's A Small World attraction at the 1964-65 New York World's Fair was the assistant manager brought in to teach the proper Disney way of doing things to the hotel people.

As Sully told me in a 2007 interview, "I came out in 1969. John Curry was the hotel director at that time. His family ran the hotels in Yosemite and they were very guest-oriented as we were. That was an easy mix.

"We had leased the Hilton Inn South. It was 110 rooms down here. It was a new hotel, the only hotel on International Drive at the time. We went down and we staffed it and we hired people to run it and all that good stuff.

"I didn't have any hotel experience. None at all. But they didn't have any Disney experience and my job was to teach them how Disney did it.

"We taught them about training. We taught them about working with people. We taught them about scheduling. Just mostly about how we wanted our guests treated.

"The only one that was a minor problem was the guy that was made the general manager, Dan Darrow was an old-time hotelier and we just had to teach him the Disney way. Dan eventually accepted it and learned it and did quite a good job.

"We wanted to see what was available like laundries and what food was available and employees that were available. We did all that and it proved to be very beneficial for us because we learned where we could buy good meats and where we could buy good vegetables and stuff like that for the hotels. We, of course, did our own laundries, but we hired some great people."

Although it had been operating since 1968, The Hilton Inn South opened May 1970 under Disney management and was the location where Disney executives stayed, as well as Disney transfers who had not found a permanent home yet.

It was also open to the general public but the standards were extremely high because Roy O. Disney himself and other top Disney executives visited frequently and did not hesitate to comment on flaws in service and accomodations. The staff for the resorts was being trained to serve as if everyone staying there was a V.I.P. It was a hospitality training laboratory.

As *Orlando Magazine* writer Edward Prizer later wrote, "The Hilton South was not only a training ground for Disney hotel employees but a social headquarters in Florida for the whole Disney organization. Never was an inn so lavishly staffed nor so meticulously run.

"Gary Reich, one time White House chef, went to work with a team of sub-chefs in a gleaming new kitchens on the dishes that would be served at the World. For $3.50 you could partake in the candlelit dining room of a buffet that would have done credit to a transatlantic liner.

"The first time we ordered a steak here, we asked for knives. 'You don't need them,' the waitress said. And so right she was. Never had such steaks been served in Central Florida.

"Those were exciting nights at the Hilton South. After an arduous day at the project, the tanned young Californians flocked in and jammed the lounge. Frequently, we joined them and sat under a cypress mural listening to the ragtime of Jim and Marthat Hession...the folk-rock of Don and Sam...the jazz of Norm Schooping. A moveable feast --- fondly remembered forever."

Contemporary Resort chef Joe Mannke and Polynesian Village chef Garry Reich (the personal chef of President Lyndon Johnson) used the kitchen to develop their distinctive menus.

Oddly even though he was an attorney, Hamilton was so excited to be working with the Disney Company that the running of the Hilton

Inn South was just a “handshake” deal. No formal lease contracts have ever been located.

Hamilton claimed in a letter to Disney President Donn Tatum that he suffered an estimated loss of over $50,000 in revenue during the time Disney managed the hotel. Among other things, Hamilton’s Hilton Inn South staff was also servicing the five Bay Hill houses that Disney owned especially for parties.

In addition some Disney executives ran up tabs but never paid them, perhaps assuming the company would take care of the bill.

Hamilton never collected nor sued because he felt that Disney would be a great source of future business and he was in the process of building yet another hotel. In addition, Disney personnel stayed on to help manage and train new employees for several months after WDW opened.

The Hilton Inn South no longer exists but it was originally in the same general area as the big McDonald’s and entrance to Quality Inn on Sand Lake Road is today.

Disney Archivist Dave Smith recalled to me, “To train the cast members who were going to manage our hotels, we leased the Hilton Inn South, on International Drive near Sand Lake Road. At least I assume it was a lease--I have never seen the actual documents. I stayed there on my first trip to Orlando, in June, 1971. They put up most of the traveling Disney executives there, but, of course, at that time there were few other choices nearby.”

WDW Publicist Charlie Ridgway told me that for the opening of Walt Disney World, “I was staying at the Hilton Inn South on Sand Lake Road. The Disney Company had leased the place to train cast members that were going to work at the Contemporary and the Polynesian and that’s where they put up the Disney executives.

“I was going to wake up at 5:00 so that I would have plenty of time to be there (at WDW on the morning of October 1, 1971) before the media got to the Polynesian. I overslept.

“I woke up about ten minutes before 6:00am. I also had to check out that day so I was rushing to get dressed and pack. As I rushed through the lobby I literally threw my room keys 60 feet to the desk and gave them a piece of my mind for not waking me up on time. I didn’t properly check out and they still send me a bill to this day.”

While on his trips to Orlando, Roy O. Disney initially stayed at the Hilton Inn South but he and his wife later spent most of their time in a cottage at Bay Hill that the Walt Disney Company built for him.

Recreacres Incorporated was formed around 1968 to help The Walt Disney Company buy property for the Walt Disney World Resort. Disney built five virtually identical two-bedroom, two-bath ranch-style homes in a cul-du-sac on Lake Tibet at Tibet Bay Drive.

Roy and Joe Fowler's homes were 1,490 square feet each while the other three homes were 1,252 square feet. Both of their homes were the only ones to share a large common driveway as well and their professional relationship and constant interaction developed into a close friendship.

Roy and his wife Edna's home was at 8922 Tibet Bay Drive and Joe and his wife Marguerite's home was next door at 8928 Tibet Bay Drive. The other houses were at 8910, 8916 and 8934.

These houses were used by Card Walker, Donn Tatum and other Disney executives when they visited from California.

Roy would occasionally host backyard barbeques for Disney executives to improve morale and reward them for their hard work. The chefs, maids and other support staff for the Bay Hill homes were borrowed from the Hilton Inn South.

On October 31, 2001, the Walt Disney Hospitality Recreation Corporation sold all five homes to TBHC Inc., a holding company for the Arnold Palmer Bay Hill Country Club and Lodge.

Two other Central Florida hotels are significant in Walt Disney World history.

The official confirmation to the press that the Walt Disney Company was building something in Central Florida came on November 15, 1965 at 2 p.m. in the Egyptian Room of the Cherry Plaza Hotel in Orlando, Florida, with Walt Disney, his brother Roy, and Governor Burns in attendance.

By 8:30 am on April 30, 1969, the parking lot at the luxurious new high-rise Ramada Inn on Highway 50 in Ocoee, Florida, was already filled with cars. News media from all over the world mixed with prominent Florida officials and corporate executives waited for the big event of the Disney Company revealing exactly what was to be built in Florida and when.

The Walt Disney Company had rented out the entire Ramada Inn, not just a conference room or two. They set up a big circus tent outside filled with models and artist renderings of Walt Disney World for a three-day event to reveal the plans for the Florida property.

Ten female Guest Relations hostesses had been flown in from Disneyland to serve as guides. They stayed in the hotel for two weeks.

"My first time in Florida was here to help with the unveiling of models and plans for Walt Disney World Phase One to an audience of over 350 out-of-state editors and reporters plus local press and dignitaries," Walt Disney World Publicist Charlie Ridgway told me in an interview. Roy O. Disney spoke to the group and showed a special seventeen minute film of the plans for the property.

The Contemporary

October 1971

The Contemporary Resort is both an architectural and artistic marvel standing approximately 150 feet high. Its unique fourteen story triangular, A-frame shape became a dynamic icon of the WDW resort with the futuristic-looking monorail amazingly zipping through its atrium core.

The exterior retro-futuristic design was inspired in part by a building in Walt's model of Progress City for Epcot that would have been a shopping center between the center of the city and the green belt.

Early pre-opening postcards in spring 1971 featuring concept art of the resort hotel stated "Tempo Bay – the world's most contemporary resort hotel...guest journey by monorail over the 'Highway in the Sky' for a spectacular tour of the Vacation Kingdom."

While some assumed the name was changed to the Contemporary because Tempo Bay sounded too similar to Tampa Bay, it was actually that Roy Disney preferred the original placeholder name for the resort. It was the name that had been used to identify it during planning and construction but Imagineers always hoped to come up with a more striking, modernistic name.

Roy felt calling it The Contemporary Resort was simple and captured the feeling of it being a modernistic location. He felt that calling it Tempo Bay sounded pretentious and phony.

Walt was always fascinated by new construction methods even as far back as the Monsanto House of the Future at Disneyland made from nearly indestructible plastic.

United States Steel Corporation, through its then newly-formed subsidiary company, U.S. Steel Realty Development, was eager to use and publicize a unique construction method called "unitized modular construction."

For the Contemporary, they built a revolutionary superstructure of thirteen steel-trussed A-frames resembling a skeletal honeycomb.

Into the honeycomb, they fitted the individual guest rooms manufactured at a 150,000-square-foot floor-space factory just a few miles away from the Contemporary, just north of where today's Port Orleans Riverside Resort area resides. The building where all of that work took place still stands at 1500 Live Oak Lane just south of the softball field.

This type of construction was attractive to the Walt Disney Company because, in theory, it would cut the building time in half since both the infrastructure and the individual rooms could be constructed at the same time. The company was battling tight deadlines to get the Vacation Kingdom built on time. By 1970, all the available 1972 convention dates for the Contemporary had already been booked in advance, so a delay was unthinkable.

Traditionally, a hotel framework would be built and then the rooms. By doing both at the same time and then combining them, it would supposedly save both time and money. It ended up doing neither. U.S. Steel estimated the cost for each room would be $17,000, but the final cost was over $100,000 a room.

The rooms were formed on an assembly line, much like automobiles, at the rate of about forty a week. As they passed through each station on the way to completion, the electrical, mechanical and plumbing facilities were added to the room.

Each room designed by California architect Donald Wexler was nine feet high, fifteen feet wide and about thirty feet long and had air conditioning units, piping, lighting and mirrors and bath fixtures in the bathrooms installed in the process.

The modular guest rooms were assembled, finished, furnished, fully equipped down to Gideon Bibles and toilet paper, and their doors locked, on the ground. They were installed at an average rate of fifteen per day.

Disney executive Tom Moses who was in charge of the Reedy Creek Improvement District hired Underwriters Laboratories who took the first unit off the assembly line for a full-scale burn test. They stacked ten pounds of wood carvings on the floor and set up half rooms on either side.

They ignited the room and filmed the result. Only one minor change around a connecting door was needed to be made to ensure optimum safety.

Every room already included a fire sprinkler, something that would not be mandatory in Central Florida hotels until the 1980s, and that sprinkler was linked to monitors in the RCID fire stations to alert them to send a unit.

Each nearly nine-ton room was placed on a truck and hauled to the Contemporary where it was lifted into place by massive cranes and fitted into the steel frame.

Supposedly, they were to be set into the frame easily, but they often didn't fit into those exacting openings on the first try, and because of the structure, they had to alternate installing rooms on the opposite sides to prevent the framework from becoming off balance and tipping over.

Of course, this was all done under the best of controlled conditions. Imagine trying to duplicate all of that once the building was completed and there were people inside and other interior additions.

The paperwork from U.S. Steel and Disney including the numerous press releases during the building of the Contemporary never make any mention of the rooms sliding back out like drawers in a dresser. That is a persistent urban legend. If there was meant to be a rotating element that would have been incorporated into the name to generate future clients.

Walt's original concept for the Epcot project was that the 20,000 residents wouldn't own their apartments and houses so that would allow various companies from American industry to come in every five or ten years and re-do the entire kitchen or the wiring so it would feature the latest technology to showcase to visitors.

This idea may have been the beginning of the urban myth of the replaceable rooms at the Contemporary.

Once the rooms were in place and hooked up, they "settled" thanks to movement in the building, gravity and other factors so they sank just below the original slot. To be removed, among many other challenges, they would have to be lifted up before being pulled out.

After the room modules were installed, they were permanently enclosed in the structure by exterior walls and balconies. When it's time to replace the wallpaper in the rooms, it makes much more sense to send in a few wallpaper hangers than to remove the exterior walls of the Contemporary, lease an expensive crane, bring in a highly skilled crane crew, disconnect all utilities including sewer connections, carefully remove the rooms (each time leaving a hole in the side of the building), swap out the room, reconnect everything, and rebuild the exterior walls and balconies.

After the rooms were installed, the structure was covered by a specially designed sun-resistant glass called "Solar Bronze".

The central opening beginning on the fourth floor was called the Grand Canyon Concourse. It was longer than a football field with a ceiling height of nine stories. Basic earth colors were chosen to be reminiscent of a pueblo village and were reflected on the costuming of the cast members and interior room design as well.

The main focus was the impressive mural on the exterior of the elevator shafts done by artist Mary Blair. She started working at the Disney Studio in 1940 and was known for her unique color and design work especially on the It's A Small World attraction as well as the Las Posadas segment of the animated film *The Three Caballeros* (1945) that both featured the playful exuberance of her distinctive ethnic children.

A massive ninety-foot tall mural encircles the elevator shafts, each wall telling a different part of the story of the children, animals, flora and geology of the Grand Canyon. Blair called the mural the "Pueblo Village".

Previously she had created murals for Walt Disney for the Jules Stein Eye Institute in Los Angeles and the new Disneyland Tomorrowland that opened in 1967.

Her final project for Disney was this mural on the elevator shafts that celebrated a Southwestern theme. The architect Welton Becket originally planned for the shafts to be encased in shiny metal, to capture a modern contemporary feeling.

Instead, Blair's artwork provided a warmer, more welcoming feel to the cavernous space. In 1971, restaurants and bars had names like the Grand Canyon Terrace Café, El Pueblo Room, Mesa Grande Lounge and Outer Rim to suggest the Grand Canyon.

In 1974, the Fiesta Fun Center debuted with a snack bar and arcade games as well as an elaborate shooting gallery. It included Bill Justice mural artwork on the walls of the Disney characters enjoying a Mexican fiesta including Mickey, Minnie and the Three Caballeros: Donald Duck, Jose Carioca and Panchito. The area survived with modifications until around 2007.

In the early years, the Mexican band, Mariachi Chaparral, played five days a week for guests enjoying one of the 4th floor restaurants or lounge areas.

Each balcony was painted a different shade of earth tone to suggest the different layers of the canyon. It took eighteen months to design, produce and install the final mural that "hid" the elevators.

Blair was inspired by prehistoric petroglyphs, pueblo murals, Navajo ceremonial art and sand paintings. The colors were meant not just to suggest Native American art but earth and sky tones associated with the Grand Canyon.

Near the upper right of the mural that faces the monorail is a five-legged goat while all the other goats clearly have four legs. In their art, the Navajo have the concept of "purposely imperfect" to indicate that nothing man makes should be perfect because doing so would be an affront to the Great Spirit.

Blair used over 18,000 individually hand-painted, fire-glazed, one foot square ceramic tiles. She was assisted by Joyce Carlson who had worked with her on the It's a Small World attraction.

High quality prints of her original design paintings for individual scenes were reproduced, framed and hung throughout the hotel, sometimes over the beds in each room. The prints were removed when the resort underwent a renovation in the early 1990s.

Three-dimensional dioramas featuring artwork inspired by Blair were on the walls in the dining area near the elevators.

The tiles were shipped from California to Florida on special air-suspension trucks. When she saw the finished mural in Florida, Blair told writer Ross Care, "I walked into that giant concourse. My reaction was 'Oh, wow!'"

Blair did no further work for the Walt Disney Company because of the jealousy some Imagineers had over the favoritism shown her while Walt was alive. With the death of Roy O. Disney in 1971, she no longer had a champion to protect her or to offer her any new work and the alcoholism that had long plagued her and her husband got out of control so this was her last work for Disney.

The resort underwent many changes over the decades. The Convention Center annex was built for a 1991 opening in a section of the original parking lot. The Bay Lake Tower part of the Disney Vacation Club is a fifteen story addition that officially opened on August 4, 2009. It is located on the former location of the demolished North Garden Wing rooms.

The Convention Center annex addition was not just to address the need for more convention space on property but a chance to update the resort hotel into a warmer, more inviting location under the direction of Wing Chao. Gwathmey Siegel & Associates was hired for the transformation.

As architect Charles Gwathmey said, "Since the Contemporary hotel was of a certain ilk, it had a kind of icon perception and needed only a minimal amount of theming."

One of the changes was to transform the rather forboding approach to the hotel with a new landscaped plaza with rows of rhythmically placed trees to look sleek and modernistic as they lined a patterned walkway.

The strip directly outside the entrance was landscaped to resemble a gigantic Mickey Mouse wristwatch that was only visible from looking from the upper floors at the design.

Spare modern furnishings and prints of modern paintings in guests rooms once again made the hotel reflect its name as the Grand Canyon theming faded.

The new convention center with a barrel-tiled roof was to blend with as well as complete the hotel and looked somewhat like a giant Quonset hut meant, as architect Charles Gwathmey said, to make the buildings seem like a complete collage as seen from "the water, from the road and from the monorail."

The color palette was to invoke both earth and sky tones in broad bands of color. Inside, the floors seemed to be in a giant checkerboard fashion referencing grids and stripes both inside and outside the building to provide a pleasing patterning for gatherings.

Bay Lake Tower, a fifteen story DVC resort, opened August 2011. It is considered an addition to Disney's Contemporary Resort as they both share the same current theme "where tradition touches today".

The Sky Way Bridge connects the two resorts and takes Guests from the fifth floor of Bay Lake Tower directly to the fourth floor Grand Canyon Concourse of the Contemporary.

The top floor of Bay Lake Tower is named the Top of the World Lounge as an homage to the original Contemporary Resort's top floor. The level includes an observation deck with views of all four WDW theme parks from various parts of the building.

Stories of the Contemporary

OPENING DAY

For logistical reasons, parts of the NBC musical special *The Grand Opening of Walt Disney World* were filmed before the park was open, so cast members were costumed as tourists inside the Contemporary for comedian Bob Hope to give his monologue to an appreciative audience.

Tom Nabbe, who was in charge of the monorails during the opening of Walt Disney World told me in an interview:

"For the filming of the opening special, we drove Bob Hope into the Contemporary Hotel concourse on the monorail to do his bit. I was standing on the platform waiting for him when one of the coordinators came up to me. These were the days when the monorails had individual air conditioners in them and they made quite a noise.

"So this guy says, 'Tom, the noise is drowning out Bob's monologue. Can you do something about it?' And I went over and hit the power button. Then I picked up the phone and called the monorail roundhouse and said, 'You'd better get over here because we've got to haul Bob Hope out of this building in fifteen minutes and you need to re-set the rectifiers because I just turned them off.'

"And they got over and were standing by so that the minute Hope finished they could re-set the rectifiers. The only way I could shut off the air conditioning units on the train was to kill the power to the train which I did. Then I had to get it started back up so we could take Hope on his merry way back to the Polynesian."

On Thursday, September 30, 1971, the Contemporary Resort looked austere as it rose above the empty landscape. There was no grass, no bushes or trees to be seen. Disney executive Dick Nunis took charge and shortly before 5 p.m., about fifteen hours before the Magic Kingdom would open to guests for the first time, Nunis began directing like a general a ragtag troop of people to make Disney magic.

As remembered by landscaper and Disney Legend Bill Evans, "Planting a few palm trees would be no problem, but we also figured it would take about four-and-a-half acres of sod just to make the place look presentable. Given the timetable, most everyone thought it an impossible task.

"Everyone but Nunis. He made the calls to have the sod trucked in, hired about a hundred extra men, none of whom knew anything about laying sod, grabbed anybody else that was standing around and began turning the brown earth green."

It grew dark as the precious hours ticked by and the workers (some of them cast members who were "volunteered" for the task including the first WDW Ambassador Debbie Dane) lugged heavy clumps of grass across the vast expanse. However, for decades, the one thing that people remembered about that night was Nunis in a loud and hoarse voice proclaiming, "Green side up! Remember, green side up!"

"Everyone's heard that story but it's true," WDW publicist Charlie Ridgway who was there told me, "All the landscapers were too tired. They were worn out trying to get ready for opening so we got some kids from Rollins College and they had never done anything like this before. No, Dick wasn't saying it with a smile in his voice. He was serious. We were battling against time."

Nunis recalled, "Before we were finished, we saw we weren't going to have enough sod. Bill Evans drew a big circle and said, 'We'll leave this bare. People will think it is a planter.' Guests walked around the circled area as if it had been planned that way."

By six in the morning the Contemporary was ready for the guests and the press just like magic although most of the media activity would take place at the Polynesian Village Resort. Three weeks later, the area was more formally landscaped and most of that last minute sod was thrown away.

PRESIDENT RICHARD NIXON

Every U.S. President has an audio-animatronics doppelganger in the Hall of Presidents attraction in the Magic Kingdom but some presidents have actually visited Walt Disney World.

Former President Richard Nixon had many memorable moments at Disneyland including inaugurating the Monorail attraction in 1959 but his most unfortunate experience happened at the Contemporary Resort November 17, 1973 in the Ballroom of the Americas B.

In an hour-long televised question-and-answer session in front of 400 Associated Press managing editors, Nixon defended his record. He has flown to Orlando that evening from his Key Biscayne, Florida home for a defining moment in his presidency.

The Watergate political scandal involving a break-in of the Democratic National Committee headquarters at the Watergate complex in Washington, D.C. and subsequent attempted cover-up by the Nixon administration was very much on the minds of the U.S. people. Nixon asked for the resignation of two of his aides who were convicted and sent to prison.

There were serious questions about Nixon's direct involvement and knowledge of the incident. During the conference, Richard Smyser, from the *Oak Ridger* newspaper in Oak Ridge, Tennessee asked about the pressures on a president and if that might explain how something like Watergate could happen.

Nixon famously and solemnly responded, "And I want to say this to the television audience. I've made my mistakes. And in all of my years of public life I have never obstructed justice. And I think too, I can say that in my years of public life, I welcome this kind of examination. People have got to know whether or not their president is a crook. Well, I'm not a crook."

That last sentence, "I am not a crook", came back to haunt him many times over the years. It became part of Nixon's legacy and was parodied on television shows, in print and more and it was said on Walt Disney World property. Nixon was finally forced to resign in August of 1974, the first and only president ever to do so.

MONORAIL

Monorail spiel from 1972: "In a few seconds, we'll be passing directly through the center of the Contemporary's Tower building for a look at the spectacular Grand Canyon Concourse.

"As we ride through the Grand Canyon Concourse, you can see one of the largest ceramic murals ever created. It's nine stories high and it's made up of 18,000 hand painted tiles. Elevators running through the center will carry you high above to the Top of the World restaurant, where famous stars entertain."

Top of the World was a dining location that provided a breathtaking and panoramic view from the fourteenth floor. It seated up to 312 guests in a posh environment with expensive food and was a popular location to view the evening fireworks over the Magic Kingdom.

In the evening, there were performers like Mel Torme, Jimmie Rodgers, Kay Starr, John Gary, The King Sisters, Alvino Ray, Shari Lewis, Diahann Carroll, Rosemary Clooney, Sammy Davis, Jr., Phyllis Diller, and Steve Lawrence & Eydie Gorme and more.

Reservations were necessary for the 6:30pm and 9:30 pm shows with a cover charge of five dollars. Gentlemen were asked to wear a coat. This type of Vegas-style supper club entertainment was replaced in July 1981 by a sparkly musical revue show entitled *Broadway at the Top* that ran until 1993.

Disney promoted it to travel agents as "two seatings nightly, this sophisticated show features a medley of Broadway hits from productions that span three decades. Gentlemen are required to wear coats. No smoking permitted." In 1995, the area became the California Grill.

As the monorail spiel continued, "You can see many of the guest rooms high in the sloping walls overlooking the restaurant terrace and shopping plaza below. In addition to the Towers building, the Contemporary Resort also features lakeside living. Additional guest rooms are located right on the shores of beautiful Bay Lake.

"You're invited to return to the Contemporary Resort anytime by simply taking one of the local Monorail trains from the Magic Kingdom. They'll drop you off right at the Grand Canyon Concourse station."

Perhaps the most dramatic and often used image in publicity and media for the opening of Walt Disney World was the monorail rocketing out of the Contemporary Resort. Concept art of this image had been drawn by Imagineer George McGinnis.

It was meant to represent that Walt Disney World was much more than just an amusement park but a vacation destination and, in addition, on the cutting edge of new technology.

When the Magic Kingdom was built, instead of having a parking lot and ticket booths mere feet from the entrance like at Disneyland, they were placed on the other side of a man-made lake called the Seven Seas Lagoon to separate the Magic Kingdom from the realities of the mundane world.

According to a Disney press information released in 1969: "The principal means of travel from the parking center and main entrance to and from the theme park and hotels will be aboard the Walt Disney World-Alweg Monorail trains. Current plans call for the building of six five-car trains, some to stop at every hotel on the way around the circuit, while others carry passengers nonstop directly to the Magic Kingdom."

The newest monorail, the Mark IV, designed by Imagineer Bob Gurr, would be the best version with a high-capacity design that could hold up to 210 guests in the 171-foot long, five-car train. There was improved air conditioning (considered vital in the Florida heat and humidity) and new door systems. These newest monorails were designed in Burbank under the direction of Gurr and built in Orlando by the Martin Marietta Corporation.

The seats in the Mark IV were a rich royal blue in color with four aisles of guests facing each other going across each car. Each car had four doors, except for the middle car that had a special double door type of setup to allow guests in wheelchairs.

The doors opened automatically but had to be closed manually by the monorail attendants attired in polyester jumpsuits (men wore blue jumpsuits with green turtlenecks while women wore the reverse in colors) and a hard blue helmet with an iconic monorail emblem.

Although the monorail would only be traveling at less than ten miles per hour entering and leaving the building, vibrations tests had to be done to make sure the building would not be affected. Gurr drove the monorail at forty miles per hour through the building as a test with no issues.

Polynesian Village

October 1971

The Polynesian Village resort has undergone many changes over the decades including in 2014 with the removal of the volcano waterfall in the lobby of the Great Ceremonial House and the reimagining of the space as a Polynesian fishing village.

The interior is now a more open social space with chandeliers suggesting floating fishing buoys. It includes shops like BouTIKI (a play on the word "boutique") that has wooden Tiki statues scattered around the merchandise displays. The statues were made in Bali and weigh up to 1,000 pounds each.

A small Tiki representing Maui by a mini-waterfall in the lobby is an homage to the former iconic landmark of the massive waterfall that in the early years also included colorful live parrots on perches. The resort also saw in 2015 the addition of Bora Bora Bungalows as part of a DVC expansion.

In 2021, it was announced that the resort will once again be refurbished with a new porte cochere and elements inspired from the Disney animated feature *Moana* (2016).

However despite all the changes over the decades, the thirty-nine acres remained styled as a South Pacific paradise, complete with beaches, tropical landscaping, waterfalls, and bamboo tiki torches among other things.

According to a 1971 publicity release, "The Polynesian Village Hotel offers our guests excellent accommodations in a peaceful village atmosphere. Nestled in luxuriant landscaping on the southern shores of the Seven Seas Lagoon, its motto is 'Aita Peatea' which means 'There will be another day tomorrow like today'.

"Maui, the god of vacations, slows the sun down to make the days longer so that our guests may enjoy the slower-paced, more casual atmosphere of this delightful South Seas resort."

When this resort was being planned, The Enchanted Tiki Room attraction at Disneyland was at its peak of popularity and the fascination with South Seas Tiki Culture was rampant in Southern California.

"One of three resorts to have opened with the Walt Disney World Resort in 1971, Disney's Polynesian Resort reflects Walt's love of Polynesian culture and his desire to extend the Magic

Kingdom experience beyond the parks," stated Ken Potrock, Senior Vice President and General Manager of Disney Vacation Club and Adventures by Disney.

The Polynesian Village Resort was open on October 1, 1971, but not all the rooms were yet available. WDW Publicist Charlie Ridgway told me, "Anyway, the only resort that had rooms completed (on that opening day) was the Polynesian. It had something like 500 rooms and we had maybe 100 that were ready. We decided to have the press office there."

Actually, the resort's official grand opening was celebrated on October 24, 1971, and according to The Walt Disney Company that should be considered the official anniversary.

The resort opened on time, which was amazing since construction on it began a mere eight months before guests set foot in it. While the Contemporary Resort opened at the same time, not all of its rooms were available and construction on it continued until November with a large crane hovering outside.

The opening celebration of the Polynesian featured a spectacular nighttime luau with authentic island delicacies served on the lagoon shore to more than a thousand media and celebrity guests. The entertainment by dozens of native dancers concluded with the debut of the Electrical Water Pageant starring King Neptune and his nautical subjects of the deep.

The resort was meant to be an homage to an American interpretation of Polynesian culture primarily reflected in West Coast restaurants like Don the Beachcomer and Trader Vic's as well as an extension of Magic Kingdom's Adventureland.

The peak of American interest in all things tropical was after World War II, when returning military personnel who had served in the South Pacific wanted to recapture the memories of that exotic experience.

When designing Walt Disney World, it was decided that the Seven Seas Lagoon would represent the seven major seas of the world and that there would be a series of resorts associated with those bodies of water, like the Asian, Persian and the Venetian.

Originally, the resort was to look like a triangular island volcano twelve stories high with a South Seas restaurant at the top. Guest rooms would have been in this structure. Surrounding this main building would be smaller longhouses to also accommodate guests. It seemed more reminiscent of a modern Hawaiian hotel.

That design was later modified by the architectural firm of Welton Becket and Associates into the current two-story structure of a smaller main building known as the Great Ceremonial House (modeled after a Tahitian royal assembly lodge). The two levels were named the Lobby Sea Level and the Bay View Terrace Level.

The limit of three stories tall for the longhouses kept the silhouette long and low to be reminiscent of a Polynesian village. The pitched roofs were covered with a special tin covering called "Cor-Ten" which weathers to a rich, natural, earth-toned patina. All the steel structures were covered with wood.

The back of the resort's postcard stated, "A tropical island adventure awaits guests at the Polynesian Village resort. Entertainment, food, decor and shopping all blend into a South Seas vacation atmosphere. Palm-lined sandy beaches are just a barefoot stroll away, while the 'rest of the World' is reached by outrigger, sailboats, old-fashioned side-wheel steamboats and swift monorail trains."

The resort opened with 492 guest rooms in eight longhouse buildings: Bali Hai, Bora Bora, Hawaii, Fiji, Samoa, Tahiti, Tonga, and Maui. The names were meant to assist guests in identifying which building had their room. Resort rates in 1971 were approximately $22 to $44 a night, depending on factors like the floor, view, size, location and season.

The Polynesian rooms were stacked on top of each other rather than slid into place like at the Contemporary's A-frame structure, but the basic process of construction of the individual rooms was similar.

At a facility on the upper east end of WDW property roughly four miles away from the resort, U.S. Steel workers produced hundreds of modular rooms weighing 8.5 tons each that were finished and furnished in an assembly-line process for both the Contemporary and the Polynesian. The building where all of that work took place still stands at 1500 Live Oak Lane just south of the softball field.

For decorative purposes, real bamboo had been used in the resort, but it quickly split and rotted, forcing a last-minute replacement of fiberglass bamboo in many areas.

At first, elaborate outdoor luaus were held on an outdoor stage on the beach, but the unpredictable Florida weather caused so many cancellations that in 1972 the sheltered Luau Cove was constructed to house the festivities.

The original pool at the resort in 1971 was the Nanea Volcano Pool, where guests had to go under a waterfall to get to the stairs to get to the top of the water slide. That pool was replaced in March 2001 with the current pool featuring a larger volcano. The resort would change constantly starting in the 1970s.

The color scheme was primarily green and orange, featuring a green quartz registration desk and white revolving ceiling fans. A green-and-blue checkerboard tiled floor was in the Great Ceremonial House.

As many as eight guests could pile into a 40-foot Polynesian War Canoe and paddle off to the islands in the Seven Seas Lagoon or enjoy a cocktail on the Chinese Junk known as the Eastern Winds.

The Eastern Winds, a cocktail lounge aboard an authentic 65-foot Chinese Junk, was docked at the resort from 1971 to 1978. It was available for charters, and took a crew of two to operate; a pilot and a deckhand.

The ship included a galley on board for dining as well as a full wet bar. Often during charters, the crew would also include a chef, a server, a bartender as well as a cocktail waitress. The large wheel was located in the stern of the 50,000-pound boat and took 22 turns from lock to lock.

It was built in Hong Kong in 1964, and was later purchased by a Texas oil baron. Football player Joe Namath did own it at one time as well.

In addition, cocktail cruises departed nightly at 7:30 pm from the Polynesian Village marina. For an hour and a half complimentary cocktails were served on one of the Chris Craft yachts or Aqua Homes. The cost was ten dollars per person including drinks.

In 1971, Kau'i Brandt, better known as "Auntie Kau'i", moved from Pearl City, Hawaii on the island of Oahu to California for eight months to perform in the Polynesian show at Disneyland. Shortly afterwards, she moved to Florida with her husband Pono to open the Kau'i Pono Polynesian Revue at the Polynesian Village Resort.

She was the master of ceremonies for the show and still remains as a cultural representative at the resort many decades later, often sitting in the lobby making flower leis for guests.

As she told me while making a flower lei, "When Pono and I learned that the Disney organization was looking for a company of Polynesian artist to perform at Walt Disney World in 1971, we decided to put together a show that would be both authentic and exciting."

Their company had twenty-eight young dancers and musicians and more than one hundred dances in their repertory. At that time, the company appeared three times nightly in the Papeete Bay Verandah restaurant and at the evening luaus on the beach where guests paid ten dollars per person to attend.

Theatrically, a raft used to bring the luau cast over from an island in the lagoon at the start of the show. The show was performed on the beach in approximately the same location where the Luau Cove is today.

The Luau Cove structure with a canopy (in case of rain) was built and seated 550 guests with a portable kitchen brought from the Great Ceremonial House in May 1972. By using the outside facilities, it helped alleviate the food service challenges inside the resort for the packed restaurants.

Luau Cove is the name of the structure not the actual cove. The actual cove was originally Beachcomber Cove. Dressing rooms were added in October 1972 and more modifications were made in June 1975. Restrooms were added in 1979.

Guests are invited to join the festivities including an all-you-can-eat buffet in the open-air but covered theater in Luau Cove. The Polynesian Village Resort show was inspired by a similar show at Disneyland's Tahitian Terrace that opened in 1962 in Adventureland.

In January 2003, the original luau show closed and in February of that year the Spirit of Aloha show premiered. It is now the story of Auntie Wini is who hosting a fun-filled luau to say goodbye to one of the local girls who's headed to the "mainland" for college. In the process, more rehab work was done on Luau Cove.

Disney executive Dick Nunis, a surfer himself, wanted to provide a surfing experience in that same location and perhaps spark a professional surfing competition to attract greater attendance in much the same way a golfing championship would.

At a cost of approximately $400,000, a wave machine was installed near the west side of Beachcomber Isle but it only lasted sporadically through 1972 when it was shut down.

Unfortunately, it generated several problems from beach erosion to making the area unsafe for watercraft traffic, and constantly breaking down every few hours requiring engineers in wet suits to swim out and fix it resulting in escalating costs.

According to a November 1971 issue of *Eyes and Ears* newsletter, "The wave machine in the Seven Seas Lagoon is now undergoing further testing. It is located on the west side of Beachcomber Isle and will create waves from four inches to four feet breaking on to Surfrider Beach. Surf Boards and instructions will be available through the hotel Recreation and Reception Desks."

Nunis' window on Main Street at Disneyland lists "Wave machines a specialty." Besides the one in the Seven Seas Lagoon (which was tested again in 1985 before being permanently shut down), Nunis lobbied for one at River Country and later Typhoon Lagoon.

The resort was renamed Disney's Polynesian Resort in 1985. It reverted to its original name in 2014. The resort saw two major rehabs in 1978 and 1985 with the addition of more buildings and the renaming of some existing structures.

In 1999, most of the Resort's longhouses were renamed: Bali Hai became Tonga; Bora Bora became Niue; Hawaii became Samoa; Maori changed to Rarotonga; Moorea became Tahiti; Oahu became Tokelau; Pago Pago became Rapa Nui; Samoa became Tuvalu; Tahiti became Aotearoa; and Tonga became Hawaii.

The names were changed to better reflect a more accurate geographical position of the islands to each other.

Stories of the Polynesian

BREAKING UP THE BEATLES

Politicians, sports stars, television and movie performers and other celebrities have enjoyed the amenities offered at the Walt Disney World resort hotels since they first opened in 1971.

Although in September 1969, John Lennon privately informed the other Beatles that he was leaving the group, there was no public acknowledgement of the break-up until Paul McCartney publically announced in April 1970 that he was leaving the Beatles.

There were many reasons for the break-up including convoluted business problems that delayed the official legal dissolution of the group for several years.

During a lengthy separation from his wife Yoko Ono, Lennon hooked up with his female personal assistant May Pang and they were officially in a relationship for eighteen months. Attorneys had finally put the final touches on the contractual paperwork necessary to legally dissolve the band.

In the February 9, 2008 *Orlando Sentinel* newspaper, Pang revealed what happened next:

"At the end of 1974, after three years of court battles and acrimony, the final dissolution of The Beatles was about to happen. The meeting was scheduled for December 19 at New York's Plaza Hotel—ironically, this was the first place the group stayed in America in 1964.

"George Harrison was in New York on his Dark Horse tour. Paul and Linda McCartney came in, and of course John and I were already in the city. Only Ringo was missing, but he had signed the documents in England.

"Julian (John's son who was eleven years old) was with us for the Christmas holiday and all was calm; all was bright. Gathered around a huge table were George, his lawyer and business manager; the McCartneys, with Paul's in-laws and lawyers; Ringo's lawyer and business manager; Neil Aspinall, of Apple, with two sets of company lawyers (one for America and one for Britain); and John's lawyer Harold Seider and his team.

"I was with John and it was up to me to tell Harold he had decided not to attend the meeting. Although John was concerned with shouldering a major tax burden because he lived in the United States, I could sense there was a bit more on his mind. His official reason for not showing was 'the stars aren't right'.

"John, Julian and I left New York the following day to spend Christmas in Florida. On December 29, 1974, the voluminous documents were brought down to John in Florida by one of Apple's lawyers.

"'Take out your camera,' he joked to me. He looked wistfully out the window. I could almost see him replaying the entire Beatles experience in his mind.

"He finally picked up his pen and, in the unlikely backdrop of the Polynesian Village Hotel at Disney World, ended the greatest rock 'n' roll band in history by simply scrawling 'John Lennon' at the bottom of the page."

Lennon had booked a room at the Polynesian Village Resort at Walt Disney World and gazed out at the Seven Seas Lagoon before he signed the document that broke up The Beatles.

Although Disney is unable to confirm which room Lennon was in, it is apparent that it was a ground floor corner room in the Samoa longhouse (formerly Hawaii) that looked out on the Seven Seas Lagoon with Cinderella Castle clearly visible in the distance. Both John and Julian were excellent swimmers and enjoyed the pool at the resort.

Pang also wrote about that incident in her book *Instamatic Karma: Photographs of John Lennon* (St. Martins Press 2008). There is a photo of Lennon standing by Cinderella Castle and another in front of his room at the Polynesian which is how it can be identified.

THE KUKUI NUT TREE

The Polynesian Village Resort has a unique Kukui Nut tree. It is the only one of its kind in the state of Florida and the tree was brought here from its native Hawaii. It is often mentioned in Hawaiian literature and still flourishes on the islands in Polynesia.

Since 1959, the Candlenut tree (Aleurites moluccana), known more commonly as "kukui", has been the official state tree of Hawaii. It can grow to over eighty feet tall. The kukui nut was used for many things including a natural medicine remedy for a variety of ailments, different dyes, moisturizing cream, body oil and lotion, shampoo, polish, children's toy (a spinning top called a "Hu"), food and light among other functions.

Torches made from placing nuts in a hollow piece of bamboo or in leaves on top of a pole were used to light pathways and homes. Today, the kukui nut is more commonly used not as a source of illumination but in the making of various types of ornamentation like necklaces, bracelets, and earrings.

The kukui tree was brought to the islands more than a thousand years ago by migrating Polynesians and proved to be incredibly versatile. Canoes were carved from its buoyant trunks, and its oily seeds were strung together and burned as a sort of primitive candle. Each seed would burn about two to three minutes. Oil pressed from nuts could be burned in stone lamps, and the residual material, or "cake", was used to feed cattle and for crop fertilization.

Dyes produced by crushing the covering of the nuts were used in tattooing, and another type of dye made from the root became a black paint for canoes. The bark of the tree provided a red dye for clothing.

Two prominent ancient uses of the kukui continue today. First, a relish spice, popular at luaus and other celebrations, is made from the roasted and chopped nuts. Second, some of the festive leis that greet the many visitors to Hawaii every year are made of beaded kukui nuts.

Traditionally, the tree is regarded as a symbol of protection and peace and is given as a precious gift between friends.

An old Hawaiian belief was that a person should not plant a kukui tree near his own house, but it was all right for a stranger to plant it for him as a gift. That stranger could plant it in the back of the house or "hale" but not in the front.

At Disney's Polynesian Village Resort, the kukui tree is located behind the Great Ceremonial House just off to the right of the pathway. Following the dictates of the popular legend, it was planted by a hotel guest on April 25, 1997 to celebrate the 25th anniversary year of the resort that opened in 1971.

Remarkably, the tree has survived a lightning strike, almost being uprooted by a hurricane and being frozen in an unseasonable Florida cold snap. A time capsule is located at the base of the tree.

The leadership team at the resort wears a lei of black kukui nuts to symbolize that they are lighting the way as a living torch for cast members to share the magic of Polynesian culture and the spirit of aloha to the guests.

Leis made of kukui nuts were considered to be highly prestigious and sacred and were only worn by the reigning kings of Hawaii. Unlike a flower lei that will disintegrate in time, a kukui nut lei was meant to last forever.

AUNTIE KAU'I

In 1971, Kau'i Brandt, better known as "Auntie Kau'i", moved from Pearl City, Hawaii on the island of Oahu to California for eight months to perform in the Polynesian show at Disneyland. Shortly afterwards, she moved to Florida with her husband Pono to open the Kau'i-Pono Polynesian Revue at the new Disney Polynesian Village Resort.

She was the master of ceremonies for the show and remained as a cultural representative at the resort for decades. Among other things as a cultural representative, she would sit in the lobby as she does today and create the authentic leis from real flowers to give to couples celebrating honeymoons or anniversaries as well as stopping occasionally to give children Hawaiian cookies and hula lessons.

She was born during a Hawaiian thunder and lightning storm in 1932 and was named "Kauihealani" which means "thundering voice of heaven". She uses the shortened version "Kau'i".

Her grandmother was Hawaiian and she was shown the stories of Polynesia told through hulas before she was able to speak. By the time she was seven years old, she was telling the stories herself at luaus.

"I studied the dances of Samoa, Tahiti, Tonga, Hawaii and the Maori dances of New Zealand," said Kau'i. "My teachers were always from the islands where the dances are still performed and knew the legends and traditions told in each dance. I taught and I learned. Many of my teachers were from the Mormon Church College on the island of Oahu in Hawaii.

"When we were looking to put together a company of Polynesian artists to perform at Walt Disney World, it was natural that we would select some of our young dancers and musicians from among the students at Church College.

"We wanted the best performers, of course, but we also wanted eager, happy, young people who would best express the spirit of aloha – generosity, joy, and good will toward everyone.

"Guests ask us if we miss our islands, if we ever get homesick for our flowers, waterfalls, mountains and rolling waves. I tell them that we bring the islands with us in our songs, in our dances and especially in our spirit of aloha – the gift of the islands to all who enjoy life."

On April 20 2007, Kau'i returned briefly to Hawaii to receive the prestigious Duke's Ho'okahiko award presented by the Duke's Waikiki restaurant to an individual who exemplifies the finest traditions of Hawaii. She was able to spend time reuniting with people she had not seen in fifty years.

Another Disney cast member, Rose Monahan, accompanied the elderly treasure. Monahan dances with Kau'i at the nonprofit organization Kau'i started called "Na'o piopio I Orlando" (Children of Orlando) that teaches children for free how to dance the hula and raises money for competitions and costumes.

Monahan stated, "She is an inspiration to everyone. She is truly the definition of aloha, and when you meet her, you fall in love with her. She is welcoming to everyone and teaches everyone to love one another."

DOLE WHIP

A cult following for a soft-serve frozen dessert created by the Dole Food Company known as Dole Whip has created such a frenzy in Disney theme park fans that many suspect that the treat is only available at Disney. It is not.

Of course, it has been served for decades at the Dole Plantation three miles north of Wahiawa, Hawaii but in recent years thanks to the ease in creating it, a variety of popular venues now offer it from sporting events to zoos to state fairs and other amusement venues. Outside of Disney, vendors are strongly encouraged to use the term Dole Soft Serve instead of Dole Whip.

"Disney has literally created Dole Whip devotees," stated Jamie Schwartz of Kent Precision Foods Group that licenses the product. "Disney built [up] the brand."

When Walt Disney's Enchanted Tiki Room opened in June 1963, it was sponsored by United Airlines promoting its flights to Hawaii. In 1976, the Dole Food Company took over sponsorship and opened up a food and beverage stand at the entrance to the attraction called the Tiki Bar.

Disneyland's Concept Manager of Food Operations Karlos Siqueiros who has worked at Disneyland for over thirty years recalled that in the beginning the little stand only sold pineapple juice and pineapple spears. "Pineapple juice had always been served at the tiki stand, but we didn't have anything to add to it literally until the Dole Whip came in."

The soft-serve pineapple dessert can also be purchased as a "float" with pineapple juice or as a swirl of pineapple and vanilla. While most Disney fans associate the term "Dole Whip" with pineapple soft serve, it also comes in several other flavors like orange, strawberry, lemon, raspberry and mango.

In 1997, Kent Precision Foods Group in St. Louis, Missouri began to license the Dole Whip product. While it used to contain a dairy derivative, in 2013 the formula was changed and it became certified as vegan and gluten free. They sell the Dole Whip Mix which is a dry powder online. To make it just like at Disney, all that needs to happen is to add water and pour it into a home soft serve ice cream machine.

It is estimated that conservatively park guests at Disneyland and Walt Disney World consume 1.4 million Dole Whips each year. (Disneyland consumes a minimum of 600,000). It is not served at any of the other Disney theme parks worldwide. At the Aulani Resort in Hawaii, it is offered at the Lava Shack.

At WDW, it can be found at Aloha Isle, located outside of the Enchanted Tiki Room in Adventureland and at Pineapple Lanai just outside the back of the Great Ceremonial House at the Polynesian Village Resort.

Starting in 2013, the Pineapple Promenade Booth at the Flower and Garden Festival sold Dole Whip where guests could order it with Siesta

Key Spice Rum. Subsequent years had the option for including Coconut Rum and Sammy's Beach Bar Red Head Macadamia Nut-flavored Rum. An alcoholic version with dark rum or coconut rum can also be purchased at Tamu Tamu restaurant in Disney's Animal Kingdom.

Kent Precision Foods explains it as such: "Dole Soft Serve Mix is a lactose-free dry mix that is reconstituted with tap water and frozen down in a soft serve machine. Marketed under the popular Dole brand name, this unique product delivers an intense, natural pineapple fruit flavor, yet is fat free and cholesterol free.

"Although the Dole Food Company originally created the Dole Whip soft serve mix, they licensed the brand to Kent Precision Foods Group who now has an exclusive agreement."

TRADER SAM'S GROG GROTTO

Trader Sam's Grog Grotto opened in April 2015 as part of the rehab of the Polynesian Village Resort. The new bar was the work of former Imagineer Brandon Kleyla, now a member of Universal Creative, who was also responsible for Trader Sam's Enchanted Tiki Bar that opened at the Disneyland Hotel in Anaheim in May 2011.

The character of Trader Sam is a cannibal salesman prominently located near the end of the iconic Jungle Cruise attraction since Disneyland opened in 1955. He is the "head salesman" of the jungle, trying to get ahead by offering two of his shrunken heads for "one of yours" because "his business is shrinking".

Kleyla prefers that they be called "explorer's bars" because they incorporate so many different Disney adventure elements like the mythology of Indiana Jones and *20,000 Leagues Under the Sea*.

As Kleyla told me when I interviewed him in 2019, "Anaheim Trader Sam is the true Trader Sam. This came up several times when we started working on the Florida Trader Sam's. At one point it came up to remove the Marc Davis Sam from the Jungle Cruise attraction and replace him with Anaheim Sam, which I think the majority of us opposed.

"So I simply came up with the fact that the Florida Sam is Anaheim Sam's cousin, and he runs the east coast. Simple and we get the best of both. And I concreted that idea by creating a black and white photo of the two of them standing together and posted it on the wall.

"Sam's expertise in head-shrinking potions grew into an interest in mixology. Bitten by the bartending bug (just one of thousands he's been bitten by), Sam sailed the Seven Seas. Countless tropical locales were explored for mystical ingredients to mix into his delectable libations.

"Along the way, he picked up many of trinkets and artifacts that you see around here. In the tiki bar business, it's a jungle out there.

But once Trader Sam began serving his exotic elixirs to his guests, the word really spread!"

The Enchanted Tiki Bar in Anaheim is set during the time period of 1930-1950 while the Grog Grotto reflects 1950-1970. It includes more elements of the extinct Magic Kingdom *20,000 Leagues Under the Sea* attraction because that was an iconic Walt Disney World ride.

THE BOU-TIKI SHOP

Connie Blowe who was Manager of Retail Sales for the resort when the Bou Tiki shop first opened said, "All of the tikis were hand-carved in Bali and we're all proud of the natural finishes and level of detail in the shop. The project team had a lot of fun choosing a name for the shop. We had several to choose from and we decided on Bou Tiki because it's a play on the word 'boutique'."

Walt Disney Imagineering created a storyline of a group of mischievous tikis who magically awaken from their slumber during the day and decide to frolic at night causing chaos in the shop.

These naughty tikis rearrange tables and racks, play with the shop's offerings, pose with new hats and shirts and send the postcard rack spinning. They are unexpectedly caught in the act of this mischief when the morning comes and they are frozen wherever they have been playing. They might have been trying to hide merchandise, push carts and more while disrupting the area.

One is caught looking through a window, another has a finger to its mouth to try to encourage Guests to keep the secret of their behavior and yet another has eleven triangle-shaped teeth broadly displayed. WDI managed the project, including the fabrication of fixtures and theme elements.

Murray Forester, Publisher and Editor of the magazine Chain Store Age described the shop as "an exotically themed design drawn from Polynesian culture that updates the main lobby gift shop at Disney's Polynesian Resort, marrying its theme with the other shops in the resort.

"Intricate, authentic Polynesian textures and details give the 5,100 square foot shop a unique ambience. Eight-foot-tall tiki statues, hand-carved in Bali, add authenticity and an underlying character story to the shopping experience. Merbau hardwood flooring, bamboo surfaces, shells, carpet resembling silver moonlit beaches and hand-woven and painted wall-coverings inspired by authentic Polynesian culture work together to engage Guests in a fun, fantastical experience that is pure Disney."

Fort Wilderness Resort & Campground

November 1971

Walt Disney's original 1966 sketch for the Florida property included a campground to the right of where the park and hotels would be located.

Near Disneyland, there was a very popular Vacationland RV campground that people driving by the park often saw off of West Street. It was part of the Disneyland Hotel and highly successful.

Besides 280 spaces for travel trailers, motor homes, pick-up campers, and tent trailers, the location had a large recreation hall, a heated and filtered swimming pool, children's playground, sanitation stations with showers, convenience store, a large laundry room with coin-operated washers and dryers and many more amenities.

Next door to Vacationland was a Kampgrounds of America (KOA) location that was not part of the Disneyland Hotel but also offered spaces for campers.

Walt felt that a similar campground would not only take advantage of the natural wilderness on the property but also provide less expensive accommodations for those wanting to visit. In addition, he realized that many tourists had previously traveled to enjoy Florida in similar vehicles to vacation and visit roadside attractions.

As building began on the land, a location had been selected for the Disney campground but all the attention was on getting everything else like the park and the resorts ready for the opening. The campground was considered low priority.

Disney executive Dick Nunis received an unexpected phone call one day from Disney CEO Card Walker in California asking how the campground was coming along. Nunis assigned Keith Kambak to research existing campgrounds, make recommendations on best practices and then help design and build it.

Work on clearing the land for the campground did not begin until spring 1971 and money, staff and equipment were severely limited because everything was devoted to finishing the park and the two resort hotels by the October first deadline.

Eventually, Nunis had to even pull the construction workers away from the campgrounds to finish the park and hotels which is why the campground did not open until November 19, 1971, roughly a month and a half after the rest of the vacation destination.

Fort Wilderness (named after the fort on Tom Sawyer Island at Disneyland Park) was larger than most campgrounds around the country, so trams, bicycles and busses provided guests with transportation options to get where they needed to go around the area.

Guests were forbidden from driving their own cars to locations inside the campground itself because of lack of parking, even if they just needed to go to the Trading Post to quickly pick up something.

From the very beginning, there were plans for a "campground railroad" to provide transportation and add to the rustic "theming" of the area, but it was not considered a priority, so it did not debut with the opening of the resort and didn't appear until 1974. When it did, it made Fort Wilderness Resort & Campground the only Disney resort hotel that ever had an actual ticketed attraction.

A clever example of re-using existing assets to save money for the resort was demonstrated by installing trash cans designed to look like tree stumps that had previously been used at the Indian Village area at Disneyland before being shipped to Fort Wilderness.

Advertisements proclaimed, "The natural beauty of a Florida cypress and pine forest has been preserved at Fort Wilderness on the shores of Bay Lake. The campsites....more than 400 in number...accommodate trailers, campers, tents, and motor homes. Each site is fully equipped with electrical outlets, charcoal fireplace, water, picnic table, and sanitary disposal system.

"Comfort stations provide private showers, telephones, laundry facilities and restrooms. The Fort Wilderness Trading Post offers complete camping and food supplies. Complimentary transportation is provided to the Magic Kingdom, and other areas in Walt Disney World.

"Guests can travel inside the camping area on the Yellowstone Wagons which make regular stops at the recreation areas. Each night there are special activities for Fort Wilderness guests including nature films and campfire programs.

"Nearby at the Tri-Circle-D Ranch, guests can take a wilderness ride by horseback in the surrounding forests."

Recreation options included swimming, sailing, water-skiing, recreational watercraft, canoe excursions, fishing, bicycling, volleyball, horseshoes, archery, nature hikes, campfire programs, and a playground.

Tri-Circle D refers to the three circles that make the famous Mickey Mouse head silhouette and, of course, "D" stands for "Disney."

Some Disney fans get confused and think the name refers to the ranch in the *The Adventures of Spin and Marty* serials for the original

Mickey Mouse Club television show. That ranch was actually called the "Triple R."

The Tri-Circle-D Ranch had two sections that were located roughly a mile apart. Horseback riding took place at the Trail Blaze Corral located just inside the main entrance next to the Outpost area. Guests could take the reins for a 45-minute guided trail ride through the resort.

The remaining Tri-Circle-D Ranch areas with the Draft Horse Barn, Blacksmith Shop, Carriage Rides and Pony Rides (the ponies are adults and weigh on average 500 pounds; pony riders have to weigh less than 80 pounds and be under 48 inches tall) were located at the Settlement area, next to where Pioneer Hall is today at the rear of the Campground.

The Tri-Circle-D's roots trace back to a man named Owen Pope. Pope made the first harnesses for the horses at Walt Disney World when he was living in and working at the Pony Farm in Disneyland. At the Magic Kingdom, a window on the Car Barn proclaims "Owen Pope. Harness Maker."

Owen Pope and his wife Dolly made their living exhibiting horses. In 1950, at the suggestion of Imagineer Harper Goff, Walt Disney caught one of their shows at the Pan Pacific Auditorium in Los Angeles.

He was especially impressed by their galloping small ponies that pulled a miniature stagecoach (built by Pope himself) around the arena at breakneck speed. In March 1951, Walt asked them if they would be interested in training horses for Disneyland.

A week after Thanksgiving that year, Pope moved his 30-foot long trailer onto the Disney Studio lot. The Popes became the only people to ever live at the Disney Studio in Burbank, California, where they built ten stalls for the horses. The Popes stayed at the Studio for about two-and-a-half years, with Walt visiting them every day to ask questions.

Once the horses were moved to Disneyland, Owen trained the horses to get used to the expected crowd noise and gunshots (due to the shooting galleries) by setting up loudspeakers cranked up to the highest volume.

In addition, Pope supervised the building of Frontierland vehicles like the stagecoach and Conestoga wagon. As work was beginning on the construction of Disneyland, one of the houses on the land was moved to a 10-acre location behind Fantasyland dubbed the "Pony Farm" (known as the "Circle D Corral" since 1980). The house had belonged to the Witherills who were walnut growers on Harbor Boulevard.

The Popes moved into the house three days before the opening of Disneyland and were the first and only people who actually resided in Disneyland. At one time, the stray dog that was the live-action reference model for Tramp (from the 1955 animated film *Lady and the Tramp*) lived with them as well.

In January 1971, Pope and his wife moved to Florida, where Owen helped supervise the building of the Tri-Circle-D Ranch and the training of the horses. The Pope House at Disneyland became the administration offices for the Pony Farm. It was relocated to a parking lot off of Ball Road in 2016 to make room for the Star Wars: Galaxy Edge expansion.

An authentic example of one of those original 1971 antique harnesses by Pope was on display at the Draft Horse Barn at the ranch in a small one-room museum called "Walt Disney Horses," devoted to Walt Disney's love of horses. Another was showcased in the Car Barn on Main Street at the Magic Kingdom.

The Popes retired in 1975, but continued to visit at least once a year until their deaths. Actually, when Dolly retired in September 1975, she became the first Walt Disney World cast member to ever retire. Owen retired in October 1975 and died in 2000 at the age 96. Dolly died in 2003 at age 89.

Generally, 80-90 horses are maintained at the ranch. Roughly 30 of them are draft horses, which can get to be 18 hands tall (or 72 inches). They weigh approximately 2,000 pounds each.

The horses that are chosen to work in the Disney parks go through a probation process, during which they are observed as to how they interact and whether they are comfortable around people and activity.

The staff at the ranch (approximately 30-35 cast members) names the animals. One horse was black and white and they wanted to name him "Mickey" but had to settle for calling him "Oliver," from the animated feature *Oliver and Company* (1988).

When Walt Disney World opened, there were four horse-drawn trolleys and it cost a dime or an "A" ticket to go one way either up or down the street.

The horses that pull the trolleys on Main Street U.S.A. at the Magic Kingdom no longer wear plastic shoes as they once did. They are shoed on the front and barefoot on the back and that is done to help prevent slipping. Mineral oil is put on the hoofs to prevent wear and tear.

While the trolley is heavy, especially loaded with guests at about 4,000 pounds, it is so well balanced that once it gets moving, it takes only minimal effort (now weighing closer to 100 pounds). That's one of the reasons that Disney has started to grease the track just outside the car barn to help it get started.

Today only one operates and soon after the 1 p.m. trolley show (that was first performed in 2002) it is pulled off the street to avoid congestion because of the parades and crowds.

The chrome and brass on the show harness for the trolley horse is cleaned and polished every day it is used. The carriage harnesses are wet down as needed during the week before a cleaning.

The horses are now considered service animals, so guests are asked not to pet them without supervision. Horses are naturally curious animals so fingers too close to a mouth sometimes are reminiscent of carrots so the horses may want to take a nibble to find out.

Also, while the horses enjoy the attention and petting, too much can be overwhelming at times, so cast members have tried to be considerate of that fact.

An outside veterinarian visits every Thursday, which is why guests might find the area at the barn blocked at that time.

Guests sometimes misunderstand behavior about the horses. For instance if a horse is drooling, he is not uncomfortable. A well-hydrated bit lubricates the mouth causing that drool.

What is a day like for a Main Street horse? They are fed and bathed in the morning. Around 8 a.m. they are loaded into a trailer and taken to backstage Main Street U.S.A. where they are put in harness and hooked and ready to go by 9 a.m.

They are kept inside the Car Barn during the "Welcome Show" at the front of the train station because of the noise and pyrotechnics and then brought out just as the guests enter the park.

They have gone through a lengthy training program, including being introduced to the music. The next step is to be introduced to the costumed characters backstage to get used to seeing a five foot tall mouse. Then, they are put in the stall in the Car Barn so they can watch the parade and other activity.

The horses are part of Disney's AZA accredited Animal Programs department, the same one that oversees animal care at Disney Animal Kingdom and Living Seas with Nemo and Friends. The manager is now the manager of the horses at the Disneyland Resort, Walt Disney World Resort and Disneyland Paris, so there is consistency.

The manager loves Clydesdales, which is why they were introduced to Walt Disney World. In the past, there were reasons for not using them, including some concerns about temperament, the larger proportionate size and the fact that they were most commonly associated with Anheuser-Busch (Budweiser) who were operating competing entertainment venues like Busch Gardens. That official connection ended when InBev sold off its amusement parks in 2009.

Did you know you can adopt a Walt Disney World horse when it retires? There is an application process that is intensely scrutinized and the waiting list is very long. Disney is very particular who the horses go to, including investigating whether the person is financially capable of taking care of the animal, and Disney will take back horses if they find out that the horses are not being well treated.

When the Disney Cruise started, there was discussion of having horses on Castaway Cay for trail rides but it was decided that it would become an issue if the horses needed to be evacuated from the island. Horses can swim but not for great distances.

Stories of Fort Wilderness Campground

FORT WILDERNESS RAILROAD

From the beginning, there were plans for a "campground railroad" to provide transportation and add to the rustic "theming" of the area, but it was not a priority, so it did not debut with the opening of the resort.

The railroad was not solely for transportation because free trams and buses continued to operate even after it was in operation. The railroad was considered a ticketed Disney attraction, and was promoted accordingly on marketing material, charging guests a minimal fee to use it when it officially opened in January 1974.

It lasted roughly six years and one month, and images of it in operation appeared on magazines, guides and posters.

The railroad consisted of four steam trains, each pulling five cars, around a circular route through the campground at a maximum speed of ten miles an hour. Each engine ran on steam and used diesel fuel to stoke the fire. The track was approximately twice the length of the track at the Magic Kingdom Park.

This strikingly beautiful train was decorated in a strong color palette of forest green, red and gold. Imagineer Bob McDonnell created that color scheme along with the distinctive logo, detailing and the attraction poster.

A single train was roughly about 150 feet long and could seat up to 90 guests.

The trains were smaller than the ones at the Magic Kingdom and were based on the traditional Baldwin "plantation locomotives" popular in the Hawaiian Islands, where they were used to haul material like sugar cane and pineapples through the jungles to market.

The railroad used a smaller gauge track (30 inches between the rails on the track) than at the Magic Kingdom (36 inches) which may have influenced people into thinking that the train itself was scaled smaller. The engine was full sized, not the 4/5th scale usually cited, but it was smaller than the engines operating at the Magic Kingdom.

Smaller gauge was common for railroads used in logging because it helped negotiate tighter curves easier just like the narrow turns at

Fort Wilderness. So, the smaller gauge and smaller size of the engines gave the illusion of the railroad being smaller than a "real" railroad when, in fact, it was indeed full size for the type of railroad it was.

Unlike every other Disney train (even the ones operating on Big Thunder Mountain Railroad), none of the engines were ever named. They were only numbered, and each of the four engines had a distinctive icon on the headlamps: elk, bison, deer and ram.

During 1972, the locomotives were built in Glendale, California, by WED (Imaginering) and its manufacturing arm, MAPO, at a reported cost of more than $1 million. Simultaneously, Buena Vista Construction was installing the track at the campground.

While at the time it was assumed that this was done to save time (like the building of hotel rooms being done separately from the construction of the framework for the Contemporary Resort), later research has confirmed that this was merely a cost-saving effort.

Buena Vista Construction had no experience in laying track, which caused major problems that eventually led to the death of the railroad.

Lack of gauge rods and tie plates, incorrect placement of ballast, rails not curved with a rail-bender, and the wrong size rail immediately caused operational problems that continued to plague the running of the railroad during all of its existence.

"The money spent putting the track in was minimal," Imagineer Bob Harpur, who was the railroad technical foreman in Florida, told historian and author Michael Broggie. "The roadbed wasn't properly prepared. We had trouble maintaining the track. The locomotives were sensitive. Other than that, they ran fine."

Roundhouse foreman George Britton and his crew tried to fix some of these issues from January 1976 to May 1976 before the opening of River Country, but, despite their efforts, the basic problems still remained, because the money was not available to completely re-do the entire track correctly, just some "quick fixes."

All that could be accomplished were some adjustments to try to address some of the more obvious issues that continued to reoccur.

The trains were shipped by flatbed trucks to WDW during the spring of 1973 and went through a trial and adjustment period, during which guests were sometimes able to ride the trains. By late November, the trains started running on a fairly regular schedule in what was considered a "soft opening."

The official opening and dedication ceremony was January 1, 1974. Mickey and Goofy, along with the WDW Ambassador, drove a "golden spike" into the rails to declare the train line operational for all guests.

Originally, the train was free for guests staying at Fort Wilderness with others (including guests staying at other WDW resorts) being charged fifty cents per day (two cents of that was for taxes). That fee increased in later years to a full dollar.

In the beginning, the train ran from 8 a.m. to 9 p.m. everyday causing some complaints from guests who disliked the fact that at all the grade crossings the extremely loud whistle would sound. Eventually, the trains would cease operation around 5 p.m. eliminating that problem.

In 1974, Pioneer Hall (with the Hoop-Dee-Doo Musical Revue) and Treasure Island (later to become the bird sanctuary Discovery Island) opened, increasing guest traffic at Fort Wilderness.

However, the heyday of the railroad was the opening of River Country in May 1976, where the train became the favored mode of transportation.

The railroad ran three trains at the same time and, during the busy times in the morning and afternoon, added a fourth train. At one point, the Disney Company tried adding an additional sixth car to each train to increase capacity, but with all trains operating that addition was quickly abandoned as unnecessary.

New cast members were added to help operate the four trains. Six full days of training were devoted to each new cast member, often running into the evening hours. Running a railroad was much more complex than operating the typical amusement rides.

While the first female fireman on the Disneyland railroad did not appear until the 1990s, roughly half of the crew members of the Fort Wilderness Railroad were women in the 1970s. They proved themselves to be more reliable and diligent than some of their male counterparts.

With the opening of River Country, a new addition did have to be made to the train cars: rubber floors, because of the dripping wet guests who had enjoyed Disney's first water park.

Why did the railroad close in February 1980? Over the years, in lieu of the Walt Disney Company giving an official explanation or even an official closing date (the railroad was just put on "hiatus"), there were many speculations.

Some claimed that safety was an issue and that the nearness of the tracks to the guests made Disney Legal fearful. Some claimed that the train produced too much noise and it disturbed guests. Some claimed that there were challenges with the engines that required constant refilling with water. Some claimed that it was just too expensive to operate and could never recover its costs.

The bottom line is that since the track was not laid correctly in the first place that even with attempts to make adjustments, the basic problem still existed that could not be overcome.

Literally, the entire length of track needed to be re-laid correctly and the estimated price tag for this work was over three million dollars. At one point, the Disney Company looked to General Electric as a possible corporate sponsor to help defray all or most of the estimated cost.

Dick Nunis, who was in charge of WDW, loved the railroad and made every attempt to try to save it by trying to manage costs.

In the early 1980s, he brought out to Florida the Nature's Wonderland trains from Disneyland Park that were no longer in use because they have been removed to make way for the Big Thunder Mountain Railroad.

These were battery powered so would save fuel costs and had proven dependability. Unfortunately, the train was much too slow on its trial run around the campground and the plan was abandoned.

The Fort Wilderness Railroad almost came to life again in 1992 with the announcement of the building of Buffalo Junction (sometimes referred to as Wilderness Junction). There were plans to connect Fort Wilderness, Wilderness Lodge and the new Buffalo Junction with a small operating railroad.

After years of being outside and subjected to Florida heat and humidity, the engines and the coach cars were sold off to private collectors who restored them. All of the engines are now in California. Former Disney Executive John Lasseter has an engine and a couple of coach cars in his backyard railroad in Northern California.

Two of the coach cars were modified and placed temporarily at the entrance of Pleasure Island as ticket booths, one of those coaches is now at the front of Typhoon Lagoon, and the other was auctioned off. Four of the cars and 3,000 feet of track were donated to the Brevard Zoo in Melbourne, Florida, but over the years those coaches found other homes.

The look of the Fort Wilderness Railroad coach cars inspired the street cars for Disneyland Paris designed by Imagineer Bob Harpur.

THE DRAGON CALLIOPE

For the 1955 Mickey Mouse Club Circus parade at Disneyland, Walt Disney purchased some authentic turn-of-the-century circus wagons and very carefully restored them. In fact, anything removed from a wagon during the restoration, Walt had preserved.

Walt purchased nine authentic circus wagons from Dave Bradley who was using them as decorations outside the entrance to his kiddie park, the Beverly Park Amusement Center at the corner of Beverly and La Cienga in Los Angeles where Walt would take his young daughters on Sunday outings. In this purchase was a 1907 twenty whistle steam calliope that was in disrepair.

Its first appearance was in the Mugivan and Bowers shows in England, circa 1907, after which it was sold to Ken Maynard's Diamond K Circus in 1936. At a cost of $50,000, Disney redesigned the calliope to resemble the others in the collection, and adorned its wagon with decorative pieces from some of Disney's other circus wagons transforming it into the Dragon Calliope.

Take a close look at the calliope car behind the engine of Disneyland's Casey Jr. train. The dragon is an exact re-creation of the one on the calliope since it is a circus train.

Many of the circus wagons, as well as the calliope, appear in the Disney live-action film, *Toby Tyler or Ten Weeks With a Circus* (1960).

Starring young Kevin Corcoran and based on the well known novel of the same name by James Otis Kaler, the film recounts a young boy running away to work in a circus and becoming a circus star after befriending a mischievous chimp.

The film's world premiere was held January 21, 1960, at the Florida Theater in Sarasota, Florida, the winter home of the Ringling Brothers and Barnum & Bailey Circus (now owned and operated by Feld Entertainment, who also produce the *Disney on Ice* shows).

Just as the parade and the credits are ending in the movie, the Dragon Calliope comes in to view, followed by the eager Toby Tyler, as music and steam billow from the colorful wagon.

In 1962, Walt would donate the wagons (including the pieces that had been removed) to the Circus World Museum in Baraboo, Wisconsin, where they are taken care of and displayed to this day. However, he kept the Dragon Calliope.

Besides being part of the short-lived Mickey Mouse Club Circus parade, the calliope went on to appear in many Disneyland parades through the park's 25th anniversary.

It was repainted silver and blue and pulled by six black Percheron horses the following year when it was relocated to Florida for the Walt Disney World Tencennial celebration in 1981. Since then, it was seen in numerous parades at Walt Disney World, including several Christmas broadcasts until it was retired from parade duty.

One of the last times the Dragon Calliope was used publicly was January 2, 2007 in Tallahassee, Florida where Mickey and Minnie Mouse were participants in the inaugural parade for newly-sworn in governor, Charlie Crist. Mickey and Minnie in the calliope were pulled by a team of eight black Percheron horses.

It is still maintained and appeared in July 2013 as part of the Limited Time Magic promotion on Main Street at the Magic Kingdom.

The Tri-Circle-D Ranch at the Fort Wilderness Resort and Campground at Walt Disney World is now the home for the famous

Dragon Calliope. It is easily accessible to be viewed behind plexiglass by guests and it is free to do so. It is even rigged so that by pushing a button, it briefly plays a tune.

It is located near another free hidden treasure, a small exhibit, named "Walt Disney Horses" dedicated to Walt's love of horses and to the different roles horses perform at Walt Disney World.

RIVER COUNTRY

"River Country! Big River Country.
It's a hoot. It's a holler! It's a water jamboree!
River Country. Big River Country.
If you're hot around the collar it's the cool place to be!"

That is the opening verse of a 1977 song written about a forgotten Walt Disney World popular attraction.

Walt Disney World defined the concept of a themed water park with the opening of Disney's River Country on June 20, 1976 as part of the Fort Wilderness Resort on the shore of Bay Lake.

Originally, this water park was going to be called "Pop's Willow Grove" and was meant to be reminiscent of "an old fishing hole" from the time period of Tom Sawyer and Huck Finn with items like rope swings enhancing that story.

River Country was about one-fourth the size of Typhoon Lagoon since the Walt Disney Company had no idea whether such a then radical idea would be successful.

Attractions included a 330,000 gallon clear water pool called Upstream Plunge, Slippery Slide Falls, two sixteen foot rock slides with faux rock work (scattered with pebbles from streambeds in Georgia and the Carolinas) done by Imagineer Fred Joerger who did rock work on everything from the Jungle Cruise's Schweitzer Falls to Big Thunder Mountain, and the Ol' Swimmin' Hole dedicated by President Gerald Ford's daughter, Susan.

The Ol' Swimmin' Hole had Whoop-n-Holler Hollow, two long winding chutes that ended with a splashing entry into the water.

Water from nearby Bay Lake was pumped through the inside of River Country's artificial mountain to the top of the flumes and raft ride at the rate of 8,500 gallons a minute and then eventually through the miracle of gravity spilled back into the lake.

There was a natural soft sand beach underfoot the massive pool rather than a concrete bottom which was a unique innovation at the time.

Even with the filtration system, the water from the lake was not completely purified and that caused some red flags for Disney Legal.

Its huge popularity resulted in many sold out days since the Walt Disney World water park had limited capacity. It became apparent that a larger water park facility was needed but it took just over a decade for it to become a reality.

Typhoon Lagoon opened on June 1, 1989 just across the street from the newly built Pleasure Island and was home to the world's largest outdoor surf pool (not just a wave pool). That new water park also proved popular so in 1995, Blizzard Beach was opened to accommodate the demand.

These new options led to a drop in attendance at the more difficult to access River Country. In 1998, the water park tried to compete with the "All-American Water Party" promotion where every day was celebrated as the Fourth of July with games, Disney characters in country costumes, live country music and good old fashioned barbeque.

In September 2001, River Country quietly closed at the end of the summer season and never re-opened. In 2002, Walt Disney World spokesman Bill Warren told the *Orlando Sentinel* newspaper that River Country could be reopened if 'there's enough guest demand".

Supposedly, River Country could not claim the honor of being America's first water park, a designation given to Wet and Wild that opened in 1977, because it was considered not a separate park but an extension of the resort.

HOOP-DEE-DOO MUSICAL REVUE

"Whoop-de-doo", and its variant "hoop-de-doo", is an old-fashioned expression meaning frenzied activity or excitement. That phrase became the cornerstone of one of Walt Disney World's most beloved nighttime entertainment experiences, the Hoop-Dee-Doo Musical Revue.

The show opened June 14, 1974, and continues to be performed in Pioneer Hall at the Fort Wilderness Resort and Campground to this day.

It was inspired by the success of the South Seas Luau at the Polynesian Village Resort and the need to find a project for the Walt Disney World Fine Arts College Workshop that supplied an inexpensive and eager cast for the new show.

The musical was developed by Robert Jani, Ron Miziker, Tom Adair, Paul Suter and Larry Billman. It was a highly collaborative effort, including contributions from the original performers as well. Billman was the director and Forrest Bahruth was the choreographer.

The premise of the show is that a stagecoach of performers on their way to another engagement (and an actual stagecoach used to be positioned outside of Pioneer Hall to support that storyline) had broken down.

They come inside the dining hall to entertain while their stagecoach is being repaired and the guests enjoy an all-you-can-eat meal of fried chicken, ribs, strawberry shortcake and more between the corn-pone vaudeville acts.

When Pioneer Hall officially opened April 1, 1974, it was called the Fort Wilderness Dining Hall. The area was intended to be used as a dining venue for breakfast and lunch as an extension of the adjacent Trail's End restaurant.

The original plans were that at night there would be animal lectures and demonstrations from animals brought over from nearby Discovery Island. Guests would also be able to play games and perhaps enjoy some musical talent like a washboard band.

In addition, a huge screen would show some of the True-Life Adventures documentary films made by the Disney Studio in the 1950s and 1960s.

Built with 1,283 hand-fitted Western white pine logs from Montana and 70 tons of rare ebony stone for pillars from North Carolina, the two-story building was modeled after a Northwest Territory Lodge from the late 1800s.

Walt Disney World had no expectations for the show other than trying to temporarily fill an operational need. In fact, many people involved in the show felt it would be cancelled in the first few weeks or simply cancelled after its initial eleven weeks when the students returned to school.

By the end of summer, it was such an unqualified success that the roles were staffed with professional performers beginning September 5, 1974.

Over the years, a few changes have been made in the original show. For instance, in the beginning and until 1979, it was apple pie and not strawberry shortcake that was served as dessert. As a result the song *Apple Pie Hoedown* was replaced with *Strawberry Short Cake Walk*.

However, the most significant change happened in 2011. The song *Hoop-Dee-Doo* (sometimes called the *Hoop-Dee-Doo Polka*) used in the show was composed by Milton DeLugg with lyrics by Frank Loesser, and was first published in 1950. When the song was used in the Hoop-Dee-Doo Revue, the lyrics were rewritten to reflect the show, but the upbeat tune remained intact.

The only problem was that in the rush to put together a temporary patchwork show, it had not occurred to anyone at Disney to get proper clearance for the use of the song. When the situation came to light, during the late summer of 2011, the popular theme song was replaced with one written specifically for Disney that still included the phrase Hoop-De-Doo.

DISCOVERY ISLAND

The Walt Disney Company bought Riles Island in Bay Lake in 1965 along with some surrounding property. Originally Walt intended it to be called Blackbeard's Island to theme in with the upcoming movie *Blackbeard's Ghost* (1968).

In early 1973, the Disney Company announced that the island would be named "Treasure Island" after the 1950 Disney live action feature film and would have walkways, small lakes and waterfalls available to "explorers and picnickers."

There were plans to build Ben Gunn's fort, Benbow Inn and the wreck of the ship *Hispaniola*, as well as other physical aspects from the film and novel. There would be nearly 600 real and rare tropical birds on the island.

On April 8, 1974, after the Walt Disney Company used 15,000 cubic yards of soil and 500 tons of boulders and 500 tons of trees to transform the landscape, "Treasure Island" opened to the public. It was a sanctuary for dozens of birds, reptiles, mammals and other non-avian species.

There was also a beached ship, but not the *Hispaniola*. It was the remains of Captain Flint's ship, the *Walrus* according to the original map.

That early Walt Disney World map of the island for guests proclaimed: "Sail the Seven Seas of Walt Disney World to an island filled with tropic beauty, colorful birds, and the mystery of Ben Gunn's buried treasure!" Cast members wore appropriately themed pirate wardrobe and the name of locations around the island included Jolly Roger Wharf, Buccaneer's Cove, Doubloon Lagoon, Mutineer Falls, Skeleton Island, Black Dog Swamp, Scavenger Beach, Rum Point and the Mizzen Mast.

The reverse side of the tri-fold map claimed that some of the future attractions would include:

- Billy Bones's Dilemma: Captain Flint's first mate falls prey to the perils of the open sea.
- The Blockhouse: Site of the battle for the treasure map. "Though fully armed... we were still out-numbered by Long John Silver's buccaneers!"
- Spy Glass Hill: A fantastic group of rocks in the heart of the island. In this primeval playground, you'll discover the secrets of this treasure isle!
- Ben Gunn's Cave: As mysterious as the strange hermit himself. Its exact location is unknown even today... but we know it's someplace on the island!

- Wreck of the *Hispaniola*: This seagoing vessel led by Captain Smollet, once anchored here in search of buried treasure... only to be overtaken by her mutinous crew, headed by the self-appointed captain, Long John Silver! She was later run ashore by the brave young Jim Hawkins... never to sail again!

In some aspects, the island would resemble a more adult version of the iconic Tom Sawyer Island in the Magic Kingdom with plenty of "natural" wonders to explore, as well as a mystery or two to be solved.

The island could be accessed for a half-day experience by either taking a direct motor launch from a resort dock or as part of the Walt Disney World Cruise, a tour of the Seven Seas Lagoon and Bay Lake that stopped at the island.

The pirate theme for the island was eventually abandoned and the island was renamed yet again. It was called Discovery Island roughly three years later, around 1977, and became an official zoological park accredited by the American Association of Zoological Parks and Aquariums.

It closed to the public on April 8, 1999, and during the next three months the wildlife was relocated to Disney's Animal Kingdom in a hub area that was rechristened Discovery Island. Disney claimed that lagging attendance, some maintenance issues and the fact that DAK was better equipped to handle the welfare of the animals contributed to the island's closing.

MINNIE MOO

Mickey Moo, a white Holstein cow with a black Mickey Mouse head silhouette shape naturally occurring on her side, was housed in Big Thunder Ranch at Disneyland's Frontierland in 1988. Mickey Moo was a part of Mickey's 60th birthday celebration that year but became instantly a popular attraction for guests.

The unusual marking on the side of the cow was not quite as unusual as it was originally assumed. A Midwest farmer contacted the Disney Company with photos of his own cow that had the same type of Mickey Mouse silhouette head.

Minnie Moo, the white Holstein with a similar black Mickey Mouse head silhouette, came to the Walt Disney World Resort from Edgerton, Minnesota, in 1990, living first in the Magic Kingdom.

Grandma Duck's Petting Farm operated at Mickey's Birthdayland/ Mickey's Starland from 1988-1996. In 1996, the area was transformed into The Barnstormer at Goofy's Wise Acres Farm.

With this change in the area, Minnie Moo and the other animals were moved to a Petting Farm at the Tri-Circle D Ranch in Disney's Fort Wilderness Resort and Campground. Minnie Moo died in August 2001, at the age of fifteen, a little more than the average lifespan for a cow.

The Disney Company did not release a notice of her death, because John McClintock, the Disney spokesman at the time, said "it was too sensitive" a subject. Just as Disney never officially revealed to guests that the 400-pound spotted grouper named Orson at Epcot's Living Seas pavilion went to the big seafood buffet in the sky.

The animals were sequestered in their pens for the health and safety of both the guests and the animals but were clearly visible.

The petting farm was officially closed early in 2005 with the animals relocated to Disney's Animal Kingdom's Affection Section.

To debunk a Disney Urban Myth, there was only one Minnie Moo (and only one Mickey Moo). Many people claim that there were multiple Minnies over the years, but that is not true. When they died, the Disney Company did not contemplate replacing them.

It was estimated that millions of adults and children visited Minnie Moo, petted her, talked to her and took her photo. She was prominently used in publicity material, although she was occasionally confused with Mickey Moo.

A memorial plaque for Minnie Moo was placed on the wall on the right-hand side in the trophy room (now the Walt Disney Horse Museum room) at the barn at Disney's Fort Wilderness Resort & Campground but was removed quite a few years ago. Below it were photos of some of the animals at the petting zoo, including goats and "Chester" the pig that have also been removed.

"Minnie Moo brought much joy to both our guests and our Cast Members," said Tom Hopkins, animal operations director for Animal Programs, at the time of her death of natural causes. "We will miss her greatly."

The popularity of Mickey Moo and Minnie Moo sparked a short-lived frenzy where the Disney Company was inundated with offers of various animals that had a Mickey Mouse type marking on them, from pigs and dogs to even inanimate objects like potatoes.

In January 1991, Walt Disney World purchased an Iowa pig named Mickey from Tom and Teresa Reuter of Monticello that had three linked black spots that resembled the silhouette of Mickey Mouse's head. They also took a brother piglet with similar markings.

Mickey Pig and Mickey Piglet joined Minnie Moo. Teresa Reuter did say she and her husband wouldn't lose any money by not sending the six month pigs to market, where they would have fetched about $130.

LAWNMOWER TREE

For several decades, a natural wonder delighted guests who came to Fort Wilderness Resort and Campground. Every time guests would visit they would seek out this living curiosity to see how it had changed over the intervening time since their last visit and were always surprised.

Years before Walt Disney World ever opened some one who lived in the area had leaned an old, push-style blade lawnmower up against a tree and left it there. No one seems to know who that person was or why they left the lawnmower there.

The tree grew through the tool so it was absorbed and became part of the tree's gnarled roots above the ground with significant rusting parts sticking out prominently.

When a tree is growing, and it encounters something that gets in the way of its growth, it can do three things: stop growing, grow away from it, or grow around it.

As the area was being developed for the campground, it was discovered by WDW Imagineers who thought it looked interesting and decided to leave it as a hidden treasure curiosity rather than remove it.

It was located just off the sidewalk about five feet from the path about halfway between Pioneer Hall and the marina about a hundred feet off the lake.

The Imagineers even decided to create a back story to explain its existence and integrate it into the lore of the campground. They installed a sign next to it that read:

"Too long did Billy Bowlegs
Park his reel slow mower
Alas, one warm and sunny day
Aside a real fast grower".

So the lawnmower tree was a popular landmark at the resort since its opening in November 1971.

As the decades passed, more and more of the lawnmower disappeared into the tree as it expanded until roughly 2007 when just a few rusting blades were still visible at the foot of the tree.

By then, the tree was dead, either through natural causes or having most of the upper half of the tree cut off. Anyway, only about twelve feet of the trunk remained and the tree had stopped absorbing the remains of the lawnmower.

Disney Legal determined that the rusty remains provided a possible safety hazard since guests sometimes would go up and touch the parts.

The Walt Disney Company hired an outside contractor to quietly remove the tree in late October 2013 without alerting the guests.

The tree was so well known that it was listed in the earliest

Birnbaum Official Guides to Walt Disney World as "a point of interest worth hunting down" and continued to be listed into the 21st Century editions.

The Disney Company itself promoted the lawnmower tree as a "fun fact" on official handouts to the media and it appeared on the earliest campground maps.

ALLIGATOR ATTACK

In 1986, eight-year-old Paul Santamaria was bitten on the leg by a 7-foot-4 inch long female alligator, which had been lurking in the shallows of a pond at Fort Wilderness Resort and Campground.

Two years after the attack, the Santamarias filed a lawsuit claiming that Disney had failed to warn visitors about the alligator, which had been known to seek people out for food after "losing its fear of humans". The suit was settled out of court.

Santamaria now lives in Hebron, New Hampshire and was interviewed by a local ABC affiliate when two year old Lane Graves was taken by an alligator at the Grand Floridan Resort in 2016.

"It was pretty terrifying at the time," said Santamaira. "Under the water, where you couldn't see, there was an alligator."

Santamaria had been watching ducks waddling out of a small pond, located on the grounds of the resort, when he was snatched up by the sharp-toothed creature.

Fortunately for him, his 12-year-old sister and 10-year-old brother were there to save his life.

"Instead of just freezing, they decided to fight, to help me to fight to get away, and I'm here because of it," Santamaria recalled.

"It came out of the water, knocked me down, grabbed my leg and started to throw me around and try to pull me into the water. My sister grabbed me under the arms and started pulling me away from the alligator. My brother started hitting it with whatever he could find and trying to get it to let me go, and with my free leg, I started to kick it and try to get away from it."

While he managed to escape with his life, he was left with large gashes in his leg and a gator tooth lodged in his thigh.

Santamaria added that while it would be wise for Disney to have signs that warn of alligators, people need to remember one thing: that creatures like alligators are commonly found in Florida and small children usually can't read very well.

"It's hard to say what can and can't be done," he explained. "I don't want to paint this as Disney is wrong or the parents are wrong. All I know is that as a child, at eight-years-old, there could have been signs there and I wouldn't have noticed them.

"Children can't read signs or just don't pay attention to them. And parents who are trying to watch their kids might not notice those signs, either. They could have all the signage in the world there, and people could still not notice it.

"While attacks are rare, they do happen and people who live up north don't even think about the possible danger. While it won't affect my decision for bringing my children to Walt Disney World in the future, it will definitely have me more alert of the surroundings."

CROCKETT'S TAVERN

Davy Crockett was a real 19th century American folk hero noted for his life as a frontiersman. In 1954, for his new weekly television show, Walt Disney dramatized the life of Crockett, who was played by actor Fess Parker, in a three episode installment.

Across Walt Disney World, there are American Amusement Machine Association Non-Violent rated Arcade Games that use rechargeable play cards.

At Fort Wilderness Campground, Daniel Boone's Wilderness Arcade is located near the Meadow Swimmin' Pool while Davy Crockett's Wilderness Arcade is over by Pioneer Hall. Both feature a variety of classic and contemporary games.

The finale of the *Hoop-Dee Doo Musical Revue* at Pioneer Hall includes a sketch accompanied by the singing of the famous Disney Davy Crockett theme song.

However, a hidden treasure missed by most guests is Crockett's Tavern. Opened in 1985, it is an extension of the Trail's End restaurant but is only open in the afternoon and early evening. It is a nostalgic full-service bar capturing the spirit of the untamed wilderness of the late 1880s and its famous namesake.

It offers adult beverages like beer and wine as well as a variety of snacks like pizza, nachos, and chicken wings.

The tavern is made of natural wood and glass and while it has indoor seating, many guests prefer the outside covered porch and the oversized rustic rocking chairs.

Dale Moore, Manager of Resort Design, who was given the job for creating the tavern, was a huge Davy Disney Crockett fan, so he included a lot of "Crockettana" for observant fans.

A small replica of the Gully Whumper keel boat from the TV show, and paintings of Fess Parker as Davy and Buddy Ebsen as Davy's friend Georgie Russel can be found, as well as a replica of Crockett's famous rifle, Old Betsy.

An imposingly terrifying stuffed grizzly bear stands next to a glassed-in display featuring the classic 1843 portrait of the real Davy Crockett, a coonskin cap, letters and other items.

The portrait of Andrew Jackson, who Davy served under during the Creek Wars, was painted by Priscilla Russ, a Senior Artist at WDW Marketing. She wanted to do it in dark brown sepia tones to capture a sense of the era but neither acrylics or water colors would resist fading with time.

Even her attempts experimenting with Doc Martin dyes weren't satisfactory, so she ended up creating an ink that had a secret ingredient, coffee grounds, and her likeness of Old Hickory has stood the test of time.

Golf Resort / Disney Inn / Shades of Green

December 1973 / February 1986 / February 1994

The Golf Resort was originally a building located in the middle of the Palm and Magnolia golf courses and was meant as an amenity for golfers using the courses in 1971-72. It was designed with wood and volcanic rock to look like a two-story country clubhouse and did not have any guest rooms.

Guest wings totaling 150 rooms were added in 1973 as part of Walt Disney World's Phase 2 expansion that was also meant to include three other Magic Kingdom resorts that were never built. It retained the name The Golf Resort, but was not generally considered a WDW resort because of its small size and not being on the monorail loop among other things.

Guests preferred staying at the Contemporary Resort or the Polynesian Village Inn resorts, which were often booked to capacity and guests usually only booked The Golf Resort if they couldn't find lodging in those two larger resorts. In February 1986, Disney expanded the resort and renamed it The Disney Inn in hopes of attracting more than just golfers, promoting it as having the intimate and rustic charm of a quiet country inn.

One of the travel brochures described the resort as:

"Tucked away in a quiet corner of the world is an enchanted inn of incomparable delights. The Disney Inn boasts all the luxuries of the more famous Walt Disney World resort accommodations with an equally renowned location minutes from the Magic Kingdom and EPCOT Center.

"In the mood for tennis? Fine dining? A siesta poolside? We've got it all. In fact, we've become the Inn place to stay at the World's Greatest Resort. Just ask any of our guests who return to us again and again."

It was lightly re-themed to *Snow White and the Seven Dwarfs* in hopes of reinforcing the Disney connection. However, the resort still could not match the popularity or attendance of the other WDW resorts.

The U.S. military was looking for a continental America location to build an Armed Forces Recreation Center (AFRC) and surveys showed that Orlando, Florida was the highest-ranking location for its service members.

To Disney's delight because of the declining attendance at the resort, on February 1, 1994, the U.S. Department of Defense leased the entire resort and the land it sits on with a 100-year lease to use for the MWR (Morale, Welfare and Recreation) program and limited the resort to eligible active and retired military personnel.

In 1996, the resort was purchased outright by the DOD for $43 million due to its high popularity and success with the military personnel. Disney still owns the land on which the resort sits. The resort was renamed Shades of Green because, at the time, all military fighting uniforms had some shade of green.

Eligible guests are exclusively active and retired members of the U.S. military, National Guard and Department of Defense as well as their families. Others who are on vacation with an eligible sponsor are also allowed. Room rates are based on rank and pay grade.

The resort was completely remodeled and expanded during 2002-2004. Those renovations by KBJ Architects included a new five story wing featuring an additional 299 rooms, a 500 seat Magnolia Ballroom, a fitness center, pools, tennis courts, new restaurants and dining areas and a new lobby featuring a vaulted ceiling, fireplace and veranda.

The front entrance overlooks a large, natural pool with plants, rockwork and five waterfalls, with each flume representing a branch of the U.S. military.

The architects designed the new building and surrounding area to blend with the existing resort to create the feel of a Floridian lodge. Its new five story parking garage was a first at a WDW resort.

The U.S. military funded the expansion project, coordinating its efforts with Walt Disney Imagineering and Walt Disney World leaders.

Shades of Green guests have full transportation to all Walt Disney World theme parks and attractions. Shades of Green is considered a Disney-owned resort for purposes of Extra Magic Hours/Early Entry Hour at the theme parks.

When I worked as an instructor at the Disney Institute, I became friends with a fellow instructor named Rich Cullen who still works for Walt Disney World today.

Rich worked at the front desk at the Disney Inn for roughly the three years before it closed and he was generous enough to answer some of my questions about the too often forgotten WDW resort and help clear up some of the misinformation that is out there.

Jim Korkis: When did you start at the Disney Inn?

Rich Cullen: I started working there in 1991 and spent almost three years there. I began my Disney career at the Fort Wilderness Resort and Campground front desk and, at that time, Disney resorts had an ancient computer system (Sperry) which was confusing and really not-so-user friendly.

The monitors were huge and the screen was mono-chromatic. When I was trained on them, my trainer, Jim Sator, jokingly said to not get used to Sperry because a whole new system called HRGS was going to be installed at all of the Disney resorts.

It was a huge improvement over Sperry. We pronounced HRGS, "har-guess." My HRGS instructor was Mike Lambert. Great guy. He eventually became a front desk manager at the Disney Inn, so long story short, he brought me over from doing the night audit at Fort Wilderness to working days at the Inn.

JK: What was your role at the Disney Inn?

RC: I worked at The Disney Inn at their check-in front desk. What was cool about working there is that you had a chance to do a little bit of everything. You could do ticket sales/dining reservations at a desk in our lobby. You could also help at dispatch out at the bell stand so some of the staff there could break for lunch.

The resorts at Disney now are so big and compartmentalized that this most likely doesn't happen anymore. Our back office was not big at all. Maybe it was a little larger than our space in the trailer where you and I worked at the Disney Institute, so not big at all. We handled all hotel account practices in the back, as well as "room assignment."

For a while, I worked a lot of graveyard shifts on the front desk. I did the night audit. This is what you did when you were the low-man and were a "Relief Lead." That's how you earned your wings. It wasn't easy working those crazy hours and doing the accounting, etc. I was by myself but there were a few people who made it better.

I used to chat and joke with two of the restaurant managers, Ruben Alvarez and Baha Sidani. Great guys. They let me have all of the cappuccinos I wanted when working the overnights. Also, there was the late Felix Rivera. He was the houseman on third-shift and he would bring me coffee at 3 a.m. or mind the front desk so I could go outside and get some air. Lovely guy. It really is the people that make working at Disney different.

JK: What were the procedures for handling a guest reservation?

RC: For example, two days out, we would look over a computer-printed roster a few times a day and try and weed out duplicate reservations and look for special requests that people might need like a crib, mini-fridge, connecting rooms, smoking/non-smoking rooms, etc.

We would also by hand (!) put together guest ticket packages. This was a project and a half. You might have a family of five with a specific plan. This would include park tickets, dining tickets, recreation tickets, etc. etc. These tickets came in packs like decks of cards in steel strong boxes twice the size of a lunch box. I always joked that they looked like the boxes that Marley's ghost was chained to in Dickens' *A Christmas Carol*.

Whoever was assigned "packages" for that day would set up at a vacant desk in the back and you had to make sure the right tickets went with the right plan. Since the tickets came in packs, like a deck of cards, you also had to date-stamp the tickets for when they expired. They could not be "open-ended." So you could be sitting there trying to figure it all out and putting this all together and whoever was doing it we knew not to disturb them...well, not too much. (*Laughs*)

Whenever any of us were doing this and went to lunch we would just say loudly before we left: "I'm doing packages so don't move anything..." or something to that effect. It was like working on putting a ship in a bottle. It wasn't bad really, but you didn't want to make any mistakes.

Disney then also had what was called "The Gold Key" package/plan. This covered EVERYTHING: Room, meals, park admission, etc. In this case, the guest received a plastic card like a credit card with their name embossed on it and their check-in/check-out dates.

This was a very expensive plan, maybe $4,000 for a week's stay back then. We had the blank stock cards and an embosser where we made up the cards in the back.

At the Inn back then, we started selling ticket media to the hotel guests so they didn't have to bother with a hard ticket. The name for it was "Length of Stay."

So let's say the guest is staying for three nights, if they were interested, we would modify their resort ID card with ticket media.

The guest name for the ticket media was called, "Be Our Guest." Our backstage name for it was "Length of Stay" or "L.O.S." When it started, I would say that most people did not want it only because we sold a "hard" multi-day ticket at our Guest Service desk that was open ended. It didn't expire.

The adult ticket was a blue bar-coded sticker and the kid's ticket was an orange one. Once purchased, they could scan their way into any one of the parks during their visit. That seemed pretty advanced in those days, but seems so ancient today.

Some of the systems at The Inn back then were really not that sophisticated. I was always astounded at how we had to count the ticket boxes to make sure the count was correct, like counting a lot of cash. It was tedious work. We did not have voicemail then. That came much later. So, like in an old movie, a guest would drop by the front desk to see if they had any messages. If someone called for a guest, we had a machine that was like a typewriter/telex.

We would receive a phone message from someone who wanted to leave a message. We would look up the room number to make sure the person was staying with us. We would take down the message, type it in and it would print on a stock that you could fold over and seal it like a letter.

Every hour or so, one of us from the front desk would deliver these messages to the various rooms and slide them under the door. This all seems so quaint now and hard to believe with e-mails and texts today!

JK: Actually it sounds pretty complicated especially having to do everything by hand.

RC: Another thing we did when a guest checked in is that we would ask if they had stayed at The Disney Inn before. Let's say they had stayed there twice before, we would print on their resort I.D. with 'RG 2', meaning 'Return Guest' and the number signifying the number of previous visits.

Those guests were put on a list for their check-in night and, later on in the evening room service would deliver to them a complimentary order of chilled milk and warm Toll House chocolate chip cookies. This was a great "welcome back" touch and it always made an impression.

I think the longest I ever saw the list of returning guests was a dozen names or so for a night, so it wasn't crazy for the kitchen to do this. Anyone who was a VIP received the milk and cookies nightly, as well. With the size of resorts now and the number of people staying there, this would be impossible to do but at the time, it was one of the things that made the Disney Inn feel more intimate, friendly and special.

JK: I had heard that Imagineer John Hench liked staying at the Disney Inn.

RC: My buddy who I worked with, Todd Merrick, is/was a HUGE Disney fan who told me all about John Hench. One day, Todd pointed out Mr. Hench to me in the lobby of the Disney Inn. You know, he really did resemble Walt Disney! There was a likeness. Over the time I worked there, I exchanged small talk with him.

I remember seeing him a couple of times wearing his Disney Imagineer name tag in the center of his shirt. Just clipped on. I thought this was very avant-garde! See, back then, all cast HAD to wear their tags on their upper left.

I also remember him sometimes wearing a blazer and an ascot. Now, not many people can get away with that look, but it suited him. He looked great. He enjoyed staying at the Inn. I once casually asked him why he didn't stay at The Grand Floridian. He mentioned that he liked the quiet atmosphere of The Inn, etc.

Of course, when he stayed there, he received the fresh milk and Toll House cookies nightly. Many years later, I was wandering around the area of Pleasure Island that was being expanded. About 100 yards away, I spotted John Hench touring around with a couple of younger Imagineers, I went up to Mr. Hench and said "hello" and told him that I had worked at the front desk at The Inn some years back.

He brightened up and said, "I sure do miss those milk and cookies!" I thought that was so cool that he remembered that. That was the last time I saw him.

JK: Do you know why the name changed from Golf Resort to The Disney Inn in the 1980s?

RC: It is my understanding that when people heard the name "Golf Resort" they thought they had to be golfers to stay there. The story goes that when the name was changed to The Disney Inn and a Snow White theme was created, occupancy went up significantly.

I was told that when it was the Golf Resort that the occupancy was maybe 60 percent or slightly higher, usually with people who couldn't get into the Contemporary or the Polynesian.

We had plenty of sell out nights as The Disney Inn, especially Thanksgiving and Christmas. We had slow periods, as well, as any hotel does, so there was a "value season" with a lesser price. We were always booked solid for the Disney Pro/Am Golf classic, which took place in October.

At Christmastime, the lobby was decked out in very tasteful holiday decor. The lobby was not very large and the sitting area would remind you of an upscale living room. From what I remember, Dopey and Snow White would make nightly appearances with the kids and I believe warm cider was served. The lobby always smelled so good during the holidays. I also remember that Mrs. Claus would make appearances to read a Christmas story.

JK: Did the rooms change much when the resort was renamed?

RC: When I started there, half the rooms were still the old décor of the Golf Resort. The rooms were large compared to other Disney resorts, a little less than 500 square feet as I recall. They made the rooms at Wilderness Lodge look tiny when I started working there later. The old decor reminded me of a Marriott. Nothing really special with what I would call a masculine color scheme.

The newer rooms were brighter and the decor had a cottage charm with details like an oak headboard but nothing crazy in terms of a

Snow White/Dwarfs theme. There were just subtle touches that didn't hit you over the head. The wonderful sign at our entrance was a yawning Sleepy holding a candle as if he was going off to bed.

T-shirts in the gift shop had this logo. So did the matchbook covers and other things. It was cute, but other than a publicity photo or two, Sleepy wasn't at the resort.

A guest once called me at the front desk and inquired about Dopey and Snow White tucking their kids in at night. I told him I would get back to him. I mentioned this to our front desk manager, John Formica, and John suggested I call up the Entertainment department at the Magic Kingdom and see what they had to say.

I mentioned the situation and the request didn't seem to surprise them. This sort of request apparently was not that unusual. The cast member mentioned that it would be a four-hour appearance minimum. It entailed costs in terms of wardrobe, make-up, transportation to and from the venue, cost of the performers and stage attendant, etc.

I believe the fee was a few-thousand dollars. So, it was possible. I called the gentleman back who inquired and told him about the cost logistics. There was a long pause and then he said, "Oh, well...thank you. I think we'll pass."

Most of the remodeled rooms had a framed original muted color print that included some images on a shelf that included a picture frame with a drawing of Snow White, an antique cuckoo clock, a candle holder, a beer stein, Doc's glasses, the key to the dwarf mine, a dwarf hat and strangely, the box that was supposed to have held Snow White's heart and behind it the crown of the evil queen.

I had never seen the image anywhere else and have never seen it since. There was no label on it to help explain what it was and the artwork was not signed. Fortunately, my sister took a photo of it when she stayed there and recently sent it to me, so it jogged my memory. When the Inn closed, I got her one of the framed prints and she still has it. I should have picked one up for myself, as well, but it just didn't occur to me.

I don't recall any other themed Snow White items in the rooms.

Two queen beds and a pullout love seat were in the rooms, as well as a small round table with two chairs. Some of the rooms had King beds, which we commonly reserved for honeymooners. I don't recall that we had any suites, but we did have a lot of connecting rooms. Back then, smoking and non-smoking rooms were the norm. In my experience, most guests were happy with non-smoking rooms. It depended on their requests. Double sinks in the bathrooms, tub/shower combo.

The gift shop was right across from our front desk about 20 feet or so away. Various sundries, souvenirs, beer, wine, snacks were sold there. It was a small shop but it had a lot of things people on vacation needed.

The Summer Room was the only formal meeting space at the Inn. It was small and maybe you could have less than 100 people for a cocktail party. I saw a few luncheon set ups in there. When the Americans with Disabilities Act was passed, I was recruited to facilitate a class in the Summer Room for the cast that worked at the Inn.

Once when the room wasn't booked, we arranged for a young lady who was staying there to use it as an impromptu rehearsal room so she could practice her violin in peace.

Our front desk might have had about five computer stations for check-in. Beautiful black marble tops that we always kept shiny. The back office also had a small desk where the cashiers could tally their receipts for the day. Our managers had their own room and our front office manager had a private cubby hole of a space. All of this was windowless.

Our general manager had a beautiful office downstairs with large picture windows that overlooked the landscaping. It was the nicest office I've ever seen at Disney! I even mentioned this to Ed Fox, who was our GM, and he good-naturally agreed.

The only time I really ever spent time in there was when the Inn was closing. We had parting gifts for the cast. It was a medallion with the Disney Inn logo of Sleepy. My buddy, Todd Merrick and I sat in Ed's office and sealed the coins in hard plastic covers. There were a few hundred. I still have mine. I've never seen them for sale on eBay.

When we closed down the Inn there was an evening reception in The Garden Gallery. Some of my front desk cast members donned in our *Sound of Music* Von Trapp costumes, sang the song from the show *So Long, Farewell* and the CFO of WDW at the time, Judson Green, accompanied on the piano. Great guy and great musician.

The Garden Gallery was the main restaurant right off of our lobby and it served breakfast, lunch and dinner. I think I had breakfast and lunch there a couple times but never dinner for some odd reason. It was standard fare like chicken and steak, etc. No "cute" Snow White/ Dwarfs names for the items.

Their specialty was "fried ice cream" but I never had it. Some one told me it was similar to the fried ice cream that was popular at the Mexican chain restaurant called Chi-Chi's. There was a bar/lounge right off the restaurant but nothing memorable about that really.

It was country club like in design. The Garden Gallery was light and airy with skylights. Out front where the bell stand was there were quite a few rocking chairs.

JK: I understand that the resort still focused on serving golfers.

RC: We had the golf pro shop/locker rooms and golf cart storage downstairs. You could take a couple of outdoor stairs from near the lobby area to get down there. There were actually three golf courses. The Palm, The Magnolia and a great nine hole walking course called Oak Trails. I played a lot on Oak Trails.

It was a great place to practice because a lot of people didn't know about it and would rather play a full 18, with a cart, on the Palm and Magnolia. The Disney courses were designed by "Gentleman" Joe Lee. He designed many courses including Cog Hill outside of Chicago, the Blue Monster at Doral, Pine Tree in Boynton Beach, Florida and Bay Hill here in Orlando.

JK: Weren't there also two swimming pools when it became The Disney Inn?

RC: There were two swimming pools at the Inn. The smaller, quieter one you could see from the windows of the Garden Gallery. This pool was never crowded. There was a small snack bar area set up around here, the Sand Trap, so the golfers could grab hot dogs, drinks, etc. as they headed to the back nine.

The pool did have three "blooming water"-type fountains. Chaise lounges and umbrella tables were around this pool. Life guard always on duty at both pools, of course. The large family pool in the back was very popular. It was in the shape of Mickey Mouse's head. There was a mill and a stream connected to the pool for decoration that was charming.

The building for the mill was the room for the pool pumps and supplies, etc. The snack bar by this pool was then called, "Happy's Hollow," after the dwarf Happy. That area also included the Diamond Mine Snack Bar. There were some arcade games, as well.

There were two lighted hard court tennis courts near our cast parking, and people could play on them at night. Once in a while I saw people playing. Never busy. The lights went off automatically and there might have been a sign-up in the golf pro shop to use them. People could rent racquets in the Golf pro shop.

JK: What did the resort look like when you drove up to it?

RC: The resort was three stories and I think we had maybe 287 rooms or so. It was originally about 150 as the Golf Resort. Three types of room view categories: Garden View, Golf Course View (both of which were roughly $185 during the regular season) and Pool View (that was $195 during the regular season). A standard room could accommodate five people. All rooms had a balcony/ small lanai.

The Inn itself was small enough that we got to know all of the people who worked in the gift shop, room service, golf ops, housekeeping, etc.

I would swear that the great John Hench had something to do with the exterior color scheme of the resort. The drive up approach with nature on both sides seemed to blend into the front design of the hotel.

Lots of wildlife lived in the area. The deer would often graze in the front open lawn and sometimes walk right up the circular driveway! Fearless. I guess that related to Snow White and being in the woods.

There was also a large enclosure of flamingos and a large pond to the left as you drove up the main drive. They were well taken care of. I wonder what happened to them? Maybe they eventually ended up at Animal Kingdom?

JK: Did guests complain that the resort was not on the monorail loop?

RC: Guests knew that we were not on the monorail line and I never heard a complaint. A Disney bus came by every 15 minutes, so there was transportation.

Some guests elected to walk to the Polynesian to catch the Monorail there. It wasn't that far a walk. I spoke with many guests who liked the fact that the Inn was tucked away and quiet rather than the hustle and bustle of the Contemporary or Poly.

It was one of the things that appealed to Disney executives, being close to the parks, but still secluded. I've read that supposedly some guests were upset that it wasn't on the monorail loop but my personal experience there in three years is that I never heard that complaint.

JK: Did you wear a themed outfit?

RC: Our front desk costume originally for guys was a blue blazer, gray slacks, white dress shirt, and print red tie. I liked being "professionally dressed" after having to wear the non-flattering, silly, bolo-tie outfit at Fort Wilderness. The women wore navy skirts, white blouse and reminded me of a classic flight attendant look.

The guys wore red hankies in our left breast pockets. I tried to fold mine "just right" but it never looked "just right"! A friendly guest checking in and I were chatting about it and he made a suggestion about how to fold the hankie. I took his advice and voila! The hankie looked "just right". He was a haberdasher.

JK: Was it fun to work the front desk at the resort?

RC: One of the best things about working the Disney Inn front desk was that every guest had to walk by through the lobby when returning back to their rooms. You would get to know their names, their kids' names, so you could engage with them by saying stuff like, "How was the luau, Mr. and Mrs. Francis?" ..."How did you do out at the Magnolia today, Mr. Tyson? "and similar things.

People would often stop by to chat if the desk wasn't busy. It was a perfect environment for that and people were impressed when you remembered their names. It made it seem more family friendly which is one of the reasons we had repeat visitors.

JK: Did you meet any celebrities?

RC: One day, actor Robert Conrad stopped by to see if he had any messages. We were the only two in the lobby. He was wearing mirrored sunglasses just like the stereotype of a celebrity. I was chatting with the guys who worked in the golf pro-shop later that week and they said the couple of times Conrad played golf, he requested to play by himself. This is an unusual request but they obliged. Usually when you play, you are paired up with others and hence that is why golf is referred to often as a social game.

One day I was working at the front desk and a kid came out of the Garden Gallery restaurant with one of the linen napkins. On it were drawings of Chip & Dale. It turns out that animator Bill Justice was eating there and spending time entertaining people with his drawings, etc. One of the girls from the front desk got one of those lucky napkins. I thought that was pretty cool.

There was the rock band, Kansas, famous for the song *Dust in the Wind*. They were friendly. Each band member came down to the desk individually to settle their incidental charges. I think they were at Disney playing a private event at that time.

I used to chat with a guy named Samuel E. Wright. He used to stop by the desk around 11 p.m. to midnight when things were quiet and I could talk. He was an actor from NYC and he told me that he was the voice of a crab in a new Disney movie, *The Little Mermaid*. I hadn't seen it so I didn't know. What I thought was cool about Sam was he was one of the "Fruit of the Loom" fruit guys that used to appear like magic in the ads. I think he was the grapes! Funny!

Oh yeah, a magician/illusionist named Franz Harary stopped by the desk for messages, etc. I recognized him only because he had been on the cover of the magician magazine *The Linking Ring* a few months earlier and I had always been interested in magic and had a subscription. I think he was consulting with Disney on some show where Mickey was doing a magic show in the Magic Kingdom.

The late Joe Shapiro stayed with us quite a lot at The Inn. He was a very busy man who seemed to have a lot on his mind. He was always flagged as a VIP. He always stayed in the same room off the lobby and he clearly was not on vacation. He was working. He seemed quite stern and mysterious.

(Note: Joe Shapiro, the husband of tennis star Pam Shriver and the former general counsel for the Walt Disney Company, died September 23, 1999 after a long battle with non-Hodgkin's lymphoma. He was 52. Known to

wear a Mickey Mouse tie in court, Mr. Shapiro aggressively pursued those who used copyrighted Disney characters without permission—including the Academy of Motion Picture Arts and Sciences, which apologized for using the Snow White character in an Academy Awards broadcast.

Shapiro who oversaw the company's early lobbying efforts in Washington and famously declared that "Mickey Mouse is not a Republican or a Democrat" told the Congressional Quarterly that Disney's reluctance to discuss its lobbying activities was linked to its desire to protect its family-friendly brand image. Shapiro was the chief negotiator for Disney in the construction, financing and operation of Disneyland Paris. Shapiro additionally recruited top lawyers to work in Disney's law department. He was lured to the Walt Disney Company by Michael Eisner personally in 1985. When he was first diagnosed with cancer he left his role as vice-president in 1994.)

One of my managers told me that Mr. Shapiro was a Harvard trained attorney and was handpicked by Eisner to work for the Walt Disney Company. Joe Shapiro was the chief negotiator when it came to putting the deal together for what was then EuroDisney.

Back then, we would receive faxes for guests and then deliver them to their rooms. We would constantly get legal faxes and Fed-Exes for Joe regularly. These were important legal documents. I suggested privately to our front desk manager that we really shouldn't be seeing these faxes and perhaps we should set up a fax machine in Joe's room so he could have instant access. That was eventually done. In fact, a type of mini-office was set up in Joe's room.

Joe always seemed to wear the same clothes: jeans, Gucci loafers and the type of white Disney sweatshirt that had a large image of Mickey face on the front and the back of Mickey's head on the back. I don't remember him wearing anything else! I would also see him carrying a full pot of coffee much of the time acquired from the Garden Gallery. He would take it back to his room and no one complained or questioned it.

So, one day, The Disney Inn came into the way of modern communication and the whole phone system with voice-mail was installed throughout the resort. Joe's room was the first to be installed. We were constantly receiving Fed-Ex letters for Joe and it was customary to deliver them right as we got them. We just slid them under the door.

I did this one time and as I was heading back to the lobby, his door opened and he called after me: "Hey, kid!" (I was probably 27 at the time and thought that was pretty funny) He waved me over and invited me in.

"What in the world is THIS all about?" I thought. See, we were all a little intimidated by Joe. He brings me over to his phone and there was a blinking red light. He asks, "What does this mean?"

I explained that he had a phone message and showed him how to retrieve his voice-mails. I was standing there while he was listening to his messages. He started laughing out loud and said something to the effect of..."If that bitch thinks I'm calling HER back she's nuts!"

I stood there like a statue. Afterward, whenever I saw Joe passing through the lobby, I always gave him a smile and a "hello" and he always responded. Many years later I learned that Joe had married the tennis great, Pam Shriver. They were married maybe a year and then Joe passed away. I believe he was 52 or 53.

I would have sworn he was much older than that. He did not seem like a guy in his forties when he regularly stayed at The Inn. Perhaps he was not well then. Another thing that dawned on me later was that Joe most likely stayed at The Disney Inn because of the negotiations between Disney and the U.S. government regarding the creation of Shades of Green resort from The Disney Inn.

JK: Any personal adventures you had at the resort?

RC: I once caught a snake by the back area pool! It was a quiet afternoon on the front desk and a guest called from the pool deck via the house phone. We mulled it over in the office and all of the ladies I worked with were squeamish and wanted nothing to do with it. We should have called Disney Pest Control but who knows how long that would have taken?

I volunteered only half-believing there was a snake down there. I got a canvas bag from housekeeping and a set of grabbers and off I went. It was a hot day and I was wearing our new corduroy costume. I went over to the snack bar area and some little kids took me over to some bushes by the deck.

I looked around and didn't see a thing. I shook the bushes and sure enough, a black racer short of three feet slithered out onto the manicured lawn. I got him with the grabbers with one shot! All the kids "oohed" and "ahhed" in unison. Funny! I put the snake in the sack, got in a golf cart and released it way back in the woods.

A couple of weeks later, a kid was walking through the lobby with a rubber snake that he got in Adventureland. I asked to borrow it and nonchalantly took it into the back office to remind people of the snake I had caught. I showed it off and there was a shriek of horror! I had NO IDEA people would be that frightened. I apologized up and down. I figured they would all know it was fake from the get-go.

We had an elderly couple that stayed at The Inn for almost a month... Mr. and Mrs. Dick Francis. They were from the UK. Very nice to chat with. They really didn't go to the parks but just enjoyed being at the Disney Inn. One day when he was in the lobby I quietly asked him if he was the mystery writer, Dick Francis. He chuckled and in his delightful accent said, "No, No but Dickie is a good friend of ours!"

Mr. Francis once gave me a bottle of champagne one time when they left. We were not permitted to accept gifts of alcohol as cast members so I told my manager and he told me to take it home. I brought it months later to our Cast Xmas party and we had a toast to Mr. and Mrs. Francis.

I believe they came back the following year, again for three or four weeks. When they checked out, they arranged for every cast member who worked at the Inn to get complimentary ice cream bars. They insisted and worked out the payment with our manager. A very nice gesture to say the least. The guests who stayed at the Inn were always extremely nice.

JK: Thanks for taking the time to answer my questions. I am sure people will be interested since so little is known about the Disney Inn.

RC: It was great fun trying to remember those days. Reviewing this interview brought back a flood of memories and images. I loved working at the Inn but it seems like another lifetime ago

Swan and Dolphin

January 1990/June 1990

The Swan and Dolphin resort hotels are the only hotels on Walt Disney World property carrying the Disney name that are not operated by Disney and do not offer the same amenities as the other Walt Disney World resorts.

By the time Michael Eisner became Chairman and CEO of the Disney Company in 1984, the company's connection to innovative architecture had faded and it had not built a new hotel on WDW property in over a decade.

"(The Walt Disney World Company) had a 14,000 room expansion plan for the property in the mid-80s," Imagineer Wing Chao told writer Ryan March. "There was a camp within the Company that wanted to create a joint venture with an outside hotel partner, lowering our financial risk and benefiting from an industry expert's experience."

When offered the opportunity for an outside company to build two new hotels near Epcot, Eisner rejected a plan to build two rather ordinary hotel towers that he referred to publicly as "refrigerator boxes".

After some legal wrangling with the Tishman Corporation, Eisner hired the award-winning Princeton architect Michael Graves to do the design. The hotels were necessary to accommodate the convention groups who were staying at off-property hotels that had greater convention space than the existing Disney resorts.

When the two hotels opened in 1990, they offered the largest hotel convention space in the Southeastern United States.

Eisner, former chairman and CEO of the Walt Disney Company, coined the term "Entertainment Architecture" to define the concept that he wanted the architecture outside the boundaries of the Disney theme parks, but still part of the Disney real estate, to embody the same fantasy and sense of story as the structures in the park.

An amateur architecture and design buff, Eisner understood that a company like Disney ought to have a distinctive physical presence in any building associated with the company. Such architecture he felt would bring attention and even future partnerships from others including filmmakers like George Lucas and Steven Spielberg.

In the 1990s, Eisner began enthusiastically commissioning these type of buildings from Robert Venturi & Denise Scott Brown, Aldo

Rossi, Arata Isozaki, Charles Moore, and other champions of postmodern design especially Michael Graves.

Eisner knew architect Robert A.M. Stern, whom he'd met years earlier when Stern worked on a renovation of Eisner's parents' Manhattan apartment, and Stern connected Eisner with postmodern architect Michael Graves, fresh off the triumph of Portland Building, and a perfect match for Eisner's idea of buildings that would grab attention.

"The best design, like the best of any art, needs to be challenging and provocative, even a little threatening at first," Eisner wrote in his memoir *Work in Progress*. "At the same time, we tried to never take ourselves too seriously. As important as it was to design buildings that were aesthetically pleasing, they also had to be fun and entertaining."

Michael Graves is often described as putting the frequently controversial concept of post-modernism on the map. His works range from large projects such as buildings to whimsical designs for furniture, teapots and other household items.

The Swan and Dolphin hotels on Walt Disney World property in Florida were designed by Michael Graves in association with Alan Lapidus and the interior design firm Wilson and Associates. Graves had never designed a hotel before he worked on the Swan and the Dolphin.

In his memoir, Eisner stated about the two resort hotels that they had "two huge swans for one and two dolphins for the other. The idea of using these creatures—icons that had classical antecedents but were also lighthearted and accessible—it seemed a perfect solution for a Disney hotel."

Graves was born in Indianapolis, Indiana on July 9, 1934. An architect in public practice since 1964, he was also a professor of Architecture at Princeton University. He directed the firm of Michael Graves Architecture & Design. When he died in 2015 at the age of 80, the causeway connecting the Swan and Dolphin hotels across the lake was renamed the Michael Graves Causeway.

For the Walt Disney Company, he was responsible for the Swan and Dolphin hotels in 1990, the Team Disney Building in Burbank, California in 1991, the Hotel New York in Disneyland Paris in 1992, and, finally, the post office in Celebration, Florida in 1996.

The exterior of Hotel New York is a stylized skyscraper filled skyline that echoes the feel of New York City. The post office in Celebration was influenced by a post office found in nearby St. Petersburg, Florida where the "open air post office" which dates back to 1917 is an important historical landmark.

The Swan and Dolphin hotels were conceived as a single set piece, facing each other across a lake and designed to accommodate convention business at the Walt Disney World resort.

Graves intended the larger Dolphin hotel to represent according to him "a mountain coming out of the Everglades". He also designed the light sconces, the chairs, the carpet pattern and even the china for the restaurants. However, there have been many changes since the original opening.

At the Swan hotel, guests walked down Graves designed lily-pond carpets to rooms whose doors were painted to look like striped beach cabanas.

Graves created a storyline for the resorts to support his design choices. Graves once said he had to design something that would attract "the serious conventioneer, as well as the 8-year-old."

His designs for the two iconic hotels earned him an Award of Merit from the New Jersey Society of Architects in 1990.

Graves' architecture met with severe criticism from his peers. Pritzker Prize-winning architect James Stirling didn't like the idea of renowned architects designing for Disney at all.

"We're not very sympathetic to the theme idea," he stated in the *New York Times*. "To me, it seems demeaning and trivial and somehow not profound or important. It's overly commercial."

Project architect for the Swan and Dolphin Patrick Burke said: "Thirty years later, this project remains an important and memorable experience for visitors and Disney fans alike – and one of the most memorable projects of my career. Rather than a literal replication of a historic building type or style, as evident in some of Disney's architecture, we looked more broadly to the history of art and architecture for themes, trying to create an exuberance that complemented Disney's properties and their location in Florida.

"The Walt Disney Company coined the phrase 'entertainment architecture' to describe what we had created. The Walt Disney World Dolphin and Swan Hotels were early, groundbreaking ventures into considering design as an important part of the hospitality experience."

During March 1997, Graves did a presentation at the Disney Institute Performance Center on his projects for the Walt Disney Company. As with many of the guest speakers at the Disney Institute, a small group of animation instructors were able to meet with the speakers at the Seasons restaurant that was across from the Performance Center for dinner or drinks after the presentation.

I was fortunate enough to be a part of that group that was able to meet with Graves that night and asked a few more questions. I was the only one who took notes apparently as I did with all the other speaker interactions and I am sharing them here.

Jim Korkis: What got you interested in design?

Michael Graves; I spent countless hours drawing. The more I did, the better I got. I really wasn't good at much else. My mother panicked when she discovered I wanted to be an artist and told me that unless I was as good as Picasso, I'd starve. (laughs) However, she did suggest I consider engineering or architecture and I chose architecture.

JK: Do you have a design philosophy?

MG: I want to put Humpty-Dumpty back together again. Others want to pull it apart.

JK: Can you tell us how you came up with the design for the Team Disney building in Burbank where the Seven Dwarfs seem to be holding up the roof?

MG: Michael (Eisner) told me, "Look, everyone here will have some design priorities for you but I only have one priority. When I come in to work each morning and go up to my office, I'll probably have very little to smile about. So do something that will make me smile when I arrive."

My first designs were rejected but I eventually came up with the concept of having the Seven Dwarfs as caryatids (caryatids are sculpted figures serving as an architectural support taking the place of a column or a pillar supporting horizontal bands). I made that choice because *Snow White and the Seven Dwarfs* was truly the foundation of the Disney Studios and supported the growth of the company just as the dwarves look as if they are supporting the building.

JK: Did it make Michael Eisner smile?

MG: Yes, I believe it did. You know since both of us have the first name Michael, I took to calling him "the real Michael". One day I was talking to Eisner on the phone and he said, "I have to call you back. On the other line is the really real Michael." It turned out to be Michael Jackson. (laughs)

JK: What was the reaction to the final building?

MG: I filled the building with references to Mickey Mouse like a silhouette of his head scattered over the table in the main conference room. One of the top executives from another company attended a meeting there and moaned to me, "There's an awful lot of Mickeys in that building." (laughs)

JK: Were you a fan of Mickey Mouse?

MG: I always loved the Mickey Mouse cartoons. I just can't relate to the three-dimensional costumed Mickey Mouses walking around Epcot. To me, Mickey is two-dimensional. I used to draw him that way when

I was six or eight years old. Seeing this three-dimensional figure who never talks, lumbering up to me and raising and lowering his hand, that is not Mickey Mouse.

JK: How did you get involved in designing the Swan and Dolphin hotels?

MG: Michael didn't like those tall, all glass buildings. He referred to them as "refrigerator boxes". He wanted the architecture to tell a story.

JK: Many people mistakenly believe the "black box" in the center of the Dolphin hotel was meant for a monorail entrance similar to the one on the Contemporary Resort.

MG: Oh, not at all. Not at all. It is the heart of the mountain that has exploded. The Dolphin is this mountain that has struggled its way to thrust out of the tropical rain forest. That's why there are banana leaves painted along the side of the building. (Note: Graves and Alan Lapidus did a lot of work on this project at the Beverly Hills Hotel in California which at the time had wallpaper decorated with giant banana leaves.)

It is a mountain that dramatically arose and in the process its heart exploded and the water cascades out nine stories down the side of the hotel, passing through the five clamshell basins to a fountain and eventually splashing into Crescent Lake. The walkway from the railings to the landscaping mimic waves that splash onto the side of the Swan.

JK: That seems like a pretty detailed mythology.

MG: Two birds were so awed by this epic spectacle that they alighted on the top of the waves to get a better look and were magically transformed into those frozen swans.

JK: Why did you select dolphins and swans?

MG: I wanted creatures that were not part of the existing Disney mythology and hoped as a result they would then be developed further as Disney icons.

JK: The dolphin doesn't look like dolphins I have seen.

MG: They were inspired by the work of an Italian sculptor, Bernini. Of course, there is one major change. Bernini's dolphins had mouths that curved downward and looked like they were frowning. Michael said that wasn't going to happen on Disney property so I curved the mouths upwards as if smiling. (Note: An example of Bernini's dolphins can be seen in the King Neptune fountain in the Italian pavilion at Epcot.)

JK: Did you do the sculpture for reference?

MG: I did the design. Gary Graham did the sculptures used for building them.

JK: While the Swan and the Dolphin are companion hotels, there seem to be some differences in design philosophy.

MG: At the Dolphin, the sculptures are three-dimensional where the guests can't touch them and two-dimensional, like in the indoor fountain, where they can be touched. At the Swan, it is reversed and the sculptures are generally three-dimensional where they can be touched by guests (except for the roof, of course) but two dimensional like the monkeys and parrots where they can't be touched.

JK: So that's why the dolphins in the outdoor fountain are two-dimensional because in theory the guests could reach out and touch them?

MG: I had designed the dolphins for the outdoor fountain to be three-dimensional but it was felt that being so large, they obstructed the view of the Swan. So I made the fountain smaller and sliced the dolphins into dolphin fillets and so I was able to keep them exactly where I wanted them but opened up the space. I made the fountain smaller so the guests might be able to touch them.

JK: The Dolphin and Swan have similarities but are very different. I find the Dolphin to be disorienting.

MG: That was a deliberate choice because it was to be a hotel for conventions and when you attend conventions, what do you want the participants to do? You want them to think differently, to see things from a different perspective. So the design is encouraging that.

JK: To really "think out of the box" as they say.

MG: Exactly. Most people are right-handed but the check-in desk is on the left. The rotunda is disorienting because there are no landmarks or icons so the person will have to really concentrate on what direction to go.

JK: The rotunda is like a circus tent or a balloon or someone said the inside of a genie's bottle.

MG: It's supposed to be fun. Both inside and out, the hotel was designed to echo the tropical Florida landscape, as well as the fun and whimsy of the nearby Disney attractions and an aura of fantasy that appeals to guests of all ages.

JK: But the Swan is very different.

MG: Yes, the check-in desk is on the right hand side and the hallways are very angular and short so that it is easier to locate where you are and where you might want to go. Something for everyone.

JK: And now the post office in Celebration.

MG: Yes, I think it is amusing that I am responsible for the largest building on Walt Disney World property (the Dolphin Hotel) and now also the smallest building on Walt Disney property (in the city of Celebration).

Designed by Graves, the swan statues (like the dolphin statues) were created from steel, wood and fiberglass, and were believed to be the largest structures of their kind in the world at the time. Since there were no existing samples to work from, Disney artist Gary Graham, following Graves' design, sculpted the swan models out of Styrofoam.

These were then computer-photographed (photogrammetry) in a process that turns the shapes into a digitized database.

The photogrammetric information was then sent on to a shipbuilding company in Wisconsin. There it was put into a computer that automatically cut the wooden ribs to exact specifications and imprinted the ribs with numbers and location directions. The ribs were then delivered to the statue site, where they were fitted to a steel frame.

Once assembled, a fiberglass covering was carefully brushed on and then covered with five layers of laminate. The swan statues were then sanded, painted and ultimately lifted into place in May 1989.

Completed, the swan statues, referred to as "heroic" statues, are each 47 feet high. And at a combined weight of 56,000 pounds, they required a multi-ton, 70-foot crane to lift them and place them atop the hotel. They were placed on specially constructed pedestals at either end of the hotel's roof, which support and display them.

The dolphin statues are each 63 feet high. All the roof sculptures are hollow inside, except for the structural beaming, and they have internal staircases and trapdoors for maintenance purposes.

Where is the entrance to the Walt Disney World Dolphin? No, it is not at the porte cochere where cars drop off their passengers. According to Graves' concept, it is facing the Walt Disney Swan.

Graves partnered with the interior design firm of Wilson and Associates to create rich beach-themed color schemes, hand-painted murals, lily pond carpets, room doors painted to look like striped cabanas, seashell light fixtures and more to capture the spirit of a playful tropical beach.

"Both inside and out, the hotel was designed to echo the tropical Florida landscape, as well as the fun and whimsy of the nearby Disney attractions and an aura of fantasy that appeals to guests of all ages," Graves told me.

The stories of the Walt Disney World Swan and Dolphin were severely readjusted in a major interior redesign that no longer supported the original story. It was felt that these changes were needed to attract a more upscale business traveler.

Both hotels have now transitioned to what is called "modern luxury," which means the design is less thematic of a playful beach story and more opulent than before. Graves was involved in the room redesign, but not in the makeover of the public space.

Both lobbies have been redesigned and the original story that Graves was attempting to tell has been retired. There was no mourning when the interior storyline shifted because neither cast members nor guests understood nor appreciated the story that Graves was attempting to tell. However, the exterior of both hotels are reminders of that original story.

Tishman Hotel Corporation Executive Vice President Dave Bagwell stated, "It's a total redesign. Entertainment architecture has had a very successful run, but it's time for a fresh new look."

The Walt Disney World Swan Reserve, a 14-story hotel offering an upscale and boutique environment opened in 2021. The exterior design seems very mid-century modern with hints of Googie architecture of the early space age. It lacks some of the clear architectural elements of its sister hotels.

The new hotel was originally called The Cove and was meant to represent the body of water shared by the Swan and the Dolphin but that attempt to connect it with the Swan and Dolphin was eventually abandoned although some of the color elements on the exterior tie in with that story.

Stories of the Dolphin

THE URBAN LEGEND OF THE BLACK BOX

Graves's original design for the Dolphin was just one side of the building sloping to create a pyramid effect with a sphere half sunk into the middle. He eventually reworked it into what is seen today.

Every since it was built, Disney guests have speculated about the black box on the side of The Dolphin with the urban legend that it was meant to be a placeholder for a future monorail station.

There was no practical way to make use of the last eighty feet of the pointy top, so fake windows were put on the outside but there are no guest rooms or floors up there. The black box area actually has real windows with permanent rooms behind it.

The urban legend is that the space behind the black area is just a big empty void. Another version of the legend claims that the area behind the black box is filled with "temporary" hotel rooms that can be removed.

Graves likes to use dark and light areas or different materials to break up building façades. Around the same time that he designed the Swan and Dolphin, he also designed the 16-story, 400-room Hyatt Regency La Jolla at Aventine that has three black squares on its façade. His 11-story office tower at Aventine only has a single black square on it.

According to Disney historian Werner Weiss, the black areas on the Swan and Dolphin are substantially different in size (about five stories tall on the Swan, and about nine stories tall on the Dolphin) and in elevation (starting about seven stories up on the Swan, and starting about ten stories up on the Dolphin). They're much taller than necessary to accommodate the Monorail.

If the beam did go through the Swan and Dolphin, there would not be a logical place to put a station because the beam would be way too high, and the buildings aren't nearly deep enough to house a monorail station.

THE DOLPHIN ORIGINAL ARTWORK

Architect Michael Graves had complete creative control over every aspect of Walt Disney World's Swan and Dolphin resort hotels from uniforms to room keys.

The murals were rendered in miniature by Graves and then the builder Tishman Realty & Construction Company commissioned Maer-Murphy Inc. (a company specializing in murals and decorative finishes) to follow those designs and execute the final full-sized paintings.

In a 4,000 square foot studio under the Manhattan Bridge in Brooklyn, shifts of eight artists worked on Belgium fireproof linen canvases up to 40 feet long to create 64 dramatic floral-patterned murals, which ranged in size from 200 to 600 square feet for the walls of the 56,000 square foot ballroom.

The artists painted in teams, each responsible for different mural elements. The fast-paced process, using more than 160 gallons of paint for the ballroom murals alone, achieved a consistent feel throughout each series without sacrificing the individual artists' touch.

As the murals were completed, they were rolled onto carpet spools and driven to Walt Disney World. Once there, they are stretched and stapled onto large birch wood frames, eight to twenty-three feet above the floor, and finished with trim molding.

Fifteen doors leading to audiovisual control rooms posed a special challenge. Workers cut out the canvas around these passageways, then re-stretched new canvas directly onto the doors. Artists then painted the doors on-site, integrating the pattern.

The Maer-Murphy team produced other murals that were painted on canvas at the studio and then affixed directly to the hotel's walls, such as a nine by one hundred and twenty nine foot floral patterned mural hanging behind the lobby reception desk, seven stairwell murals, composed of a collage of textures and geometric patterns and ten floral-patterned corridor murals.

One of the highlights, the Copa Banana Night Club, featured three giant fruit murals and three-dimensional fruits made of hand-painted wooden cut-outs which festoon the furniture. These works included a fifty foot long banana bar, watermelon, cantaloupe and grapefruit drink rails up to ten feet long and palm tree cut-outs thirteen feet high.

Some artwork was produced on site such as the three and half by two hundred and forty two foot hand painted wooden leaf valance that edged the ceiling of Harry's Safari Bar and Grille and the five foot square checkerboard patterns painted directly onto the light blue wall covering in Tubbi Checkers Buffeteria, the 1950s themed fast food restaurant.

In the Coral Café, twenty-four oversized fish (catfish, mousefish and even a school of fish sporting mortar boards) seem to "float" from the ceiling with another twenty affixed to the walls. The four to six foot long wooden cut-outs were by artist Robert Braun.

Braun painted the floral patterned mural for the rotunda lobby and also created beach scene murals, complete with palm tees, beach balls, and pails and shovels to line the corridor, while the carpet design was meant to resemble a sandy beach with beach towels, balls and suntan lotion designs.

Like Walt Disney World areas, some of these areas had back stories. Harry's Safari Bar and Grille was owned by a legendary traveler who roamed the world in search of gourmet treasure which included open-flame cooked meats, fish and vegetables flavored with exotic herbs. The staff never knows when Harry may stop in so his table is always ready and Harry's Safari Ale is always in the cooler.

In addition, over 4,500 prints of classic paintings hung throughout the hotel representing artists who had influenced Graves' style including Picasso, Matisse, Hockney and Rousseau.

The Swan was promoted to travel agents with the following statement: "Designed by leading architect Michael Graves, this resort is as much an adventure on the inside as it is on the out. Colorful hand-painted murals line the lobby ceiling, parrot lamps and seahorse chandeliers decoratively light the hallways, and pineapples stenciled on headboards signal a traditional welcome."

Port Orleans (French Quarter) / Dixie Landings (Riverside)

May 1991 / February 1992

Disney's Port Orleans Resort first opened to the public at the Walt Disney World Resort in May 1991 thanks to Fugleberg Koch Architects of Winter Park, Florida in collaboration with the Disney Development Company. The company was also responsible for the design of the Old Key West Resort and the Caribbean Beach Resort.

"In those days, we all read newspapers and they had these huge Sunday travel sections," Imagineer Wing Chao told writer Ryan March. "You'd read these great stories about visiting the Caribbean or New Orleans or the U.S. national parks. So those places became the source of inspiration for the next wave of Disney resort hotels, using our unique design approach to fulfill guests' wishes.

"We do that through what we came to call 'entertainment architecture' which is about so much more than just the design of the building. It's about colors, finishes, materials and textures. It's about artwork and landscaping, furnishings and fabrics. Everything from the roof tiles to the floor tiles. Every detail supports the story."

Walt Disney always had a fondness for New Orleans and wanted a section devoted to it on the edge of Frontierland when Disneyland first opened in 1955.

He and his wife Lillian loved shopping for antiques in that city since the 1940s and some of those treasures were purchased and included in his apartment over the firehouse at Disneyland. Finally an actual New Orleans Square opened at the park in July 1966.

In 1980, Disney executive Dick Nunis pushed for an expansion of the Shopping Village at Lake Buena Vista (better known as Disney Springs today) by creating a moderately priced, six hundred room resort themed to resemble New Orleans.

Guest rooms would have been "hidden" in buildings resembling a cotton mill or a boatwrights shop. The rooms would be on the upper floors with the bottom floor reserved for shops and restaurants like Café Orleans.

Nunis told cast members in a May 1982 issue of *Eyes &Ears* cast newspaper that "From the Empress Lilly, we're going into a New Orleans street, and you'll walk right into a beautiful New Orleans hotel".

An illustrated marketing packet was produced by the Walt Disney Company in September 1981 (and later revised in April 1982) for the project, that detailed what was called "Lake Buena Vista New Orleans Square".

While that project never developed, the theme was later incorporated into another WDW resort: Port Orleans: French Quarter.

It was themed to the French Quarter of New Orleans around the mid-1800s and was situated by the Sassagoula River, a man-made Disney waterway named after the Native American word for the Mississippi.

With its nearness to the Dixie Landings resort, it was meant to reference a journey by steam riverboat up the Mississippi up from New Orleans to Natchez.

The waterways are all man-made and were originally woodlands. They are actually a constant-level canal system linked to Lake Buena Vista at Disney Springs.

The length of the river is approximately two and a half miles, beginning upriver at the Port Orleans: Riverside region and continuing down river past the French Quarter Region and the Saratoga Springs Resort, finally ending at the entry of Lake Buena Vista.

The streets that radiate from the courtyard area are designed in a similar arrangement to historic Jackson Square warehouse district located in the actual French Quarter of New Orleans.

The architecture showcases balconies, wrought-iron railings, cobblestone streets, and courtyards reminiscent of New Orleans in the 19th century. The lush landscaping consisting of pear trees, oaks, crepe, myrtles and magnolias reinforce this theme.

Before its rehab, there were many distinctive elements that referenced New Orleans.

The registration lobby known as the *Port Orleans Mint* was themed after the inside of a commercial bank of the 1800s. The musical staff notes across the registration desk represent the first verse of the classic tune *When the Saints Go Marching In.*

The colorful jester figures located inside the food court and on the approach to the Doubloon Lagoon pool are closely based on the figure found next to the Canal Street / Algiers Ferry terminal in New Orleans.

The musical instrument playing alligator figures reference not only the iconic bayou creatures of New Orleans but the city being the home of jazz music. They are a New Orleans street band that playfully lead the guests to the pool area like pied pipers.

Blaine Kern was known as "Mr. Mardi Gras," because when the Mardi Gras parades were offering only dim shadows of past glories in the 1950s, Kern became an innovator at creating fanciful, outlandish floats that included storybook characters whose heads turned and whose eyes moved.

In 1959, Kern met Walt Disney, who was visiting Mardi Gras in search of new ideas. Walt offered Kern a job to work as an Imagineer designing floats for Disneyland, as well as working on other projects. Kern's boss, Darwin Fenner (the son of the Fenner in the Merrill Lynch, Pierce, Fenner and Smith) convinced Kern to say "no" to Walt.

Blaine Kern Artists, Inc. were responsible for collecting and creating the many Mardi Gras props, such as the jesters, located in the original food court area. Some of the Mardi Gras decorative props were purchased directly from Mardi Gras warehouses in New Orleans.

Some of those items, including a huge head, proved too intimidating for young children and became a maintenance issue and so were removed in a recent rehab.

At the food court, the bakery section was originally named Jacques' Beignets that was an aural pun on American comedian Jack Benny.

When guests checked in to the Port Orleans Resort during the first few years of operation, they received a copy of the *Sassagoula Sentinel*, a faux newspaper that included guest information including where the ice machines were located, whether a guest would be charged for making a collect call, when the boat would leave for the Village Marketplace, restaurant information, and other similar helpful directions.

This wonderful eight-page tabloid format (11-by-17 inches) newspaper was also filled with historical news stories that recounted the fictional back story of the resort. The story was a mixture of authentic history mixed with fanciful but logical additions from Walt Disney Imagineering.

According to the Imagineering back story in the newspaper:

"Elizabeth Cuenta D'Arnet, was the founder of the *Sassagoula Sentinel*. Known to locals as Ruby Rivers, D'Arnet was firmly established as 'The Poet Of The Delta', for her popular verses that highlighted the virtues of living in the Sassagoula delta.

"The *Sassagoula Sentinel* was an instant success when the first edition hit the streets in 1835. Using her knowledge of the people and their customs, D'Arnet produced a daily that highlighted the cultural, financial and culinary news of the bustling little city. But more than anything else, the *Sassagoula Sentinel* linked the people of Port Orleans together."

The text on the back of the very first postcard released for the resort stated:

> Evoking a bygone era of romance and charm, the hidden courtyards, splashing fountains and lush gardens of Disney's Port Orleans Resort create a welcome retreat. At the heart of it all is Doubloon Lagoon, where 'Scales' the sea serpent invites visitors to make a splash!

Right in the middle of the illustrated card was this massive sea serpent, who didn't look quite as dangerous as most sea serpents. Doubloon Lagoon was named for the doubloon coins (along with strings of beads) that are tossed to folks celebrating Mardi Gras in New Orleans.

King Neptune, holding his iconic trident high in the air, rides majestically on top of the head of a highly unique and popular pool slide, a sea serpent named Scales. Guests emerge from the jaws of the serpent to slide down Scales' long twisting 51-foot pink tongue into the 225,000 gallon pool.

Is there a story behind this delightful creature? Is his name just a reference to the fact that a sea serpent would have scales like a fish?

Since it was built at the time where everything at the Walt Disney World Resort had to have some type of back story, there are actually two different versions about how this monster from the sea ended up in a New Orleans swimming pool.

Here is the story of Scales from the *Sassagoula Sentinel*:

THE STORY OF SCALES, SEA SERPENT OF THE SASSAGOULA

A Mardi Gras Legend, 1882

"Folklore in the Sassagoula delta is a mix of various cultural traditions. The Indians that inhabited the area had many stories about the origins of the Sassagoula. One story they told explained how the river feared that the sea would consume all its water if the sea could find the source of the river. So in order to confuse the sea, the Sassagoula split into a thousand small rivers just before it reached the sea. This was how the delta was formed.

"The French and Spanish settlers brought many of their own cultural folklores with them and over time these traditions melded together. Most of the stories the children learned dealt with religious observances and holidays. However, one story emerged that was totally unique to Port Orleans.

"It seems that parents have always had a difficult time keeping their children away from the bayou that surrounds the city. These swampy marshes have inherent dangers such as alligators and snakes. So in order to frighten their children away from playing in the bayou, a story emerged of a large serpentine creature that lurks beneath the surface of the dark and still waters, waiting to eat unsuspecting children.

Many people, it was said, met their demise while wandering in the misty depths of the murky swamp.

"Some of the older children were not frightened by the myth. So a group of fathers decided to do something to scare them. In a cabin near the bayou, the men constructed a large dragon-like serpent made of fence wire and bedsheets.

"They painted it with whatever they could find, so the finished product was a horrendous looking, multicolored contraption that took 16 men to operate. When the unsuspecting children arrived at the bayou, the serpent emerged, howling, screaming and chasing the ashen children all the way back to town.

"Each year the serpent reappeared at the end of the Mardi Gras parade, reminding the children to stay away from the bayou. Eventually 'Scales' became a permanent fixture at Doubloon Lagoon and can been seen there today."

As with every Disney story, there is always more to the tale of Scales.

I believe that the credit for the name "Scales" should be given to talented writer Greg Ehrbar.

Over the decades, Ehrbar has contributed his writing skills to many Walt Disney World projects from providing accurate and entertaining fun facts for Regis Philbin's narration of the annual Christmas parade to the charming children's menu given out at Tony's Town Square restaurant on Main Street U.S.A. in the Magic Kingdom.

Speaking of children's menus, Port Orleans once had a full-service restaurant called Bonfamille's Cafe and next to it was Scat Cat's Club. Disney animation fans will instantly remember that retired opera singer Madame Bonfamille was the owner of the talented French cats in the animated feature *The Aristocats (1970).* Those famous felines were assisted in their adventures by a jazz band of cats led by the outrageous Scat Cat.

A special children's menu created for Bonfamille's Café was done in the form of a booklet with line art drawings that could be colored at the table by energetic kids waiting for their meal.

This coloring book was written by Greg Ehrbar and illustrated by the very talented Peter Emslie. Emslie illustrated several Walt Disney World children's menu over the years, including ones themed to *The Jungle Book* and *The Rescuers.*

He enjoyed this work during his time at Disney because he got to draw characters that he wouldn't normally be asked to do for his work in advertising or merchandise. Later, with Don "Ducky" Williams, Emslie got to illustrate a Little Golden Book story of *The Aristocats.*

To Emslie's delight, Ehrbar created a sort of sequel to *The Aristocats* in a few short pages.

In the form of a photo album journal by Madame Adelaide Bonfamille, the booklet described how the good Madame, Duchess, the kittens, Thomas O'Malley and the Alley Cat Band took a musical cruise to Port Orleans, where they were "tailed" by a jazz-loving sea serpent.

The sea creature fell in love with the jazz that Scat Cat and his band played on the voyage. The serpent was named "Scales" (a nod to musical scales and the Sherman Brothers tune, *Scales and Arpeggios* that appears in the film). The story closes with him staying at the resort to enjoy the music played by the resident "jazz gators".

Ehrbar received help from his wife, Suzanne, who grew up in New Orleans. He was among those people under the direction of Dale Stafford (who was in charge of the resort) who came up with the names for the new resort from boats to the laundry to the sea serpent in the pool.

Ehrbar was responsible for naming "Doubloon Lagoon" and "Scales". He was just told there would be a sea serpent slide in the then unnamed pool but given no further information.

However, with his vast knowledge and love of Disney animation, he was able to create a back story for a new Disney character that has delighted guests for more than two decades.

The old Bonfamille's Café restaurant is now used as a test kitchen for developing new culinary ideas for other locations around Walt Disney World, and for occasional resort cast member activities.

Port Orleans Riverside opened as Disney's Dixie Landings Resort on February 2, 1992, themed to the Antebellum South of steamboat travel, formal garden parties, mint juleps on the front porch and more.

It was inspired by rural Louisiana and nestled alongside the picturesque Sassagoula River (using the Native American term for the Mississippi).

In 2001, to try to eliminate the negative connotations associated with the Old South, including a cotton mill that suggested the slavery of the pre-Civil War era as well as the word "Dixie" itself, the resort was formally merged into Disney's Port Orleans resort to become Port Orleans Riverside.

The old Port Orleans resort was then renamed Port Orleans French Quarter.

The "Sassagoula Steamboat Company" lobby, which houses the registration desks and guest services, is themed after the inside of a departure hall for an old-style riverboat with massive ceiling fans.

The ports of call are listed around the tops of the decorative columns: Riverside, French Quarter, Gretna, Chalmette, Port Eads, St. Louis, Sainte Genevieve, Cape Girardeau, Cairo, New Madrid, Caruthersville, Memphis, Helena, Greenville, Vicksburg, Vidalia, Natchez and Baton Rouge.

Riverside is divided into two distinctly themed parishes: the stately white-columned Magnolia Bend "mansions" reminiscent of the Old South and the quaint backwoods "cottages" of Alligator Bayou themed after Cajun Country.

The Riverside Mill food court was themed after an old Southern cotton mill and houses a cotton press powered by an authentically reproduced and working 35 foot water wheel. The food court was previously known as the Colonel's Cotton Mill.

Boatwright's Dining Hall is themed after a wooden shipbuilding yard with vintage shipbuilding tools hanging on the walls inside the restaurant. The partially built sailboat hanging overhead is actually an authentic reproduction of the flat-bottom "New Orleans Lugger" that sailed the Mississippi River in the 1820s. It was constructed at the Brewers Dauntless Ship Yard.

The dockside immediately outside Boatwright's features a raised boat-ramp, just adjacent to two giant faux sliding doors hung from metal rails on the side of the building to allow newly built boats access to the river.

Fulton's General Store is named after real-life steamboat pioneer Robert Fulton who in 1807 built the first commercial steamboat, the *North River Steamboat*, later known as the *Clermont*.

The wooden Alligator Bayou guest beds were hand-carved from hickory by a North Carolina woodworker hired by Disney specifically for the resort project. The green carpeting in the rooms were meant to represent an alligator-skin texture.

When Dixie Landings opened, it offered guests a newspaper, *The Sassagoula Times* (supposedly originally printed in 1893 and costing five cents but given free to guests).

This newspaper detailed guest information but was also filled with stories that were a mixture of authentic history mixed with fanciful but logical additions from Walt Disney Imagineering.

Today, resort guests receive a generic "Directory of Services and Resort Map", a small pocket sized pamphlet containing just the basic service information but no background story or fun facts.

According to stories in the original issue of *The Sassagoula Times*, Dixie Landings was founded by a pair of brothers from Port Orleans. Colonel J.C. Peace and his brother Everette came up river to make their own home away from the hustle and bustle of the city.

Everette, the recluse of the family who often spent days on end whittling small carvings with a remarkable degree of detail, settled on a remote island in 1835 in the heart of what later became known as Alligator Bayou, to live the life of a hermit. Legends arose about this Old Man Island and its odd inhabitant.

Everette's younger brother, Jonathon, who was an honorary colonel like Colonel Sanders of KFC fame, was much more outgoing. He constructed a stately home known as Acadian House. Neighbors would pay visits on one another regularly, the cotton trade brought numerous business guests, and steamboats along the vital Sassagoula accounted for a steady stream of visitors from across the country.

Before long, a community of stately Southern mansions arose in this tranquil part of the Sassagoula, commonly called Magnolia Bend.

Over the years, Jonathon had heard tall tales of the mysterious Old Man living on Old Man Island but dismissed them as legend. One day, his granddaughter, Susie, came running to him with a beautifully carved wooden bird in her hand. She told stories of the funny old man who gave it to her as a gift.

Turning over the rustic artistic treasure, he could barely make out the tiny letters carved into the base: "Everette Peace, 1857".

Immediately, the Colonel made his way out to the island loudly shouting his older brother's name. The two embraced warmly. Despite Jonathon's offer to come live with him, Everette had no desire to leave his little island. Jonathon continued to visit his brother many nights there to reminisce until their deaths.

The three and a half acre *Ol' Man Island* is a secluded, lushly wooded island accessed via three wooden bridges and features many of the resort's recreational activities, including the main feature swimming pool, children's playground and fishing hole.

It took hundreds of people working over 48 hours to re-plant the live oak tree (Quercus Virginiana) on Ol' Man Island. It is the largest living oak tree ever to be transplanted, with an original height of 55 feet and a weight of approximately 85 tons (including box and dirt).

This live oak, and its sister tree in front of Port Orleans Riverside, were transplanted from the site that now contains Disney's Animal Kingdom theme park.

A wooden plaque on the island reads as follows:

> On Earth Day April 22, 1991 this majestic Live Oak was placed in its new home before you, The Oak and its companion at the entrance of Disney's Port Orleans Resort Riverside each weighed 85 tons and were transplanted from a wooded location 13 miles away.
>
> Cypress boxes 22 foot square were constructed around and beneath each Oak, and after months of preparation, the transportation took three days. Ol' Man Island was then constructed around this Oak as you see it now.

Old Key West

December 1991

The very first DVC resort opened on December 20, 1991 and was just known as Disney's Vacation Club Resort up until January 1996. It was renamed Disney's Old Key West Resort to distinguish it from the newer DVC resorts, Disney's Vero Beach Resort (October 1995) and Disney's Hilton Head Island Resort (March 1996).

The latter two DVC resorts were beautiful, if somewhat secluded, but Disney soon realized that its members were not as excited about different locations, as in the traditional timeshare format, but preferred ones directly connected to a Disney theme park.

Disney guests loved having exclusive access to on-property accommodations with multiple bedrooms, several pools, a general store, and various children's play areas that provided the larger units and flexibility they had been seeking for years and previously had found off property.

The theme of Disney's Old Key West Resort is the famous Florida Keys, a series of islands located off the southern tip of Florida beginning about fifteen miles from Miami. Key West is the most famous and popular of these islands and is a mere ninety-four miles from Cuba.

Legend has it that author Ernest Hemingway wrote part of his novel *A Farewell to Arms* while living above the showroom of a Key West Ford car dealership awaiting delivery of a Ford Model A roadster.

He was introduced to deep-sea fishing, got the nickname "Papa" and worked on other novels while living in Key West, including *For Whom the Bell Tolls, To Have and Have Not* and *The Snows of Kilimanjaro.*

Author Tennessee Williams was another famous resident. He supposedly wrote the first draft of *A Streetcar Named Desire* while living there in a modest bungalow. Many other famous people vacationed on the island, including several presidents of the United States. Singer Jimmy Buffet's song *Margaritaville* is closely associated with the location.

It seemed natural that the first DVC resort in Florida would try to capture the casual tropic feel of Key West in the early 1900s, with just a taste of the Caribbean.

Turtle Krawl is the location of the resort's main facilities. Turtle Krawl, sometimes spelled Kraal or Kraul, is an Afrikaans and Dutch word that refers to a corral for sea turtles that were often gathered in

Key West for export and the making of turtle soup that was once considered a delicacy for the elite. In 1971, the United States government banned the killing of Green Sea Turtles, and today turtle soup is made from regular turtles.

That reference to the turtle industry is also in Old Turtle Pond Road and the Turtle Shack at the resort.

In the early 1900s, the only way to get to Key West was by plane, boat or train. It was not accessible by car until many years later. That is why the check-in desk at Disney's Old Key West Resort resembles a train station with actual antique lampposts from Key West's Duval Street.

After a guest passes the security gate, they drive over a bridge to suggest the bridges that have to be crossed to get to each of the fabled island Keys.

At the far end of Hospitality House is Papa's Den. This is a relatively quiet place where a guest can just grab a book and sit for awhile and meant to call to mind "Papa" Hemingway and his love of books without specifically mentioning the great author.

On either side of the fireplace are sets of framed pens, authentic to the early 1900s, to suggest Hemingway's writing. The marlin fish handing overhead and vintage lures underneath suggest Hemingway's love of fishing and his famous book *The Old Man and the Sea.*

Hemingway had a great love for cats, and so there are eight small statues of cats in the den as well. The two lion statues on the shelves reference his love of big game hunting, the bull his interest in bullfighting and running with the bulls. You'll also find cigar boxes to hold his Cuban cigars and a hand bell to symbolize *For Whom the Bell Tolls.*

Old Key West is themed to be Conch Flats, a well-maintained part of Key West. Turtle Krawl's marina is located on Trumbo Canal which, in turn, connects to the Sassagoula River... the Disney man-made waterway that connects Port Orleans Riverside, Port Orleans French Quarter, Saratoga Springs Resort, and Downtown Disney.

There is a lighthouse by the pool that calls to mind the famous Key West lighthouse opened in 1848. In the years following, the lighthouse underwent a number of upgrades. In 1969, the U.S. Coast Guard decommissioned the Key West Lighthouse since there was no longer a need for a full-time keeper due to technological advancements. Today, the building is a museum dedicated to Key West's maritime heritage.

The resort's restaurant is Olivia's Cafe, a casual sit-down restaurant with some menu items that are related to the specialties of Key West. There are quick-serve eateries as well, including Good's Food To Go and the Turtle Shack. The Gurgling Suitcase bar also has some simple snacks.

For many, Olivia's Cafe is a "hidden treasure" at Walt Disney World, with its hospitable staff and tasty offerings that are suitable for the entire family. It is also a favorite location for many executive cast members who find the secluded location and good food a convenient place for a "working lunch" close to their offices.

The Imagineers came up with an elaborate back story for the restaurant. It is one that is fairly well-known by the cast members who work there, and they are quite willing to share it with guests.

The official website states: "A longtime resident of Conch Flats, Olivia welcomes diners with Island-inspired dishes. This nautical-themed eatery has the friendly, familiar feel of a neighborhood institution and is a perennial favorite of many a Guest."

Besides some more traditional offerings are Conch Flats items like conch fritters, conch chowder, Conch Republic omelet and more, including the beloved Key Lime tart dessert.

The story of Olivia, whose photo graced the menu, is much more involved, however.

Olivia Farnsworth lived in a small cottage along Turtle Krawl, upwind of the strip. She loved cooking, but did not have the money to open a restaurant of her own. She was very friendly and very proud of her cooking. Almost daily she would invite curious passers-by who smelled her cooking to come in to her dining room and pull up a chair to enjoy what she had prepared.

Soon, these visits became more and more frequent, both for the locals and for visiting out-of-towners as well. Olivia quickly ran out of room and everything else. People began bringing their own tables and chairs and even silverware, then left them there for their next visit.

That's why the silverware and the chairs in the restaurant are mismatched and add to a homey, family-type atmosphere. This was not a restaurant that was built, but it was Olivia's small cottage home which transformed into a restaurant by necessity and has been operating successfully for quite some time.

Long-forgotten and perhaps lost are the original Imagineering descriptions. Here they are to help enhance the experience even more:

"Olivia Farnsworth is 60 going on 20. She arrived in Conch Flats longer ago than you'll get her to talk about. She moved into a small cottage along Turtle Krawl, turned on her stove, and changed everything around here for the better.

"Upwind from downtown, Olivia's cooking was a hard secret to keep. Dinner traffic boomed. Soon she began doubling recipes, then double doubling. Then triple doubling, until the math got ugly. She pulled up more chairs, added more tables, and sat people on the porch, until the floor plan got all cattywhumpus. Finally, to the town's great relief, Olivia made it official, cinched up her apron and hung out her shingle."

The Imagineers even included "A Little Note from Miss Olivia" herself:

"How I came to be here in Conch Flats is a whole other story. Besides that was more than a few home-cooked meals ago and I've got other fish to fry, if you know what I mean.

"The long and short of it is, I never intended to be any kind of big-time restaurant owner. I just happened to have this cozy cottage I called home and my kitchen just happened to be on the leeward side where aromas could wander out along Turtle Krawl. Seems like every time I turned on the stove, 'specially early in the morning, folks would drop by with a friendly smile and a healthy appetite. I didn't mind. I'd just pull another chair up to the table. Then one more chair, and one more chair...

" 'Fore long, I found myself setting a second kitchen table and practically inviting passers-by to 'come on in and sit down.' Whether it's for two or twenty, I have it on pretty good authority that I can cook with the best of 'em, and I know you won't find better company to keep this side of the Dry Tortugas.

" 'Course, I admit I've sure had my share of helping hands from more than a few friends along the way. Miss Vickey, for instance, is my kind of people. She may not exactly fit into any proper pigeonhole, but she's been a true friend to me. In fact, I owe the whole look of Olivia's to Miss V's artistic eye for coordinated color combinations.

"Then there's Captain Wahoo. He often doesn't have a nickel to his name, but his fish tales have kept me laughing through some lean times, and he's always made sure I get first choice of the bounty his boat brings home to the Flats.

"There are lots of others who made Olivia's what it is — like Frenchie, who's sometimes a pest but always a pal, and Hank, and... well, I could go on, but I've a kitchen to keep up with and a passel of people to feed. So let me let you get on with your life with this closing thought — you're always welcome at Olivia's Cafe, where the food's always good and the atmosphere's always 100% Conch Flats."

Some of those references to certain people may seem a little confusing to recent patrons. When the restaurant first opened with the resort in 1991, there was a mannequin at the check-in podium that was dressed in a matronly outfit and was supposed to represent Miss Vickey, who was welcoming you to the restaurant because Olivia was busy in the kitchen and couldn't do it herself.

In the lobby that is now filled with photos of DVC members was a second mannequin of Captain Wahoo, who was dressed in a yellow rain slicker and cap and then moved to a rear booth in the restaurant where he was enjoying a cup of coffee.

He was to represent the heritage of the sea, especially with the marina just outside the windows. As additional seating was needed for guests, he joined Miss Vickey at the check-in podium to welcome guests.

Both mannequins have been gone for quite some time.

The Gurgling Suitcase Bar has a story behind it as well. During Prohibition, people would come down to Key West to purchase illegal alcohol. They would pack it using their clothes to cushion the bottles so they wouldn't break in their suitcases.

Law enforcement officers soon caught on to this practice and when they stopped people, they would pick up the luggage and shake it to see if it "gurgled," indicating that there was liquid inside.

The fictional mayor of the town of Conch Flats is Cooter Trumbo, Esquire. "Cooter" is a call-out to a slang name for a turtle (turtles are a reoccurring theme in the resort) in the southeast United States, and "Trumbo" is for Trumbo Point, a man made addition to Key West in 1912 by the Trumbo American Dredging Company to accommodate a shipping port for the railroad.

The town's logo includes an image of the city and three Latin phrases: Pro Bono Persona (For Your Own Good), Veni Vici Veni Adinfiintium (I Came. I Saw. I Stayed Forever) and Carpe Diem Omnidiem (Seize the Day Everyday.)

On the upper shelves and rafters of The Conch Flats General Store are items that reflect Old Key West's history of wrecking and salvaging from nearby shipwrecks, making it the richest city in the United States at one time. Originally, the store was supposedly owned and operated by Miss Vickey who had a great love of eclectic items and since the store was right next to Olivia's house, it was easy for her to drop over and help out.

Wilderness Lodge / Boulder Ridge Villas / Copper Creek Villas and Cabins

May 1994 / November 2000 / July 2017

At Disney's Wilderness Lodge that opened May 28, 1994, the Walt Disney Imagineers attempted to maintain a linear time lime for the entire area that is divided into three distinct-but-connected sections that were all built at different times.

The arrival of the Transcontinental Railroad in the Pacific Northwest spurred the development of rustic, residential communities housing the railroad workers and that is the story of Boulder Ridge Villas, formerly known as the Villas at Wilderness Lodge when they first opened in November 15, 2000. They were renamed Boulder Ridge Villas in May 2016.

With the completion of the railroad, grand vacation lodges that attracted visitors coming to the U.S. National Parks became hugely popular for tourists and that is the story behind Disney's Wilderness Lodge. The Lodge has design elements that are clearly reminiscent of Old Faithful Inn at Yellowstone National Park and the Awahwanee Lodge in Yosemite National Park.

Decades later, the abandonment of the railroad (in favor of cars, planes, etc.), resulted in the resourceful locals turning railroad relics (abandoned quarries, train stations, railroad-supervisor residences, etc.) into new living spaces for today's travelers and that is the tale of Copper Creek Villas & Cabins that opened on July 17, 2017.

The development of the concept of the Wilderness Lodge was inspired by the 1982 announcement of Disney executive Dick Nunis of a proposed new hotel for WDW property.

"The Cypress Point Lodge will be west of River Country and be themed as a western hotel. It'll include log cabins along Bay Lake," said Nunis. It would have been a moderate-priced 600 room hotel facility that was reminiscent of a hunting lodge secluded in a deep forest.

However, cost overruns for the building of Epcot Center resulted in Cypress Point Lodge being cancelled, and it is no longer mentioned in any documentation after 1983.

THE BIRTH OF THE WILDERNESS LODGE

When Disney CEO Michael Eisner arrived in 1984, he chose to develop both Disney's Grand Floridian Resort, in place of the proposed Asian resort, and a lodge-themed resort, similar to the announced Cypress Point Lodge, which became the Wilderness Lodge.

It was Eisner's goal to entice lauded architects, like Robert Stern and Michael Graves, to design buildings on WDW property, giving them an inordinate amount of freedom.

"In our architecture, Disney continues to produce the kind of groundbreaking entertainment that keeps the Disney name magical to people around the world. Our architecture is part of the show," said Eisner in August 1992 at the ground-breaking ceremony for the Wilderness Lodge.

Peter Dominick Jr., who headed the Urban Design Group of Denver, Colorado, and was an avid outdoorsman, had been commissioned to design the now-premium resort. He was well known for having a great passion and understanding of the building traditions of the Rocky Mountain West.

As part of the research for the Disney resort, Dominick and members of the Disney Development Company visited lodges at Yosemite, Yellowstone and Glacier National Parks.

Dominick recalled that when he presented his initial design to Eisner that "Michael Eisner leapt up from the conference table to examine the drawing more closely, challenging his creative team to accept our idea.

"During these halcyon years of Disney, when Eisner was being hailed as a modern-day Medici, we worked with one of the great creative companies of its time and collaborated with the most talented designers, working at their most creative boundaries."

Several different lodges have influences at the Wilderness Lodge including elements from the Timberline Lodge in Oregon to the Lake McDonald Lodge in Glacier National Park.

However, Dominick's primary inspirations for the Wilderness Lodge were clearly the Old Faithful Inn at Yellowstone National Park and the Ahwahnee Lodge in Yosemite National Park that are referenced several times in both the interior and exterior of the final design.

For instance, outside the Wilderness Lodge flies five flags just as they do at its inspiration, the Old Faithful Inn in Yellowstone. However, the flags at Wilderness Lodge have a Disney twist.

Facing the building and looking left to right, the flags are the Wilderness Lodge flag, the Florida State flag, the American flag, the Disney Mickey Mouse flag and finally the Disney Vacation Club flag.

"[Disney's Wilderness Lodge] does, in fact, capture the spirit and sense of place one associates with our National Parks, icons of our American heritage ...with their art, architecture and dramatic landscapes," Dominick said.

"There are romantic and endearing qualities associated with the early national parks movement—the Northwest, the Native Americans, the great lodges. All of these elements have been combined in wonderful detail, creating a unique wilderness experience."

Dominick was inspired by Stephen Mather, the first director of the National Park Service, who insisted that architects use whatever building materials were indigenous to an area in building a hotel so that it blends all aspects together and becomes more organic to the setting.

This style was known as "rustic architecture." Robert Reamer, the designer of the Ahwahnee Lodge, did use whatever building materials were indigenous to the location to make that iconic resort in Yosemite.

"We poured a ton of energy into the Wilderness Lodge Resort," said Donimick to *The Pennsylvania Gazette*. "[We] ... found that a client like Disney had resources, questions, and demands that were bigger, deeper, and more thorough than we were used to on a smaller scale."

The Wilderness Lodge Resort project was completed by Urban Design Group under the leadership of the founding Principals of 4240 Architecture. Randy Johnson and Peter H. Dominick Jr., FAIA were involved in the project

One other person who was very involved in the design process was Michael Eisner himself. "Michael reviewed the design completion and was involved in design presentations at each stage of the design process," said Randy Johnson.

Johnson added, "Models and renderings of the Wilderness Lodge were built at each phase of the project from general schematic plans through to construction, as the design was fine-tuned. The initial design presented at the competition stage remained throughout the process, and is reflected in the final design built today.

"In additionl to Thomas Molesworth and Hopi Indians, the team researched Northwest Coast Natives, Landscape Painters such as Albert Bierstadt and Thomas Moran, and architects like Mary Coulter, Robert Reamer, and Gilbert Stanley Underwood."

"Silver Creek comes from my experiences growing up and camping in Oregon. From experiencing the origin of the Metolius River, a spring bubbling out of the ground, hiking in Silver Falls State Park, and seeing the great bundled railroad support piers in the Columbia River that inspired the lobby columns."

Dominick set out to create a log hotel from the early 1900s in the Northwest Rockies, incorporating authentic Native American elements, natural lighting and, wherever possible, traditional building materials like natural limestone.

"Disney's Wilderness Lodge captures the spirit and sense of place one associates with our National Parks, icons of our American heritage ... with their art, architecture and dramatic landscapes," said Dominick Jr. "There are romantic and endearing qualities associated with the early national parks movement – the Northwest, the Native Americans, the great lodges. All of these elements have been combined in wonderful detail, creating a unique wilderness experience."

Eighty-five loads of lodge pole pines were harvested from "standing dead forests" (meaning the trees had been killed from a natural cause, like insects or volcanic soot) in Oregon and Montana to build the resort. No living trees were chopped down to create the lodge poles and Disney replanted new trees wherever they took trees. Stretched end to end, the lodge poles would be forty miles long.

The wood floor in the lobby is composed of Brazilian cherry, white oak, bird's eye maple, and burl walnut. It actually mimics a Native American Hopi rug that tells a "storm creation story".

There is the center of the earth and from it flow four rivers in a lightning pattern to the four corners of the earth where lodge poles extend upward to hold the canopy of the sky. Standing on an upper level looking down into the lobby, the design is clearly prominent.

Cast members will tell you the wooden "carpet design" also depicts the symbol of unity among the four seasons, wildlife, man, and the cosmos.

When the Wilderness Lodge first opened, and then every November annually as part of Native American Heritage Month, there would be a ceremony performed called the Blessing of the Four Directions, which is rooted in the belief that human beings are tied to all things in nature.

It is this belief which assigned virtues to the four cardinal directions: East, South, West and North. It was conducted by James Hansen (Black Wolf) and Anita Hansen (Quick Silver) and the ceremony symbolically drove out negative energy and purified the resort for the year ahead. The Hansens also told stories and answered questions for guests about Native American culture.

The last ceremony was held in 2009. Apparently, the Hansens decided they no longer wanted to travel to do it and Disney decided not to find an alternative.

The rockwork for the exterior and interior is fabricated using gunite. Real rocks were used to create molds for cement that was later spray painted to look like granite or sandstone.

Dominick's work on the Wilderness Lodge was so well received by guests and critics that he went on to also design the Animal Kingdom

Lodge at WDW and The Grand Californian resort in Anaheim for the Disney Company. Dominick passed away at the age of 67 in 2009.

THE WILDERNESS LODGE LOBBY

Located behind the Guest Services Desk is a large mounted gold key. In 1995, the resort was recognized with the grand prize for "Excellence in Hospitality Design" in the lobby/reception category at 14th annual Gold Key Awards by International Hotel/Motel & Restaurant Association. The "Mickey head" on the key was meant to remind the cast members to always unlock the magic in their hearts for the guests.

The Bright Angel Lodge at the Grand Canyon has a small geologic fireplace that was quarried directly from the layers of the Grand Canyon but the WDW Imagineers went for a more dramatic storytelling version for the Wilderness Lodge.

The fireplace is an intricate 82-foot-high replica of the South Rim Grand Canyon Strata. As you ascend the levels of the lobby, you travel upward to modern times. To see evidence of the first creatures to squirm over and under the surface of the earth, guests should go to the fourth floor and search the layers of Tapeats Sandstone for worm borrows and trilobite trails.

Paleontologist Robert Reid (who was also an artist) was sent to study the actual walls of the Grand Canyon. His studies were reproduced in a detailed book that was used to help contractors create the fireplace replete with a kaleidoscope of colors, rocks and fossils—many of which are real.

Some of the fossils of prehistoric plant and animal life are several hundred millions years old and are carefully embedded in the correct stratus for a historically accurate view. They pre-date the dinosaur era.

Due to laws restricting the removal of material from National Parks, the fireplace was constructed and sculpted in place by artisans using similar materials as found in the Grand Canyon strata.

More than 100 colors in hues of green, magenta, buff, red, black and brown are visible. From the Vishnu Schist to Bass Limestone to Tapeats Sandstone to the Redwall and Temple Butte Limestone and finally ending with Kaibab Limestone and Toroweap Formation, the fireplace represents the 1.6 billion years of the time it took for the layers of rock to form.

The variations are recreated in the same proportions as those that appear in the real Grand Canyon that range from 50-700 feet thick.

The fireplace is built to scale with the geologic layout of the Grand Canyon, complete with geologic disconformities (periods of deposition, erosion, tilting and renewed deposition on top of the older rocks).

The detail is nearly perfect with the textbook diagrams documenting the geology of the Grand Canyon.

Samples of elements from each strata are housed in glass display cases near the fireplace on each floor level. These displays describe the epoch that section of the fireplace rock represented.

One of the things that does not exist in the real Grand Canyon is a Hidden Mickey, but it does in the Wilderness Lodge fireplace.

Directly facing the fireplace, on the right hand side of the three-sided fireplace, where a lodge pole on the left is jutting out before the start of the next floor (in the reddish rock) is the famous three-circled Mickey Mouse head.

At the Guest Services front desk, guests can get a riddle clue sheet to help them locate the more than two-dozen Hidden Mickeys at the Wilderness Lodge Resort.

The Wilderness Lodge fireplace is a real working fireplace. Originally, it burned wood, which caused several challenges over the early years including, raising the humidity level in the lobby that caused problems, like cracking the wood used in the massive totem poles. It was converted to a gas burning fireplace for a number of reasons, including the fact that gas is safer and can be more easily controlled.

A variety of Native American tribes, including Cheyenne, Crow, Sioux, and Blackfoot are represented in the lobby and throughout the lodge, including the guest rooms that feature fabrics representing different tribes.

Hanging above the lobby are four massive, 500 pound floating tepee chandeliers. Made from actual rawhide that was stretched over the framework, each of the tepee shades are hand-painted with geometric Native American symbols in red and black. Inside each tepee is a 48-bulb fixture which provides 2,880 watts needed to illuminate the entire lobby.

The tepees are approximately ten feet in diameter at the base and ten feet high at the peak. Additionally, they are framed with a bronze and steel ring (with an aged finish) of silhouetted buffaloes and Native Americans on horseback. The images were inspired by photographs and the work of artist Thomas Molesworth.

Behind the front desk is a beautiful collection of reproductions of cradleboards, a wooden frame and a soft skin pouch used for the protection of a baby or "papoose" to prevent it from falling.

Within the first few weeks after a baby was born, the mother would begin to lace the baby into the cradleboard so that it could be carried on the woman's back or hooked onto a saddle. Left to right, the cradleboards behind the front desk represent the North American Indian tribes of Crow, Apache, Arapaho, Cheyenne, Ute, Kiowa, Navajo, and Comanche.

The Spirit of America Discovery statue in the show at The American Adventure pavilion at Epcot has a Native American woman with a cradleboard on her back. The statue is meant to suggest the sixteen year old Sacagawea, the Native American woman who helped guide the Lewis and Clark expedition, along with her newborn baby.

A striking and unique garment is the Elk Tooth Dress located near the lobby elevators. It is made of red wool blanket or Stroud Cloth, which was considered a desirable decorative fabric. This type of dress was typical of one that might be worn by the Kiowa and Arapaho Plains tribeswomen.

This particular dress was obviously the possession of a great hunter's wife since elk teeth are a great display of wealth. An elk only has two teeth and a dress might take hundreds of them. Most hunters saved the teeth as a memento of the hunt or traded for them with other warriors.

This rare dress, which has been determined to be from around 1875, was worn for special ceremonial occasions like a wedding, a special dance or a young girl entering womanhood. This particular dress has 161 teeth arranged in five almost even rows. Some rows have 32 while others have 31 or 33.

An authentic display of moccasins made by the Plains Indians is at the far end of the lobby near the fireplace along with other displays that bring a sense of reality and history to the lobby.

Headdresses are displayed in the lobby. Some Native Americans believed that by wearing the feathers of the eagle, one of the most respected and revered birds, it was possible to impart the characteristics and power of the eagle to the wearer.

Today, it is illegal to use eagle feathers, so the WDW Imagineers had to adapt turkey feathers when they recreated headdresses for display.

At the entrance to the Whispering Canyon restaurant are two headdresses on display.

On the left hand side is a Single Trailer Split Horn Headdress that would have been worn by a high-ranking warrior chief circa 1835. A single trailer headdress has a felt trailer hanging from the back of the headdress to the ground. The feathers are displayed on only one side of the trailer, giving it a symmetrical appearance.

This particular headdress was inspired by one belonging to Mato-Tope of the Mandan Tribe.

On the right hand side is a Double Trailer Eagle Feathers Headdress from around 1875. A double trailer headdress is named for the two felt trailers that hang down the back of the headdress to the ground. An elaborate headdress of this style would have been worn by the highest ranking member of the Sioux tribe.

This particular headdress was inspired by one belonging to Chief Red Cloud of the Oglala Lakota tribe of the Great Sioux Nation.

Located between two bundles of lodgepoles towards the back of the lobby is the Ermine-Tipped Raven Headdress that resembles a nineteenth century Crow warrior headdress. Its inspiration is the watercolor painting done by artist Charles Bodmer that is located off the lobby elevator on the fourth floor. The painting was rendered in the 1830s during an expedition led by Prince Maximillian to the American West.

Just to the right of the elevators is the Feather Duster Rooster Feathers Headdress. It was used by the Crow tribe circa 1890. The red of the feathers indicates war honor.

In addition, there is an authentic display of moccasins made by the Plains Indians. Hard rawhide soles were hand sewed to a soft buckskin upper piece. Often, they would chew on the material to make it softer and more pliable. The footwear was then ornamented with dyes, quills, beads, cloth, buttons, fur and fringe and this work varied greatly among the different tribes.

Using no measuring tools or patterns, moccasins were each one-of-a-kind made to fit a specific foot of a child or adult. Intricate designs existed only in the minds of the Native Americans making them and sometimes the design evolved as it was being worked on.

Another display case specifically showcases some actual beadwork for a variety of different articles. The "seed" bead, a small round opaque Venetian glass bead, became available to the Native American cultures around 1840 through the pioneers entering their territories. Because "seed" beads were partly handmade, they were somewhat irregular.

The delicacy of the bead pattern determined the size of the bead chosen. When settlers began to crowd into the Sioux country about 1860, beadwork became a major industry for the Native Americans that was highly popular until around 1900, although examples of this beautiful craft are still produced in smaller quantities today.

Settlers sometimes dictated the style of bead pattern for the garments they were willing to purchase or trade. Later visitors to the area brought imported Czechoslovakian beads, which were somewhat darker than Venetian beads and had a slightly bluish tinge.

THE TWO TOTEM POLES

The Walt Disney Company hired Duane Pasco to carve the two 55-foot-tall totem poles for the lobby. Though not a descendant of Pacific Northwest Indians, Pasco is considered one of the most adept among the handful of Canadian and American master carvers. His work is done for both private and civic groups.

One pole is dedicated to the eagle while the other to the raven. These animals were chosen because most Northwest Native American cultures have these birds as a significant part of their cultural mythology.

Pasco did not want the stories to depict a specific version by a particular tribe or clan but to capture a "pan coastal" interpretation. Originally, it was planned for the two poles to directly face each other but in native cultures this suggests conflict, not harmony, so they were placed slightly askew.

"These totem poles measure 3-feet wide at the top and 5-feet wide at the bottom and each is constructed of two 27-foot sections spliced together," Pasco said. "The choice of characters and their placement were the choice of Disneyworld's consultants."

"I made very detailed drawings for this project because there were to be three assistants helping me: Pat Huggins, Loren White, and Scott Jensen," he said. "I drew front, side, three-quarter views and lots of cross sections. In this way the client, the contractor and all the carvers can see exactly what the end product should look like."

"The goal in designing the totem poles was to use legend and lore that was common among many tribes of the Northwest Coast but not necessarily specific to any one tribe," wrote Pasco's wife, Katie.

"This was easy to accomplish because the figures and the stories they represent remain fairly consistent. Characters on the Disney poles are pan-coastal in nature, with a particular attempt to portray figures not associated with inherited stories or family crests."

Pasco and his assistants began cutting away material with chainsaws. For finer details they used adzes, knives and other traditional carving tools. The entire process took roughly six months. The poles are made from four old-growth red cedars each about 5 feet in diameter at the base.

The big cedars had to be hollowed out and there was considerable rot inside that had to be removed. Pasco reinforced the centers by splicing in new wood. After the poles were carved, they were finished with Thompson's Water Seal and then painted. The installation, which took place January 1994, took five days. The poles are flanked by stone walls and tied to steel I-beams.

There are plaques at the base of each totem pole summarizing each story:

> The Raven Pole like all totem poles should be read from bottom to top. It includes Whale, Cougar, Wren, the bear cub twins, Dolphin and Salmon and culminates with the story of Raven pulling the sun, moon and stars from a box to light the darkened world. The figures on this pole are common to many tribes of the great Northwest.

> The Eagle Pole, like all totem poles should be read from the bottom to the top. It includes Bear Chief, Frog, Bear Cub, Mountain Goat, Mouse Woman, Raven and Beaver. Eagle, who is a helper to all humans and animals perches on top. He is aided by three watchmen, known as Taan-skeel, who keep their eyes open day and night protecting the village. The figures on this pole are common to many tribes of the great Northwest.

Wilson & Associates (who later designed the interiors for Disneyland Paris Cheyenne Hotel) under the design team of Connie Jackson and Susan Seifert were responsible for the interior of the Wilderness Lodge.

As reference, they used the books *Great Lodges of the National Parks* by Christine Barnes and *True West* by Christine Mather.

The lobby is a tribute to Native Americans. Whispering Canyon Cafe showcases cowboys as depicted on the backs of the chairs and the fireplace grating.

The Territory Lounge is devoted to the early explorers of the West, which is why on the ceiling is painted a map of the famous Lewis and Clark Expedition. In the glass cases are authentic artifacts from the 1800s.

On the walls are a 34 star American flag from 1861 which explains why it is a bit tattered and an actual Wyoming State flag from 1890 that features an image of a white buffalo.

The paintings in the room are "inspired by Carl Clemens Runcius (1869-1959)", a renowned wildlife artist who started painting animals in Wyoming in 1895.

Artist's Point celebrates the painters who captured the images of the wilderness with murals inspired by Albert Bierstadt, who is known for his lavish, sweeping landscapes of the American West.

Throughout the resort, the furniture and lighting fixtures were inspired by American furniture designer Thomas Molesworth, who had an understanding of Native American culture and the American West. This influence is notable in the flat backed chairs in Whispering Canyon Cafe.

Other pieces in Disney's Wilderness Lodge were inspired by Charles and Henry Greene, who ushered in the American Arts and Crafts Movement that is seen throughout the entire resort. Since the furniture was inspired by deceased artists, Wilson & Associates had to custom design every single piece.

To the right of the lobby side of the fireplace is the elevated Library area of Whispering Canyon restaurant. It has both Gustav Stickley chairs and Frank Lloyd Wright tables and china cabinet. Stickley was a proponent of the Arts and Crafts Movement, traditional craftsmanship in simple forms.

The pottery and ceramics that adorn the cabinet are authentic Arts and Crafts pieces from the Arts and Crafts Movement. They are a 100 years old. Mass production by machines was becoming more common so the Arts and Crafts Movement emphasized the appreciation for hand made glass and pottery because they expressed the unique individuality of the particular artist.

THE IMAGINEERING BACK STORY OF THE WILDERNESS LODGE

It is a wonderful sensory experience to seemingly leave Florida property when guests turn off World Drive onto Timberline Drive, into a world of wildflowers, pine forests and images of bears of the Pacific Northwest on a winding road that leads not directly to the front of the resort but just off to its side so it is "discovered" in the wilderness.

The lodge was supposedly built around a hot mineral spring that becomes Silver Creek and flows toward Bay Lake, stopping briefly to ignite Fire Rock Geyser.

However, generally unknown to guests and cast members, there was a fairly detailed back story created by the Imagineers about the Lodge when the resort first opened on May 28, 1994.

According to articles in a commemorative edition newspaper titled *The Silver Creek Star* Vol. B, No. 28,928 (actually a clever way of communicating information to guests staying at the Lodge about the guest services procedures, as well as sharing the colorful Imagineering back story), Wilderness Lodge had a rich history and it centered on the exploits of one man: Colonel Ezekiel Moreland.

A magnificently beautiful valley in America's Northwest was discovered by Colonel Moreland in the early 1800s. He described the location in a letter to his daughter as "a tranquil valley along the shores of a splendid lake...a cathedral of trees that touch the sky, a stream that glitters with radiant light, rocks and minerals of every color and description...I call this sweet valley—Silver Creek Springs."

Later, he returned to settle this frontier area and make it his new home along with his daughter who was a young art curator nicknamed "Jenny".

According to the *Silver Star*: "Using the small fortune Moreland had raised from the fur trade, they brought out a crew of men from St. Louis and had a small lodge built near the fresh water spring. The Wilderness Lodge welcomed artists, scientists, and nature lovers of all kinds over the years. As the number of visitors grew, the Lodge expanded to accommodate them. Eventually, they added rooms that grew around the spring, making it part of the Wilderness Lodge."

Artist Point became a location where guests could experience the grandeur of the vistas that inspired the painters whose work decorated the dining room.

In the beginning, every location at the Wilderness Lodge had a back story, as well. The Teton Boat and Bike Rental building, located near the lake shore, was supposedly the original cabin that Colonel Ezekiel Moreland built shortly after arriving in the valley for the first time.

The Colonel learned the legend of the Fire Rock Geyser from the Indian elder known as Running Elk. During one especially bad winter, an Indian hunting party had been trapped in the valley by excessive snow.

They built a fire and were forced to keep it burning continuously. After five days, the rock beneath them began to crack and tremble. The next day, the trembling became even greater and as they placed another piece of wood on the fire, the Earth opened up and a great pillar of hot, steaming water erupted upwards, launching a nearby teepee high into the air. The frightened group fled the valley with warnings to avoid the location where they had angered the earth with their wasteful use of continuous fire.

Georgie MacGregor, an unlucky prospector, brought dynamite to aid in his mining of the area, but ended up blowing up his cabin and the huge crater that remained became the pool.

The name of the area obviously brings to mind the very famous Silver Springs in Marion County, Florida, home to one of the largest artisan springs in the world and forming the headwaters of the Silver River. The location is a famous tourist attraction (with glass bottom boat rides) and has been used as the site for filming many movies, including some scenes for the classic *Tarzan* movies of the 1930s and 1940s.

The vivid and convoluted adventures of Colonel Moreland and his friends, just like those of Merriweather Adam Pleasure for Pleasure Island, have completely disappeared from Disney history along with so many other interesting tales that should be documented for future researchers.

WILLIAM ROBERTSON

William Robertson was a Disney character sculptor before becoming self-employed. Disney hired him to build frames for topiaries, which he did in the backyard of his Florida College Park home.

One of those topiaries was the 14-foot long bison out in front of the entrance of the Wilderness Lodge that included its embedded footprints in the walkway leading to his final location. That figure has since been relocated.

Robertson was also responsible for the topiaries in the Johnny Depp film, *Edward Scissorhands* (1990).

Displayed in the lodge posts of the Wilderness Lodge lobby are many carvings by Robertson, showing along their height the four corresponding levels of animal life living in the wilderness.

At the lowest level, you find the creatures of the field and meadows, such as the turkey, raccoon, squirrel and rabbit. The animals on the next are those on the lower mountain, such as the wolf, pronghorn antelope, bison and elk.

On the third are those of the high mountain level such as the mountain goat, sheep, bear and mountain lion. The highest level has the birds of prey such as the falcon, American bald eagle, hawk and owl.

It took four tons of wood to create these creatures. On average, it was ten days to carve each animal using an electric saw, rotary saw, a chisel and a hammer.

Robertson did massive research and then rendered drawings that he used to create scale clay or plaster models as guides.

Mountain goats and some Rocky Mountain sheep look similar, so Robertson had to emphasize the subtle differences in head shapes. Disney suggested some animals they would like included but the artist said that after that point he had a free hand.

"I had to know how to fit the animals into the trees," Robertson said. "Each animal had to be carved around the limbs, knots and rotten spots. There was no way to change the tree."

Robertson said he wanted to "show the mark of the hands of the artist—not slick but a rough, human feeling".

"Disney will try and do something artificially to meet fire codes or to get it to be weather-resistant," Robertson said. "But in this instance everything was done in the traditional way, by the artist, by hand."

Every night during the six months before the hotel's Memorial Day 1994 opening, Robertson climbed scaffolds to chisel into the pine logs. "We finished the day before the hotel opened," he laughed.

Robertson's sculpture work can also be seen on the six brass animals at the check-in desk that were purposely positioned at a children's level so they could be petted by curious youngsters.

The beavers in the elevator holding a long stick that is used as a railing are also the work of the sculptor, who at one time worked with Disney Legend Blaine Gibson, renowned for his Disney sculpting.

As a bit of whimsy, Robertson also took months to carve the cedar character totem pole outside the Mercantile gift shop that features Mickey Mouse, Goofy, Donald Duck, and Humphrey the Bear. Over the years, the store has sold exclusive merchandise featuring the image of Humphrey.

"This wasn't necessarily just another traditional Disney image," he said. "That was rather exciting as an artist. I had freedom to have a little fun. I called an artist in Oregon to get advice on how to handle that kind of wood. I'd never have chosen cedar. It has to be kept sopping wet to cut it. But the other totem poles were also done in cedar."

Disney's Wilderness Lodge Resort is the only Disney resort hotel to have an official mascot, the brown bear. Images and allusions can be found throughout the resort, including bear tracks embedded in the walkways.

To make that potentially fearsome mascot friendlier for younger guests, some of the brown bear images are of the Disney animated character Humphrey the Bear, a lovable, overweight brown bear who lives in the fictional Brownstone National Park which also themes into the idea of a National Park lodge.

Only seven Disney cartoon characters have starred in their own theatrical cartoon series. Humphrey the Bear was the last one to do so, starting in 1956, before the Disney Company decided to stop making theatrical cartoon shorts.

Boulder Ridge Villas (formerly Villas at Wilderness Lodge)

November 2000

Christian Barlock of Urban Design Group under the leadership of Peter Dominick Jr. led the design for the Villas at Wilderness Lodge Vacation Club, as well as subsequent hotels with Disney.

"The site and wetlands dictated the placement of the DVC hotel," said Christian Barlock. "The site dictated the shape and position of the hotel – constrained on all three sides by two acres of wetlands.

"The form of the building mimics that of the main hotel with the four-story atrium lobby positioned close to the main hotel. By sitting the building at right angles to the Wilderness Lodge, the DVC exposes the narrowest building profile to the hotel guest of the Lodge while maximizing the views to Bay Lake.

"Additionally, the Villas' rooflines step down toward the Lodge, again lessening the impact of the Villas on the adjacent Lodge."

According to the Imagineering back story, on the land adjacent to where the Wilderness Lodge would later be built, a team of railroad workers in the 1860s found an ideal location to set up camp as they built the transcontinental railway. They built themselves a place to stay but moved on once their job was completed.

The biggest design challenge for UDG was to build a larger

building with slightly different requirements on a constrained site comprising two acres of wetlands and adjacent to a dominant and beloved iconographic building, but with a smaller budget and shorter construction schedule.

In addition they had to create the illusion that the 147 room DVC property was constructed prior to the Wilderness Lodge, even though in reality they were opening almost a decade later. So, among other things, a different color palette including the dark red clay roof and light gray shingles was utilized.

The inspiration for the villas came from the early railroad hotels developed by Fred Harvey in the early 1900s.

Randy Johnson stated, "The DVC's clapboard and shingle structure reflects the simple and straightforward approach of early railroad hotel architecture and gives the building the appearance of having been built prior to the Wilderness Lodge."

The four-story octagonal-shaped atrium, complete with log columns and central stone fireplace forms the central lobby and is reminiscent of a railroad roundhouse and serves as a transitional area to different locations.

At the second floor lobby balcony frieze, ornamental stenciled graphics and carved log beam ends depicting animals celebrate the Native American medicine wheel and the Circle of Life.

Sculptor William Robertson came out of retirement to carve the animals on those logs as he had for the lodge poles in the main lodge. He even included a hidden three-dimensional mouse in one of the log beams to serve as an era appropriate early "Hidden Mickey".

When this DVC resort opened, it featured a small, quiet room off to the right side of the lobby called The Iron Spike Room. An iron spike was traditionally used on railroad ties.

In the fall of 2007, it was renamed The Carolwood Pacific Room thanks to the efforts of Michael Broggie, co-founder of the Carolwood Historical Society and son of legendary Imagineer Roger Broggie. It referenced Walt Disney's 1/8th scale miniature railroad of the same name that he installed in the backyard of his California home from 1950-1953.

Copper Creek Villas and Cabins

July 2017

The Copper Creek Villas and Cabins Imagineer project manager Mitch Mioelli stated:

"We were pulling from different materials and objects that were indigenous to the Pacific Northwest. What we wanted to do, knowing that this resort would have been here for hundreds of years, is take materials that these settlers would have found on site and the rejuvenation and sort of re-gentrification of the area.

"Its found objects that would have almost been artifacts from the mining area from the railroad are incorporated. They would have been repurposed and built into their everyday houses and everyday construction.

"Everything was coming westward on the trains and this is really an homage to Walt (Disney) and his love of trains and the westward expansion of the United States. So we played on that to make everyone feel that this was an early settlement.

"Everything is rooted in the history of railroad and the natural environment. We wanted to make it feel like the interior expanded into the exterior so there's floor-to-ceiling windows."

Ken Potrock, senior vice president and general manager of the Disney Vacation Club said, "Our guests have told us they don't want any old hotel; they want themed hotels. They want a hotel that has a back story. They want to hear 'is there a connection to Walt Disney?' So we worked hard to give them what they wanted."

Copper Creek that continues the storytelling of Disney's Wilderness Lodge, is inspired by the "legendary mining and railroad history of the Pacific Northwest," as well as Walt Disney's love of railroads.

Where the tale of the original structures at Wilderness Lodge draw their story from the 1800s, the new Copper Creek Villas & Cabins are tied to a later period when the railroad, mining, and quarry managers and foremen brought their families out west and built homes (like the cabins) along the lakes with some of the materials and objects found in the area.

The story concept is that the units employ "up-cycling" of materials like rustic tracks and reclaimed wood, as well as giant cogs that form a wall hanging and an occasional Hidden Mickey. Light fixtures are made from shards of colored glass from the quarry and, above the dining table, a chandelier featuring a giant cog from a crane.

Artwork in the rooms (like photographs from Vancouver), plus exposed steel beams and lots of wood are all used to reinforce the story. However there are also playful references to the Disney characters Ruke and Tuke from *Brother Bear* (2003) and Chip'n'Dale.

The villas and cabins also have imitation wood flooring that according to Miorelli was "hand-scraped to make it feel like it came out of a sawmill."

According to the Disney Parks Blog:

"A sweeping re-imagination of the former Hidden Springs Pool area will help tell the richly layered back story of Boulder Ridge in what appears to have been an abandoned rock quarry.

"Such rejuvenating transformations were common in the Pacific Northwest following the mid-20th-century fading of the Transcontinental Railroad, as locals turned rails into trails – repurposing everything from bridges and tunnels to cranes and quarries.

"A nearby Boulder Ridge Railway and Mining Co. water tower will be among the pool area's landmark reminders of its pioneering past while a vintage mine cart supports the mining theme with an affectionate nod to Disney history."

The Hidden Springs pool was replaced with a significantly larger pool with a zero-entry feature, more deck space, and a lot of decorative rockwork all around that is reminiscent of the sort of natural stone quarry that may be found in the Pacific Northwest. Nearby is a crane recycled from Disney Hollywood Studios now closed Catastrophe Canyon attraction.

Stories of Wilderness Lodge

HUMPHREY THE BEAR

Disney's Wilderness Lodge Resort is the only Disney resort hotel to have an official mascot, the brown bear. Images and allusions can be found throughout the resort including bear tracks imbedded in the walkways.

To make that potentially fearsome mascot more friendly for younger guests, some of the brown bear images are of the Disney animated character Humphrey the Bear, a lovable, overweight brown bear who lives in the fictional Brownstone National Park.

Humphrey is most prominent on a totem pole on the outside of the Mercantile Store in the lobby of the resort that was carved out of cedar by William Robertson. A smiling Humphrey is at the bottom of the pole supporting frontier-garbed Mickey Mouse, Goofy and Donald Duck on top of him. Over the years, the store has sold different varieties of exclusive merchandise featuring the image of Humphrey.

In addition, Humphrey pops up on signage throughout the resort that many guests fail to notice. On the road leading to the Wilderness Lodge, just to right before the archway, is a round metal sign with silhouettes of Mickey Mouse and his bindle being followed by Humphrey.

At the entrance to the Villas at Wilderness Lodge is another metal sign with the silhouettes of Mickey walking along and Humphrey riding on top of an old fashioned penny farthing bicycle to mark the bike crossing path.

Only seven Disney cartoon characters have starred in their own theatrical cartoon series. Humphrey the Bear was the last one to do so before the Disney Company decided to stop making theatrical cartoon shorts.

Humphrey starred prominently in four Donald Duck cartoons, *Rugged Bear* (1953), *Grin and Bear It* (1954*), Bearly Asleep* (1955), *and Beezy Bear* (1955). He was so popular that Disney gave him his own series but only two cartoons were completed, *Hooked Bear* (1956) and *In the Bag* (1956), before the Disney Studio stopped making short theatrical cartoons.

In addition, Humphrey appeared in the opening credits for the original Mickey Mouse Club television series in 1955 holding the trampoline on which various characters bounce Mickey Mouse high into the air.

Humphrey the Bear does not speak but communicates through expressive grunts supplied by voice man Jimmy MacDonald who also did the voice of Mickey Mouse. Sometimes, director Jack Hannah would step in to supply some of the grunts.

Hannah directed all the Humphrey the Bear animated appearances in the Golden Age of Disney animation.

As he told me in a 1979 interview: "For the sake of something new, we tried the Duck with a bear and it seemed like an immediate success for them to play against each other, Later, when we started thinking of another picture for the bear, it seemed natural to be in a National Forest and that's how the Little Ranger came into being. The Little Ranger always treated his bears like his own pets and I always found that funny as did the audience."

Humphrey has also appeared in cartoons made for television including *House of Mouse* and *Mickey Mouse Clubhouse*. He even has a short cameo at the end of the film *Who Framed Roger Rabbit* (1988).

While Humphrey never appeared in any cartoon featuring him in the circus, he was recently revived to be included in the New Fantasyland expansion at the Magic Kingdom. He is prominent on the sign for Big Top Treats "Circus Snacks Galore" with him happily munching away on a caramel apple. In addition, that same image is used on a Storybook Circus poster.

However, while he may sneak over to the Magic Kingdom to grab a tasty treat, his official Walt Disney World home is Wilderness Lodge.

RAVEN TOTEM POLE

Stories on a totem pole are read from the bottom to the top. The pole in front of Whispering Canyon Café shares a story of the raven. Here is the complete story:

Beginning at the bottom of the Raven pole, is the image of the Whale Chief who had a beautiful daughter, Dolphin. Mountain Lion asked to marry her but was refused and, in his anger, scratched Whale Chief's throat with his claws, leaving scratches so deep they have remained on many whales ever since.

Frog is known as the great communicator and made peace between Whale Chief and Mountain Lion. As part of that agreement, Whale Chief decided to hold an archery contest and the animal that came closest with its arrow to the mark would be allowed to wed his daughter.

Wolf, Bear, Eagle, Beaver, Otter, Kingfisher and many others tried but while some of their arrows came very close to the center of the mark, none of them were perfect.

Finally, the little Wren asked to try. Because he was so tiny, he had made his own bow and arrow from two spruce needles. His needlelike arrow flew straight to the center of the mark, winning the right to marry the Whale Chief's daughter.

All the other animals roared and shrieked in fury and started to chase the small Wren, who flew up to a knot hole where he was safe and where most wrens have nested ever since.

Hootis, the Bear Chief, and his wife had two small cubs who could transform themselves into humans. They went with Wren and his new bride as their protectors when they moved to a small island.

Beautiful Dolphin would leap out of the water for joy whenever her husband sang and danced for her. However, she missed her friends the Salmon people. Wren had Frog call the Salmon people back from their journeys to the surrounding rivers and islands.

The Salmon people did return and were so happy to see Dolphin again that they leapt up the rivers and over the waterfalls. Many new salmon were born in these waters but left to grow large and shiny but vowed they would return to the very river where they had been born.

At the very top of the pole is Raven and tells another version of the trickster bird flying into the Sky Chief's house where with his beak, he cleverly untied the double cords and knots that tightly bound a painted box. Opening the lid, Raven lifted out the moon, breaking making chips of stars out of the cedar box. He flung them all into the dark night sky where they have spread their light.

Next, he reached into the box again and flung out a fiery ball of sun as a gift to all the animals, birds and humans to brighten the whole world ever since.

The final tale of the raven is another variation of the raven story told on the large cedar totem pole outside the Trading Post in the Canada pavilion at World Showcase. This particular story is central to the Northwest Indian's spiritual beliefs about the origins of the world.

EAGLE TOTEM POLE

Stories on a totem pole are read from the bottom to the top. The pole that is in front of the check-in desk tells a story of the eagle. Here is the complete story:

The Eagle pole story begins at the bottom with the Bear Chief. Frog tells the Bear Chief that he should hold a potlatch feast for his young nephew, Bear Cub. (On the pole, the Bear Cub is emerging from between the Chief's ears because traditionally, nephews were to be trained by their uncles who would educate them in the ways of the Bear Clan.)

A great painted shield of copper, the symbol of highest wealth, shows the design of Staget, the magical spirit between animals and humans. The Bear Chief plans to give this item of great value to his nephew during the potlatch feast.

Klu-kun, the Mountain Goat sits on a pole holding the copper to protect it. Mountain Goat once helped a young copper seeker to climb down the mountain cliffs by lending him his hooves.

A short section with a hole is where Ksem Wed-Zin, the Mouse Woman, lives and monitors the animals and humans around her. She is famous for helping young people, intervening when she feels that a young human or animal has been hurt or abused.

Above her are the clamshells that are another tale of Raven when there were only a few animals and no humans in the world. Raven was flying along a long, narrow arm of sand that was thrust far out into the sea. He saw a large clam lying on that beach and he opened it with his powerful beak.

In this way, Raven released the first humans who ever walked on earth. These humans were all very small, no larger than the size of the smallest finger, but as they went running toward freedom, they began to grow and grow until they reached a normal size. They built huge sea canoes and paddled along the coastlines until soon they had populated the whole world.

Beaver with a chew stick sits between Raven and Eagle because these two great supernatural birds have not always lived in peace together. Once, these two birds argued over who should grab the smaller Beaver's crest and take it for their own.

Beaver prevented this from happening by threatening to unleash a giant beaver larger than the two of them together. Beaver dove into the pond and made a hole so the water drained away revealing this monstrous beaver hiding at the bottom of the pond.

At the top of the pole is the Eagle who heard a girl crying far out to sea because she had gone away to marry one of the Undersea People but grew sad and lonely for her family and her own people. Eagle flew out and picked up the girl and started to fly her back to her family but the girl was so curious that she didn't listen to Eagle's warning not to look down and it caused both of them to fall down into the sea in front of the girl's village. They both struggled terribly to swim ashore.

Eagle likes to help which is why atop his head sits three small Taan-skeels. These are the watchmen for all humans and animals. Wearing tall, shading hats, Taan-skeel keeps their eyes wide open day and night, peering endlessly out to sea, along the beaches and deep inside the shadows of the forest to help protect the village houses.

CAROLWOOD PACIFIC ROOM

The Villas at Disney's Wilderness Lodge opened on November 15, 2000, becoming the fifth Disney Vacation Club location. When it opened it featured a small, quiet room off to the right side of the lobby called The Iron Spike Room. An iron spike was traditionally used on railroad ties.

In the Fall of 2007, it was renamed The Carolwood Pacific Room thanks to the efforts of Michael Broggie, co-founder of the Carolwood Historical Society and son of legendary Imagineer Roger Broggie.

"The Iron Spike room name fit the railroad theme, but I wanted to see the name truly represent the backyard railroad that played such an important role in Disney history," Broggie said.

From 1950-1953, Walt Disney transported friends and family through his elaborately landscaped backyard in Holmby Hills, California, on a 1/8th scale train dubbed the Carolwood Pacific Railroad.

It was named for the street where Walt lived at the time (355 North Carolwood Drive) as well as to reference the Central Pacific Railroad from the turn of the century. Walt called the engine, based on a Central Pacific 1872 locomotive, the Lilly Belle in honor of his wife Lillian.

"I vividly remember my first ride, straddling one of those freight cars as it rocked back and forth," Michael Broggie recalled. "I remember entering a long tunnel, which was absolutely pitch-black. You could hear the chuffing of the engine echoing off of this long tunnel. You could smell and taste the coal smoke. You could feel the vibration of the track. Walt had created an experience that excited every one of your senses."

From the beginning, the room was decorated with train memorabilia and framed photos related to Walt Disney's love of trains. Broggie helped the Imagineers locate the authentic artifacts that filled the room.

A cattle car, a gondola car (both hand built by Roger Broggie with Walt) and a stretch of track all from the actual backyard railroad was loaned to the area by Walt's oldest daughter, Diane Disney Miller and her Disney Family Foundation. The cars feature the Carolwood Pacific "Fair Weather Route" logo.

The rest of Walt's *Lilly Belle* is displayed at the Walt Disney Family Museum in San Francisco. Another car from the train is displayed at the Disney Barn at Griffith Park in Los Angeles, California.

A painting on display is "Walt's Magical Barn," by artist Bob Byerley created in 2001 in celebration of Walt Disney's 100th birthday and used as the cover for a book published by the Carolwood Pacific Society.

Also on display in a lucite case is a special limited edition re-creation of the CP 173 Lilly Belle locomotive, tender, gondola car and the yellow caboose from Walt's Carolwood Pacific Railroad.

It was produced in 2000 in garden gauge (1:24 scale) by Hartland Locomotive Works of Indiana. This Limited Edition (1500 Units) was only offered only through Disneyland, Walt Disney World (five locations), Disney Direct catalog and Disney Galleries. It originally sold for $595 and came with a solid oak base and an authentic piece of rail from Walt's backyard railroad.

Disney Institute / Saratoga Springs Resort & Spa

February 1996 / May 2004

In 1972, the Buena Vista Land Company was created and developed some of the acreage beyond the Magic Kingdom and its resorts.

It announced in June 1973 the construction of Lake Buena Vista, a 1,200 acre residential community located adjacent to where Hotel Plaza Boulevard is today. This project featured an 18-hole golf course; a shopping village (finally opened in March 1975); and dwellings consisting of townhouses, single family homes, and cluster homes.

The original plans called for these residences to be leased and sold to businesses as corporate retreats and to individuals as second-home vacation properties.

By May 1974, 133 town houses and 60 treehouse villas were built, but the apartments and single family homes (although four different showcase models were built as examples) were never completed because there were concerns raised that if someone owned those dwellings they would have voting rights in the area. Disney could not allow that to happen. In addition, issues about proper taxation of the residents would have caused another mess.

So the idea of selling these dwellings was replaced by the concept of them being another form of lodging that could be rented like the rooms at other resorts on property.

The resort opened as "The Village Resort" in 1985. The name was changed to "The Disney Village Resort" in 1989. The nearby Lake Buena Vista Village shopping center changed its focus for just serving the resort toward all Walt Disney World visitors and was renamed "Walt Disney World Village" and eventually became part of what is the Marketplace section of Disney Springs.

When Michael Eisner became CEO of the Walt Disney Company in 1984, he wanted to develop the unused WDW property, especially building resort hotels that could accommodate large convention groups. This goal led to the building of the Swan and Dolphin resorts. But he also had other development plans.

Eisner and his family visited the Chautauqua Institution in 1985 in upstate New York that offered lectures, performances, recreation, and, more specifically, classes designed for adults to enhance their education during the summer months.

Eisner thought that this could be a new form of year-round vacation experience that would extend guests' visits to Walt Disney World, as well as attract new guests with no interest in the theme parks.

Eisner thought that so-called similar enrichment vacations were becoming increasingly popular as aging Baby Boomers looked for ways to combine rest and relaxation with learning and exercise. Experts had claimed it was an emerging trend in travel like eco-travel that combined nature experiences with lessons on the environment.

Obviously, the word "Institute" in Disney Institute came from Chautaqua's "Institution," although other names for the place were considered and discarded. Like many of Eisner's ideas, it took awhile to put it all in motion.

At one point, Eisner wanted the Disney Institute to be in Aspen, Colorado, so it was removed from the theme park experience to emphasize the educational aspects, but the cost estimates were way too high. He wanted to appeal to those rich folks who had discretionary income to re-connect with learning and who frequented that area and be a West Coast version of the East Coast Chautaqua.

He then was going to build it in Celebration to increase the prestige of that project, but that was still too pricey to start from scratch. In order to cut costs, it was decided to convert the already existing Lake Buena Vista Villas and townhouses and just build the additional classroom facilities there.

The thought was that guests would physically stay at the resort for a minimum of three days and not need their cars because it would all be within easy walking distance of the cinema, performing arts center, health club and classrooms and would feel like a private community so there was no need for much parking. Eisner announced the project at Carnegie Hall.

Program planning began as early as 1993 with actual construction beginning in 1995. The new structures were designed by Tom Beedy and given the look of a small, friendly New England town. Facilities at the 457-room lakeside resort were designed to accommodate about 900 people at its peak, a fairly modest number considering the other resorts and attendance at the theme parks.

The Buena Vista Golf Club building was greatly expanded to include not just the Check-in Center but a small upscale shop called Dabblers (which also featured exclusive pricey merchandise related to the classes guests would take) and was so named because guests were "dabbling" in unfamiliar disciplines. A full-service restaurant was also built called Seasons, because each of its four dining rooms was themed to one of the four seasons of the year.

The food was more upscale (and the chefs constantly changing menu offerings sometimes every day) but the atmosphere was fairly casual. Its location made it awkward for those not staying at D.I. to get there to eat or to park once they did.

Just outside the restaurant was a luxurious lounge with sofas and chairs, where people could gather and relax and with a grand piano that former Disney executive Judson Green used to come in and play at night.

Additionally, other new structures included a 38,000-square-foot two-story sports and fitness center with a full basketball court, indoor pool, and a full-service spa with seaweed facial or an "aroma therapy" massage; a 225-seat Performance Center that was acoustically perfect and featured side boxes in the audience; a 400-seat movie theater without a balcony; and a 1,150-seat uncovered amphitheater (which proved to be a huge mistake when it rained or the Orlando heat was too intense so could not be used).

Twenty-eight intimate program studio classrooms generally located in a two-story building in the center of the complex between the amphitheater and the Cinema were created although some classrooms like for Culinary and Design Arts were placed elsewhere.

Also a closed-circuit TV studio (DITV) and a radio station (WALT) both located in the same building as the culinary studio were built so that visiting media crews could broadcast from the studios in addition to offering classes for guests.

Some upgrades to the Lake Buena Vista living accommodations were made, but most of these were merely cosmetic, so there was no outlet to plug in and recharge any devices like a computer. The prices were going to be the same as the premium resorts on property but without the same amenities.

For instance, the Business Center was only open during the weekdays from 9 a.m.-5 p.m., and then closed on the weekends, even though on the West Coast there was still three hours of working time during the week and business around the world continued on the weekends.

Officially the Disney Institute opened on February 9, 1996, but throughout the month of January, there were trial "soft opening" classes run for selected cast members and several dozen invited travel writers to try to work out any problems in the programs before opening.

"I think those people walked in as interested skeptics, and they left as firm supporters," said Richard Hutton, vice president of the Disney Institute. "We've always felt that this kind of vacation, which has never been done before, would build over time with word-of-mouth."

The motto was "You won't believe what you can do!" The logo featured the letter "T" in the word "Institute" becoming more and more empowered so that it literally flew into the air.

That character had a name, but none of the staff ever used it if they even knew. It was supposed to be the mascot and symbol of D.I. but guests never understood nor warmed to it either.

Animation manager Larry Lauria told me, "They paid big money for a design group to come up with that 'jumping T' in the name 'Institute'. The point was that he was to represent the guest and as the guest took more and more classes, he became more and more happy and empowered and knowledgeable and leapt from the mundane world high into the unlimited sky."

To increase attendance for the classes, it was not required that the guests physically stay in the D.I. lodgings, and since the cost was the same as a premium resort, many financially well-off guests simply stayed at Disney's Boardwalk Inn or Disney's Grand Floridian Resort & Spa, and took transport to the Institute. Others stayed at less-expensive locations locally and drove in to take their classes or see nighttime performances.

One of the reasons for the demise of D.I. was that the ratio of "heads in beds" continued to drop drastically from the day the Institute opened so it was hard to cover the necessary overhead.

Generally each classroom held approximately fifteen guests maximum. The classrooms were so small in order to provide a more intimate one-on-one personal experience that even when they were fully booked (or often overbooked with other chairs being dragged in to a class to increase attendance during the final years), it was not enough to cover the cost of the salaried instructors, the assistants, the crew that prepped and cleaned the classrooms, and the materials, let alone the cost of utilities.

As part of the opening day staff, I heard Eisner himself tell us that he didn't expect D.I. to really be profitable for about three years, and that he was committed to supporting any losses for this new endeavor in learning and entertainment during that time.

He said it would take time for people to understand what was happening since it was such a new concept and our job was to provide the best experience possible.

"The Disney Institute is stimulation for the mind. At Disney we have fun, escapism and, now, a campus for smart fun," he emphasized.

Within six months, classes like genealogy, spiritual inquiry, power baby sitting and money management, along with all the staff teaching them were suddenly cut. That started a domino effect and, by 1997, the entire Story Arts curriculum, including classes like Storytelling Journeys and As Walt Would Tell It were also gone. That last class focused on how Disney told stories in its animated feature films.

The lead instructor of As Walt Would Tell It was former Imagineer Charlie Kurts, who had been involved in the creation of the Splash

Mountain attraction. Even though I was assigned to the Animation department, I was cross-trained in teaching this class to cover when Charlie was sick or needed elsewhere. Of course, Story Arts and that class and all its staff and assistants were gone within that first year.

When D.I. opened in 1996, guests could choose from more than 80 programs in nine areas, including Entertainment Arts (which also encompassed animation), Sports and Fitness, Life Styles, Story Arts, Culinary Arts, Design Arts, Environment, Performing Arts and Youth Programs.

By 1997, in order to increase revenue, several popular Disney University programs were relocated to be part of the Disney Institute.

The very expensive Professional Development programs ("the magic behind the business") were now located at D.I., and some new programming was created that might make use of the existing D.I. instructors as "trained monkeys" (as some of the P.D. facilitators called them) to offer guests an experience in gourmet cooking, animation, gardening or video production, and then have the P.D. facilitators pontificate about business connections at various points in the class.

Disney Adult Discoveries, which handled the backstage guest tours like Backstage Magic, Hidden Treasures of World Showcase, Innovation in Action, and more, were also brought in from Disney University and crammed into a small office in the instructors' trailer across the street from the resort.

The Disney University Wonders programs, designed for children 10-16 were renamed Y.E.S. (Youth Education Series) and offered classes for kids whose parents were taking regular classes. Later, these classes were expanded to be offered to visiting school classes from around the country.

By 1997, the core D.I. program tracks had been cut severely and this remained pretty much the curriculum for the next two years until the next round of major cuts.

Individual classes were each offered two or three times a week (usually every other day) and were roughly two to three hours long.

There was a morning session offering and an afternoon session. There was a two hour break for lunch and in the evening there were events either in the Performance Center or the Cinema.

There weren't any tests, grades, or homework. The classes were designed as foolproof as possible so that every guest despite their abilities would be successful.

The 1997 program tracks and classes:

- **ANIMATION** (Animation Sampler, Animated Beginnings, Voices of Disney, Classical Animation, Computer Animation, Clay Animation)

- **CULINARY ARTS** (Taste of the World, Wine, Wonders and Song, Healthy Cooking, Romantic Dinners, Culinary Technique, Studio Bakery, Celebrations)
- **HOME, GARDEN & GREAT OUTDOORS** (Painting Illusions, Disney Architecture, Canoe Adventure, Traveling Gardener, Topiary Creations – one of THE most popular classes where people made a small Mickey Mouse topiary, Gifts from Your Garden, Container Gardener)
- **COMMUNICATION ARTS & ENTERTAINMENT** (Edit Workshop, Outdoor Photography, TimeQuest, DNN Studio Production, Exploring Photojournalism, Computers: Internet, Digital Imaging, DNN Field Production, Candid Portrait Photography, DI Deejay for Youth, Computers: Desktop Publishing, DI Deejay)
- **CAMP DISNEY** (Youth 10 years old and older) (Show Biz Magic, Swamp Stomp, The Funny Papers—Cartooning, Art Magic, Broadway Bound, Wildlife Adventure, Youth Rock Climbing, Discovery Island Explorers, Disney Island Kid Venture, Tiles, Temples and Treasure, Stealing the Show, Face Magic!, DI Art Lab, Disney's Orient Express, Art Surround)
- **SPORTS & FITNESS** (Aerobics, Golf: The Game, Tennis: High Tech, Dance! Dance! Dance!, Golf: In Depth, Rise & Shine: Walk, Tennis: On the Attack, Tennis Aerobics, Rock Climbing: First Steps, Strength Training & Toning, Rock Climbing: Hang Time, Tennis: Stay in the Pt., Relaxation Techniques, Self-Defense, Water Exercise, Stretching, Tennis Clinic)

It is important to realize that the Disney Institute right from the start had the highest rated guest satisfaction surveys on all of WDW property and maintained that until major cuts started happening in 1998.

To encourage more attendance in the classes, a special $49 one-day offering was presented, but failed to generate guests wanting to pay full price once the offering expired. When regular pricing kicked in, the rates sometimes ranged from $582-$1,986 per person, depending on the season, the number of nights and the type of accommodations.

Disney Institute offered three-night, four-night and seven-night packages to "blend learning with leisure". All of the programs were designed for hands-on experience, up-close personal attention from a highly trained instructor with previous professional experience in the subject area and physical things for the guest to take away like the meal they made or the cel they painted. However, it was still a narrow market.

On opening day, Richard Hutton told all of us on the opening staff as a costumed Mickey waved for the photographers, "This is the last time that Mickey Mouse sets foot on this property."

He felt that connections with the iconic Disney characters minimized the seriousness of the institution. In addition, no accommodations were made to allow guests to visit the nearby theme parks as part of their package and it was actively discouraged because it would be taking money away from D.I., another reason why D.I. failed since the parks were temptingly just minutes away.

Lauria told me, "Hutton came from a public television background in Washington, D.C., and New York. His staff like Bonnie Benjamin-Phariss had the same background and attitude. They were definitely not immersed in the Disney culture nor wanted to be, and I think they were given marching orders to make the place prestigious and exclusive."

People could take classes taught by experts anywhere. They were coming to D.I. to learn "how does Disney do it" which is why classes like animation and making a Mickey Mouse topiary figure were so popular and lasted the longest when things were being cut but that made no impact on the management team running the Institute. Guests wanted to meet Mickey and go to the parks. They wanted to see programs in the Cinema about Disney animation not obscure independent films.

As fewer guests signed up for classes and stayed at the resort, classes were eliminated or consolidated and more staff was let go, with only two animation instructors left out of an initial group of ten during its final year.

The fact that Eisner was under siege at the time, and had no interest in protecting the place and those who wanted to undercut him saw D.I. as one of his pet projects, didn't help either in terms of generating needed support. Eventually, the guest enrichment programs disappeared entirely and Disney Institute closed in 2002.

The Disney Institute still exists today in name. Disney claimed that the Disney Institute was so successful that it could not be limited to just one physical location, but that the entire WDW was a living classroom.

The Professional Development staff was moved into cubicles at Celebration, but only offered their standard roster of expensive business classes to corporate clients or flew out to different cities throughout the country to present them at a premium price. They are known today as the Disney Institute.

The Disney Vacation Club (DVC), like the Disney Cruise Line, was not only a healthy business division within the company but was rapidly growing so it was decided to convert the physical D.I. property into the seventh membership resort.

Many things were gutted and razed. The amphitheater was changed into a large outdoor pool. New accommodations were built and a theme of Saratoga Springs, New York was incorporated.

Saratoga Springs Resort & Spa

May 2004

The resort is the largest DVC resort in size and the volume of guest rooms. The lakeside community with classic Victorian architecture recaptures the heyday of upstate New York country retreats in the late 1800s.

Disney's Saratoga Springs Resort and Spa officially opened May 17, 2004 with a "health-history-horses" theme. The Development Manager for the project was Kevin Cummings.

Cummings was born and raised in Saratoga Springs, New York, the city that was the inspiration for the Disney Vacation Club resort. In fact, at the time, his twin brother still lived in that historic upstate New York town so Kevin would go back to visit several times during the year.

In his role as a Development Manager, Kevin oversaw the hiring of the project's design professionals, from the design architect to the working architect, to all the engineers.

"I coordinate them as a team to come up with the design for our project," he stated.

As soon as Kevin heard that the new resort was to be inspired by the tranquil towns of upstate New York in the 1800s, he told everyone, "It's got to be Saratoga! We took trips up there to look at the architecture, and I'd show my friends around since I knew the lay of the land. I knew exactly where to look, where the best architecture was—North Broadway, Union Avenue, and all the special buildings that we took bits and pieces of our design from for the resort."

Working with Boston-based Graham Gund Architects (who had worked on Disney's Vero Beach Resort, the Celebration Hotel in Celebration, Florida, and Disney's Coronado Springs Resort), the team, according to Kevin, "went up and down the East Coast looking for different elements to be put to use for our buildings. Of course, the major part of the architecture is based on Saratoga. But we were very careful to use actual design elements—it's really real, what you're seeing, we didn't make this stuff up.

"Of course, I knew the history from growing up and going to school there, the local history, and the history of the racecourse. It's *not* a racetrack—it's a racecourse—the oldest racecourse in the United States, going all the way back to 1863. In the 1920s and '30s, especially, Saratoga was the place for the upper class to summer, and they all went during the racing season. It was known as the 'August place'. Saratoga Springs used to have more hotel rooms than any other U.S. destination."

Kevin helped develop a binder filled with photos from the research trips so that the smallest details like the awnings would be accurate.

Kevin was also instrumental in naming many of the features like the High Rock Spring Pool after one of the actual "healing springs" found in the city and frequented by celebrities like U.S. Presidents.

Street names such as Union Avenue and Broadway will also be familiar with people who know Saratoga Springs. Kevin wanted to see the name of the street he grew up on included, but it didn't make the cut.

What most reminded Kevin of his hometown were the three towers. "We have three different building types, and we have three different tower designs on the Guest room buildings. They're right at the entrances, and they rise 70 feet into the air.

"Those elements really strike you. You'll see them all over Saratoga, even the colors. The blues, greens, reds, and yellows we used to paint the buildings. The greatest homes in Saratoga Springs have those colors. That's what really hit me...the colors of the buildings...and the towers. No doubt about it."

With the emphasis on horses, there are references to horses every where including horses from Disney animated films like Philippe from *Beauty and the Beast,* Maximus from *Tangled*, Bullseye from *Toy Story*, Khan from *Mulan* and more.

Phillipe's head and Maximus' head can be found on pillows and framed artwork featuring the heads of other animated horses are framed in the lobby.

Racing silks designed especially for the resort hang in the hallway between The Turf Club and The Artist's Palette including a framed jockey jacket with Mickey's head on it. The pressed penny machine has designs which include Mickey riding a horse along with Cinderella and her horse, Major.

Furlong is a horse racing term, and represents the distance of an 8th of a mile. There are furlong markers around the resort. Paintings by noted racing artist Peter Williams are featured on the wall behind the front desk. The pieces depict events that take place at the Saratoga Race Course before, during, and after the big horse race, culminating in the Winner's Circle.

The weather vane features a reference to the half-moon smiling Funmeister icon who was the mascot of Pleasure Island that was just across the water.

The resort sells items from the real Saratoga Springs including Saratoga bottled water, Saratoga Salsa, Sundaes Best Hot Fudge Sauce, and the famed Peppermint Pig from Saratoga Sweets.

The carousel horse inside the Carriage House recalls the lead horse of the Congress Park Carousel at Saratoga Springs.

Boardwalk Inn and Villas

July 1996

The Boardwalk Inn and Villas was designed to incorporate aspects of the iconic Atlantic City Boardwalk and the Coney Island playground to create an East Coast seaside vacation destination from the early 1900s.

The real Atlantic City in New Jersey is well-known as a popular vacation location, enhanced by its many conventions and gambling facilities. It was also home to the very first boardwalk in the United States that opened on June 26, 1870. Originally, that boardwalk was just eight feet wide and a mile long.

The boardwalk was created as a way to keep tourists from tracking sand into the hotels and businesses. Some visitors also did not want to get dirty by setting foot on the beach itself, even though they enjoyed the view and the fresh sea air.

The boardwalk was so effective that, over the decades, it was modified and expanded many times so that it eventually spanned more than six miles and became sixty feet wide.

Opening July 1, 1996, the BoardWalk Inn and Villas Resort was designed by architect Robert A. M. Stern, who also designed many other Disney buildings, including Disney's Yacht and Beach Club Resorts, just across the other side of Crescent Lake. The physical Disney herringbone-patterned boardwalk at Crescent Lake is roughly thirty-five feet wide and 1,300 feet long.

For the Boardwalk area, Stern utilized elements from Atlantic City and Coney Island, in particular the first Luna Park amusement park, to create a Northeast Coast seaside village that is not historically exact, but rather an attempt to capture the spirit of the early 1900s using some specific elements.

In early planning for the resort, there was discussion about having a full-sized antique carousel operating at one end of the boardwalk. Another idea discussed was having a wooden pier (a smaller version of the Steel Pier near Atlantic City's Boardwalk) going out into Crescent Lake and, among other things, have a working Ferris Wheel to entertain guests.

Stern's approach to architecture is "interpretation," meaning that he takes an existing piece or style of architecture like the Doge's Palace in Venice, Italy, and utilizes those aspects to create something new like the Walt Disney World Casting Center, across the street from the Downtown Disney district, that echoes its original source material.

Besides the hotel itself, there are restaurants, nightclubs, shops, and games, just as a person might find on this type of boardwalk but without some of the unsavory aspects that also existed on the early boardwalk areas.

Fans of the HBO series *Boardwalk Empire* are well aware that during the time period represented at the Disney resort, the Atlantic City boardwalk was known for gambling, prostitution, illegal alcohol and other vices. None of those elements are incorporated into the Boardwalk Inn and Villas, not even in name references.

Boardwalk Inn and Villas was the second Disney Vacation Club property that was built at Walt Disney World, and the first to offer the option of housing to non-members.

Ironically, it was the opening of the Walt Disney World Resort in 1971 that contributed to the decline of the decades-long appeal of Atlantic City. It became almost as inexpensive and infinitely more entertaining to journey further south for entertainment for the entire family.

The resort is filled with artifacts and references to both Atlantic City and Coney Island. Intriguingly, there are many similarities between the two locations at this time period. For instance, Coney Island also had a boardwalk, as well as a huge elephant-shaped hotel just like Atlantic City, and was a popular Northeastern vacation destination.

Fortunately, the resort does have some signage identifying these things, but, unfortunately, some items have no signs or incomplete (or sometimes misleading) information.

"We deliberately went through a process of creating virtual memories," Alix Beeny told the *New York Times* in 1996 when the Disney resort opened.

Beeny was the director of Parker Blake, a Denver design company hired by Disney Imagineering division to help explore themes and find artifacts from the glory days of both Atlantic City and Coney Island to add authentic touches to the Boardwalk complex.

In 1996, few Walt Disney World guests had any direct memories of the fabled culture of the Atlantic City and Coney Island in the 1920s and 1930s, but the purpose of actual artifacts and references was to create a hybrid of history and cinematic staging.

Just as Disney Hollywood Studios is clearly an attempt to present a "Hollywood that never was but always will be" or, more precisely, a Hollywood that was a state of mind rather than a specific geographical location, Boardwalk Inn and Villas was to capture what Todd A. Lenahan, the architecture and engineering design manager for Disney

Imagineering at the time, called a location that would "romanticize people's recollection of what a boardwalk was."

Lenahan, 30 years old when the resort opened, was many decades removed from the time period he was in charge of bringing to reality from drawing board concepts to final ribbon-cutting ceremony.

There were at least a dozen and a half contributors of historical images for use in the resort from the New York Public Library to the Atlantic City Historical Museum, as well as the Atlantic City Historical Society.

Some items came from the Vicki Gold Levi Collection. Vicki Gold Levi is a noted cultural historian and the co-author of one of the major texts used in the project, *Atlantic City: 125 years of Ocean Madness* (Ten Speed Press, 1994).

She told reporters that the book was to spotlight the golden era of her hometown and recall the Atlantic City Boardwalk of her youth where it was "a cacophony of sound, crowds, bright lights." That boardwalk was a chaos of stage theaters, movie palaces, snake charmers, big bands, roller coasters, saloons and more, all brightly advertised and competing for attention.

"I wish somebody in Atlantic City would take old Atlantic City as seriously as Disney did," Levi told the *New York Times* when the resort opened.

BALLYHOO BANNER

On the wall to the left hand side just before entering the lobby itself, is a huge, colorful banner under glass. It features a well dressed man holding a small horse in his hand and on the side, the banner proclaims: "Seeing is believing. Let's Go See It. Let's Go. Let's All Go."

The small sign near it states: "Wonderful Showcloth Banner. The showcloth banner or 'ballyhoo' is a holdover from the late 19th century when seasonal venues whose façade architecture was little more than a collapsible wall of elaborately painted canvas. The 'ballyhoo' enticed passerby to partake of a particular attraction—in this case, a jewel-size living horse. On canvas with gold and silver leaf."

These types of banners were most common for sideshows at a circus. Miniature horses, although none so tiny they could fit in the palm of a hand, were first seen in the United States in the late 1800s. However, since "ballyhoo" is a "sensationalized promotion," I am sure the banner perhaps exaggerated the smallness although today there are perfectly proportioned miniature horses only seventeen inches tall.

Below is a cabinet with four illustrated scenes from Atlantic City: the Steel Pier diving horse, Lucy the elephant building, the first Miss America and a typical Boardwalk scene with a store offering Fatima cigarettes (popular in the late 1800s through the 1940s and was a blend of exotic Turkish tobacco), and Lipschutz's 44 Cigars (popular five-cents cigars produced in Philadelphia that had opened another factory in New Jersey in 1911).

MINIATURE CAROUSEL IN THE LOBBY

Marcus Charles Illions (1872-1949) was a master carver particularly famed for his work on carousel horses and their carousels. He worked at many of the finest and most prestigious carousel companies and finally opened his own company.

He was an expert horseman and owned a few of his own. His knowledge of horse musculature, even their facial veins, translated into his creating legendary figures that are still revered today.

His style, known as the more flamboyant "Coney Island-style" of carousels, dominated the Coney Island area with at least ten of his carousels in residence during the 1920s.

In the 1920s, he created three grand machines known as the Supreme series. There is a small flag flying from the top of this miniature proclaiming "M.C. Illions Supreme Carousel."

There is a known photo (unfortunately not displayed by Disney) of Harry Illions, M.C.'s oldest son (who was only 16 years old when Illions formed his own company in 1909), with this same miniature model carousel.

M.C. Illions would take this salesman's sample to the conventions of the National Association of Amusement Parks or NAAP (formed February 1920). This group is now known today as The International Association of Amusement Parks and Attractions or IAAPA.

Disney purchased this model direct from Illions' granddaughter at auction in 1995. It had been hidden from general public view for nearly 80 years.

This sales tool featured forty four four-inch-tall horses that were each unique. No two horses were similar. The horses even moved up and down when the machine was turned on. Illions never intended that the model would be displayed publicly.

The Walt Disney Company purchased it in 1995 and spent more than a year restoring the wood, mechanisms, flaking paint and other elements that were in disrepair. The original paint colors and decorations were researched (using the still existing full size Illions' carousels and horses as partial reference).

Brass was re-plated, gold leaf applied, and miniature leather stirrup straps were attached. Even the tiny pearl-headed pins that were to represent light bulbs were replaced.

The Imagineers scaled the speed of the carousel to match that of the

King Arthur Carrousel located at Disneyland Park in California. As a final playful touch, a Hidden Mickey was added to two of the horses (You can find one of those horses on the outer circle about two horses up from the green-blue chariot).

Approximately every twenty minutes or so, the carousel springs to life playing a medley of Disney instrumental songs.

Between the two restrooms down the hall near the Belle Vue Lounge is an interesting artifact that looks like a face on an elaborate stick.

The small sign reads: "All manner of sculptural elements decorated the turn of the century Boardwalk carousel to provide sumptuous ornament for the usual feast of the amusement business. Carved by M.C. Illions this figurine originally surrounded mirrored panels and was accompanied by dozens of similar figures. Cast from the circa 1910 original, hand painted and gold lettered."

HIPPOCAMPUS ELECTROLIER

Hanging above the miniature carousel is the Hippocampus Electrolier that supposedly is a one-of-a-kind original rather than a reproduction.

The classical hippocampus comes from Greek mythology and is a sea monster with a horse's forequarters and a fish's tail, quite literally a seahorse. Poseidon was not only the god of the sea, but also earthquakes and horses. He was often accompanied by hippocampi who pulled his chariot.

Electrolier was the name for a chandelier powered by electric lights, rather than gas or candle, but the term never caught on in common usage. Reportedly, it was inventor Thomas Edison who coined the term.

The Hippocampus Electrolier Chandelier weighs 3,000 pounds and is finished entirely in 22-karat gold leaf, hand-cut Austrian crystal, and custom-blown glass. Underneath there is a glass globe that used to be filled with sand and a time capsule to be opened on the 50th anniversary of Walt Disney World. The globe developed a leak (or fell and cracked depending upon who tells the story) and the sand and the time capsule were removed and are supposedly in safe keeping.

REGISTRATION DESK DISPLAY

Above the registration desk are three carousel "rounding boards." These would be found on the outside of a carousel and traditionally feature pastoral scenes. These three paintings feature Disney Imagineers interpretations of three castles. From left to right, the Disneyland Resort, Disneyland Paris and the Walt Disney World Resort as if they existed in a real world are shown.

NANNY CHAIRS

Placed on either side of the fireplace are the scary "nanny chairs" that were originally found on 19th century European carrousels. They were intended for adults to rest upon while their children rode the moving animals. From this concept developed the more traditional "chariot" benches.

It would have been inappropriate for female nannies to even ride side saddle on a carousel horse. These reproductions were cast from circa 1889 originals, hand painted and highlighted with gold leaf. In a moment of cleverness, the two Imagineers involved in the reproductions printed their names on the back of each chair: Todd and Paul.

LUCY THE ELEPHANT

Above the fireplace is a statue of an unusual elephant and a black and white photo is framed nearby. This is one of the earliest examples of programmatic architecture which is commonly known today as "California Crazy." There are several examples at Disney Hollywood Studio, including the Darkroom on Hollywood Boulevard and Gertie the Dinosaur in the Echo Lake area.

James Lafferty owned a number of sandy lots in the South Atlantic City area (today it is known as Margate) and he needed to do something to attract attention (and property buyers) to the area. The 65-foot high elephant was constructed in 1881 at a reported cost of $25,000 (although Lafferty always claimed that by the time it was finished it was $38,000).

To protect his idea of an animal-shaped structure, Lafferty applied for and received a patent from the U.S. Government for exclusive rights for seventeen years to make, use or sell animal shaped buildings.

Lucy the Elephant is one of three such structures designed and built by Lafferty. It is the only one still intact and survived the ravages of Hurricane Sandy. Lucy's nearest relative was the Light of Asia, a 40-foot wooden elephant built on South Cape May. Lucy's other relative, the 150-foot high Elephantine Colossus, was built at Coney Island, New York, purely as an amusement attraction in 1885.

In 1887, to try to recoup after some financial downturns, Lafferty sold his South Atlantic City holdings, including Lucy, to Anton Gertzen. It was Gertzen's wife, Sophia, who named the elephant Lucy (despite the fact that it had tusks making it a male elephant) and the reason for the name is apparently lost to the ages.

Lucy was a business office, a hotel and even a speakeasy right before prohibition. She was designated a National Historic Landmark in 1976. So both Atlantic City and Coney Island had elephant shaped structures

FLIP FLAP RAILWAY

In the lobby is a glass encased model of the Flip Flap Railway which was located in Sea Lion Park at Coney Island. (This park site was later bought and transformed into Luna Park.)

Built in 1895, this early ride featured a 25-foot loop and was the world's first inverted (upside down loop-the-loop) roller coaster. Because of its design (and no seatbelts), there were neck and back injuries among other discomforts.

Atlantic City had its own version of the Flip-Flap (sometimes called the Looping the Loop) on Young's Pier from 1902-1912. So, once again, both Coney Island and Atlantic City shared similar attractions.

The Coney Flip-Flap produced 12 Gs, enough to knock riders out. To put this in comparison, Epcot's Mission: Space produces about 2.5 Gs for 45 seconds. Even the high-flying aerobatics of the Blue Angels only produces 9-11 Gs maximum.

SWAN RIDE

On a table in the middle of the room is an authentic two-headed "Swan Seat." According to the nearby sign, it "is of European origin from the period of large-themed carousels dedicated to one species of animal, bird or fish. These grand rides had dispensed with rocking gondolas or spinning tubes in favor of these more fanciful creations.

"Giant baskets carried the passengers on a 'Manege des Cochons' (ride of pigs). This swan seat originally hung from chairs and rocked on the carousel floor from the shifting weight of the children inside. Iron and tin with hand painting and gold leafing circa 1890."

MUTOSCOPES

Located in the Disney Boardwalk Inn and Villas resort hallway directly across from the restrooms near the Belle Vue Lounge are a green and a red Clamshell Mutoscope. At one time, there was also a mutoscope that was painted white with gold trim.

Mutoscopes were originally manufactured from 1895 to 1909 by the American Mutoscope and Biograph Company.

The red and green mutoscopes are authentic operating machines from this time period and you can still clearly see the appropriate markings on the front of the machines.

The cast iron clamshell was one of the most durable styles and is so named because of the clamshell design pattern on both sides.

Mutoscopes were basically a huge mechanical "flip book" with about 850 sturdy photographic prints on individual cards attached to a central core and flipped by a hand cranked ratchet.

Each coin-operated machine had a single reel, often an excerpt from a silent film but sometimes original and lasting about a minute.

The viewer could control the presentation speed but only to a limited degree. The crank could be turned in both directions, but this did not reverse the playing of the reel.

Nor could the patron extend viewing time by stopping the crank because the flexible images were bent into the proper viewing position by tension applied from forward cranking.

Stopping the crank reduced the forward tension on the reels causing the reel to go backwards and the picture to move from the viewing position; a spring in the mechanism turned off the light and in some models brought down a shutter which completely blocked out the picture.

For the opening of Walt Disney World, the Disney Company bought a very large collection of authentic mutoscopes, mechanical games and Orchestrions (music boxes like "Big Bertha" at Disney's Grand Floridian Resort and Spa) from Paul Eakin in the 1970s and moved them all from where they were being displayed and stored in Missouri to Florida. (Some machines from the Disneyland collection were also shipped out to Florida.)

Eakin's collection of machines operated for many years at the Million Dollar Museum in Sikeston and The Gay 90s Melody Museum located in St. Louis. Both Missouri museums were closed when Eakin sold the bulk of his collection to Walt Disney World.

These two particular mutoscopes were part of that collection and were enjoyed by Disney guests at the Main Street Penny Arcade until it closed March 19, 1995 to become part of Main Street Athletic Company.

A handful of the machines were eventually moved to the upper floor of the Main Street Train Station while the rest were stored under Cinderella Castle in a small, leaky room in the utilidoors. Most of the collection is no longer in storage but was sold off to private collectors in 1997.

The red and green machine were rescued from under the Magic Kingdom in 1996 and installed in one of the animation classrooms at the Disney Institute and used as an enhancement for an animation history class. One of the machines featured an excerpt from a silent Felix the Cat cartoon and the other some unnamed silent cartoon.

When the Disney Institute stopped offering individual programs to guests in 2000 and then later left the physical space in 2002, the mutoscopes found a new home at the Boardwalk where a little tender loving care may help them spring back to life to continue to delight guests.

LUNA PARK REFERENCES

Luna Park Pool is a reference to one of the most popular early amusement parks at Coney Island. Luna Park was built and operated by Frederic Thompson and Elmer "Skip" Dundy from 1903 to 1944. It was one of three major entertainment parks at Coney Island that included Steeplechase Park and Dreamland.

That's the reason why the proprietor of the "On the Boardwalk Thimbles & Threads" shop is "F. Thompson" and inside the resort's main lobby is "Dundy's Sundries—Serving the Boadwalk since 1902".

It is 1902 because Thompson and Dundy's amazing ride from the 1901 Pan-American Exposition (the name of the World's Fair held in New York) called "A Trip To The Moon" was moved to Coney Island's Steeplechase Park for the 1902 season.

It was an electrically powered dark ride where thirty passengers boarded a wooden spacecraft and were taken on a visit to the moon complete with little people dressed up as moonmen. It proved so popular that Thompson and Dundy had enough money to build their own amusement venue, Luna Park.

"Luna" is Latin for the "moon" (and also the name of the airship vehicle in their attraction). Dundy's sister was also named "Luna".

Why are there elephants at the pool?

One of the biggest attractions at Coney Island's Luna Park was its private herd of elephants, which roamed freely. Elephant rides were popular for the guests as well as a once-in-a-lifetime experience.

However, cleaning an elephant is a long, arduous task so it was quickly discovered that taking the elephants out to the Atlantic Ocean to bathe was not only easier but it was free publicity for the park.

The two-hundred-foot-long Keister Coaster is meant to be reminiscent of the many classic wooden roller coasters at Coney Island in its prime. That's why it is a seemingly wooden structure. Keister is a slang term for the human buttocks which is how guests ride down the waterslide.

However, the huge clown face at the end is not just to reference the many clowns at Coney Island, one of whom was the famous animation director Dave Fleischer who was rotoscoped in his clown outfit to become KoKo the Clown, the famous silent animated cartoon character.

One of the popular Midway games was the Clown Water Gun Balloon Game where a patron would shoot water into the open mouth of the head of a clown to build up pressure to blow up the balloon on the head to pop first so the player could win against other competitors doing the exact same thing with other clown heads.

The game still exists today and is popular. A variation of the game, an auto race, is one of the Midway games in the Wildwood Landing section on Disney's boardwalk.

In 2021, the clown head which while authentic disturbed some guests who were afraid of clowns was removed. The entire waterslide was re-decorated with friendlier artwork of the Disney Channel Mickey Mouse characters.

The nearby Ferris W. Eahlers Community Hall is not an obscure reference to a turn-of-the-century personality or an Imagineer. Said aloud it sounds like "Ferris Wheelers", a reference to the Coney Island Ferris wheels.

While most guests are unfamiliar with these connections, for those few who are it enhances an already premium experience.

Stories of the Boardwalk

THE ABRACADABAR

The AbracadaBar at the Boardwalk Resort opened in July 2016 serving elixirs and concoctions in the former SeaShore Sweets location.

According to Disney publicity, "This little lounge was a former stomping ground for the famous magicians, boardwalk illusionists, and lovely magician's assistants of the Golden Age. After a show, prestidigitators would gather to 'conjure' up new cocktails, swap magic tips and tricks, and stay up all night attempting to 'out-charm' each other with their extraordinary illusions.

"According to BoardWalk lore, it was on just such an evening that every single magician in the lounge vanished into thin air, and was never seen again ..."

Now, after sitting vacant for nearly seventy-six years, it is back in operation for the general public.

It was on a Friday the 13th in September 1940 that the mysterious disappearance happened but since this private sophisticated social club was left exactly as it was decades ago the magic still remains strongly intact, and can be seen, heard, and savored in the bar's signature cocktails including Elixir 13, a mixture of Lucid Absinthe and water that may have helped cause the magicians' disappearance.

The rich and ornate area is decorated with enchanted ever-changing magic show posters, mystifying mirrors, and vintage props and tricks left behind decades ago including displays of locks and keys, cards, linking rings and magic wands.

Even the wall paper has hidden images of interlocking rings, doves, rabbits, card suits, handcuffs and other magical artifacts.

On one wall is a framed copy of *The Boardwalk Bugle* newspaper from Wednesday November 13, 1940 telling the official back story:

"The shocking revelations of a secret magicians' lounge could point to new clues concerning the group of beloved illusionists who mysteriously vanished from our boardwalk weeks ago. Though, truth be told, we may be more perplexed than before.

"A custodian working at BoardWalk's magic club made the surprising discovery late yesterday evening when he rested his mop against a false door leading into the secret room. By the look of the room's peculiar décor – including magical accoutrements and shelves lined with curious elixirs – this is no doubt the clandestine hideout of our missing master magicians.

"But there's just one dilemma...there are still no magicians in sight!

"After investigating the magicians' hideout this morning, The Boardwalk Bugle noticed something extra out of the ordinary about this already peculiar lounge. Glasses filled with odd elixirs still sat on the countertops.

"Magic props and playing cards were scattered all about. And, stranger yet, all of the clocks in the room were set to thirteen past the hour – almost as if time froze and every magician disappeared on the spot.

"When we questioned the club owner about her knowledge of the hidden room and the possible whereabouts of the missing magicians, she repeated the same unhelpful news we've been reporting for weeks now: 'A good magician never reveals her secrets!'

"According to multiple witnesses, the missing conjurers in question were last seen entering the loading area behind BoardWalk's magic club on September 13. All wore ostentatious costumes, and were accompanied by assistants, stagehands and crates filled with small animals – including doves, rabbits and the like.

"Suspicions only arose when the touring magician Laslow the Lucky failed to appear for his much anticipated matinee performance the following day. In addition to M. Laslow, it would appear that his assistant, multiplying rabbits and every illusionist on the boardwalk vanished along with him.

"Whether a good illusion of a simple misunderstanding, The Boardwalk Bugle will be certain to keep our dear readers informed about the whereabouts of our beloved magicians."

SEASHORE SWEETS

To accommodate the new AbracadaBar at the Boardwalk Inn and Villas, an old fashioned ice cream and candy shop called Seashore Sweets was closed February 1, 2016. The shop was especially known for offering hand-scooped ice cream.

Seashore Sweets had a main story related to the Miss America Pageant that was celebrated throughout this location as well as a smaller tangent story about a well-known candy associated with Atlantic City.

Atlantic City is where saltwater taffy was created in 1883 when a clever businessman named David Bradley sold some taffy that had a hint of salt water when his shop was flooded by ocean water. Salt water is not an ingredient in salt water taffy today. Of course, salt water taffy could be purchased in the shop, usually with Goofy's face on the bag.

The main storyline was that two sisters, known as the "Sweet Sisters", who competed in the early Miss America pageant decided to stay in the area and opened the shop. Their picture is on the outside sign and the motto of the store is "Confections served with Affection" (look for the heart shapes in the letter "O" in that sign).

Atlantic City was famous for the Miss America pageant that began in the 1920s and lasted for 85 years on the Boardwalk before relocating to Las Vegas in 2007. It returned to Atlantic City in 2013.

Leanza Cornett, who was Miss America 1993, was the first actress to play a live-action version of Ariel, the title character from *The Little Mermaid,* at the *Voyage of The Little Mermaid* show at Disney's Hollywood Studios at Walt Disney World Resort in 1991.

There were many authentic artifacts like souvenir programs and tickets inside the store including in a transparent case on the right hand side of the entrance with a trophy, crown, regal cape and scepter used in an actual Miss America pageant.

Up above near the ceiling were framed photos of all the Miss America winners from 1921 through 2007 (when it stopped being held in Atlantic City).

In the earliest days, the women were not just judged in a swimsuit competition (called the Bathers' Revue) but also as part of the Rolling Chair Parade, referenced in a newspaper article on the wall.

Framed posters and memorabilia could be found in every area of the small shop. A souvenir program from the 1942 pageant would have cost twenty-five cents that year but is worth many times that price today.

The inspiration for the name Flying Fish Café next door most likely came from a classic Coney Island roller coaster called the Flying Turns. One of the ride vehicles was called the Flying Fish.

The interior of the restaurant was originally a colorful homage to Coney Island. The back of the booths resembled the curving lifts and drops of a roller coaster. On the back wall was a huge depiction of a back-lit Ferris wheel.

Fish did, in fact, fly overhead in pairs in the restarurant on a version of the famous parachute ride that was a decades-long favorite at Steeplechase Park at Coney Island. In fact one of the first images on the wall mural is of people riding the eight wooden horses on a steel track at Steeplechase.

On the cloud painted ceiling, the stars changed colors every few minutes.

The entire interior, including the addition of an open on-stage kitchen, has been recently redesigned. The new design includes images of flying fish in a chandelier of glass, the kitchen tiles and the upholstery. The restaurant also has references to the classic boardwalk with carnival art, vintage carnival games and more.

Coronado Springs / Gran Destino Tower

August 1997 / July 2019

The Blizzard Beach water park was originally going to be connected to a Disney resort across the street. Located where the Coronado Springs Resort site now stands, Disney's Alpine Resort would have overlooked the melting snows of Blizzard Beach.

The Alpine Resort would have been a moderately priced hotel and as one of the perks for staying there, guests would have been able to ride a chair lift to the water park. Several concerns sidelined that concept and a different theme was developed.

Disney's Coronado Springs Resort opened as a moderate priced resort but with convention facilities and other enhancements not typical for that level. However, by carefully doing things like having a lobby that employed millwork, vaulted ceilings, a mural and a fountain, the resort seemed more luxurious than it actually was.

It also included a fine dining restaurant (Maya Grill) that gave the impression of a more upscale resort. It is a full-service restaurant featuring a huge, wood-fired grill and seating around a Mayan temple replica.

The fountain at the entrance to the temple is themed after a Yucatanian cenote, a natural limestone pit exposing the swirling, underlying groundwater. Mesoamerican murals, dramatic ceremonial pillars and flickering torches decorate the location.

Project coordinator Cindy MacKenzie returned from a research trip to Oaxaca with three foot tall frogs, lobsters and iguanas to take up residence in the 420 seat Pepper Market food court meant to suggest an old warehouse where individual food vendors have set up shop.

The restaurant had seven different serving stations and was divided into three areas: the fire temple near the exhibit cooking, the water temple and the sun temple. It has been rehabbed into El Mercado de Coronado to resemble an open-air market.

Boll Holland who was Director of Design and Development for the resort stated at the time, "Some conventioneers see only business deals and don't want too much of a 'good time' atmosphere. However, the WDW Resort market requires more amenities. It's all very subjective and you must take into account the nature of convention business and meetings."

So the convention area is more neutral in tone than the rest of the resort. "There was a struggle between Southwestern and Mexican styles," explained Holland. "Southwest is more serious and acceptable for business while Mexico provides a fun and fanciful image.

"The architect, Graham Gund, is not a literal architect. His style is evocative and exterior details are never exactly the same as the historic precedent. He has a tendency to reconfigure historical architectural elements."

However, since it was intended to be a moderate resort, budget factors to contain costs were important. Assistant project manager Bill Hanus stated, "Economic concessions were made for a design standpoint. For example, there are open air walkways as a motel would have versus corridors.

"We used real ceramic tile in high visibility areas, while in other less prominent areas we mixed the real thing with fake. That meant that for every 10,000 feet of tile, 5,000 might be ceramic but the remainder were faux finished.

"In the rooms, the headboards are painted for texture instead of using wood molding. It all adds up when each room's savings is multiplied many times. The contractor purchased everything up front – door frames, hardware, roofing and then stockpiled the materials in site trailers which protected the project from price increases over a two year period.

"He also used 'just in time' delivery for all 'pilferable materials', a significant cost containment step."

Looking for savings in low-maintenance, fan-coil air conditioning units resulted in the elimination of extra duct work systems, a more efficient unit with less maintenance for the operator and millions of dollars in savings for Disney. Lowering overall construction costs was a key factor in realizing the resort's moderate price point.

Of course, Disney is a storytelling company so there is a back story for the resort. Francisco de Coronado left Mexico in 1540 and headed north in search of the fabled seven golden cities of Cibola.

Imagineers used that actual story as a springboard for the back story that "Coronado Springs was founded by the descendants of a Spanish explorer named Juan Francisco. Searching for gold in 1569, Francisco stumbled upon the ruins of a forty-six foot tall Mayan pyramid."

The original Imagineering story for the Mayan pyramid is that it serves as a ceremonial center in the lake. According to Disney, "The temple sits five stories above the Coronado Springs, and the water cascades down the temple's steps into the Lost City of Cibola Feature Pool.

Bas-relief sculptures, called stellae, have been carved on the pyramid."

Mayan symbols are inlaid into the bottom of the twenty-two acre Lago Dorado ("Golden Lake") pool and the pool deck.

According to an Imagineering document: "Hundreds of years later, relatives found his charts and decided to mount an expedition of their own. The rugged group liked the place so much that they built houses and put down roots."

Imagineer Wing Chao said, "We looked at a map to see where people go on vacation. After determining that they like to go to Mexico and the Southwestern U.S., we just blended the themes."

The project was actually put on hold several times for a variety of reasons after it was first proposed in 1992. The original plans did not include a convention center but studies showed that Walt Disney World did not have enough convention space. However, those WDW resorts with that space had room rates too high for many associations' budgets.

Finally, with the introduction of tunnel form cost-conscious construction with poured concrete bays, it became feasible in 1995 for an economic solution to provide convention space and moderately priced rooms. The Coronado ballroom is roughly 60,214-square-foot and is the largest ballroom in the southeastern United States.

The resort was designed to reflect three themes: Cabanas, Ranchos and Casitas. The two story Cabana buildings represent the coastal regions of the American Southwest and Gulf Coast villas. The Cabanas surround the rocky beach adjacent to the fifteen acre man-made lake, Lago Dorado.

The architecture and landscape of the Ranchos suggest the more arid, country-ranch or farmhouse parts of the region with a small stream or arroyo tumbling over a rocky stream bed. Project coordinator Mark Kohl said, "We made sure the vegetation selected would really grow next to a river in the same region of Mexico."

The Casitas were inspired by the urban areas of Mexico and the American Southwest. The Casitas are interspersed with colorful plazas and fountains and palm-shaded courtyards.

"We had to find a balance between Mexico and the Southwest when it came to selecting colors and how they relate," said Kohl. "It was a two year research process where team members went to look and bring back photos, art and books for inspiration. I have a Mexican stone calendar on my wall. The art we finally selected for the guest rooms provides a better fit for the theme of that particular area."

Palacios are decorated in shades of desert sand and sunset pink. The red tile roofs, mosaic accents, shady courtyards and sunny patios recall the grand haciendas of the Spanish Colonial era.

"In a moderate hotel there is little demand for room service, a concierge or beauty parlor so you couldn't justify those amenities," said Boll Holland who was Director of Design and Development for the resort.

The Coronado Springs team even sparked a competitive bidding war between commode manufacturers to obtain the optimum savings in toilets that provided water conservation, quiet flush and less stoppage.

Construction manager Dean Majors recalled, "The highest savings came from using Tunnel form system, a fast method of construction using two L-shaped metal forms to pour concrete room structures. The speed in which the rooms were built – twice as fast as regular construction – could not have been achieved without it. Lowering overall construction costs was a key factor in realizing the resort's moderate price point."

Executive Vice President of Architecture and Design Wing Chao said when the resort opened, "The theme is attractive. It's something you can't find in other places in America. We offer our guests the opportunity to escape to a different geographic and time period. This resort was purposely designed to perform at the same level as a luxury class hotel with the individual products of the same quality because the expectation level of our guests remains high."

As might be expected, the resort has references to the Disney animated feature *The Three Caballeros* (1945) and its three stars: Donald Duck, Jose Carioca and Panchito the Mexican charro rooster from artwork to topiary to "Panchito's Gifts and Sundries" gift shop that includes a large three-dimensional figure of the character singing.

A statue of Little Burrito, a flying donkey, from a segment in the film used to sit outside the gift shop.

Gran Destino Tower

July 2019

The Gran Destino Tower opened along with renovations of existing rooms at the Coronado Springs Resort. The new tower adds 545 rooms to the resorts existing 1840 rooms and includes a unique two story lobby.

All of the rooms throughout the resort were updated according to Disney to "celebrate the daring spirit of the great Spanish explorers, artists, writers and architects".

The name of the tower was inspired by *Destino* ("Destiny") that began in 1945 as a seven minute, experimental, animated short. It was a collaboration between Walt Disney and the famed surrealist painter Salvador Dali that was never completed during their lifetimes. It was the beginning of a long friendship between the two visionary artists.

Dali's idea for the story was inspired by a melancholy love song entitled *Destino* that Disney had purchased but never used for the animated feature film *The Three Caballeros* (1944).

Walt teamed the Spanish artist with John Hench to help guide him through the mechanics of animation for several months with Hench creating some artwork for the film as well.

The pre-production artwork of Dali and Hench was rediscovered by Roy E. Disney in 1999 when he was working on *Fantasia 2000* (2000). He later championed the finishing and releasing of the film in 2003 that was shown at several international film exhibitions.

Hench who was still working at the Walt Disney Company at the age of 95 consulted on the work and Dali's wife loaned her late husband's notebooks on the film.

The *Destino* film plays on several screens in the main lobby that is designed to be an homage to the Catalan Modernism style, as well as in the rooftop Dahlia Lounge.

The Dahlia Lounge on the 16th floor of the Gran Destino Tower is inspired by Spanish surrealism and features a wall full of photos of Walt Disney with Salvador Dali from over the years.

The Dahlia Lounge is named after the heroine of the film, a young woman who struggles through the fluidity of time and unusual transformations to be united through destiny with her one true love.

Dandelion imagery and metal bell accents (at one point in the film she becomes clothed in the bell's shadow) all around the tower including a massive mural on the wall all draw inspiration from the film and its heroine.

Disney Imagineer David Stofcik said that the tower pays homage to the Spanish origins of the stories of Mexico and the American Southwest already told at the resort. He said that the resort's fourteen acre lake, Lago Dorado, ties it all together and that the tower's ribbon-patterned lines on its exterior (which are illuminated at night) represent water that flows through the building and into the lake.

Stofcik said some of the Spanish influences in the architecture were extended to provide opportunities to allow more light into spaces in the building, and that the decorative panels around the lobby itself were inspired by five specific Spanish tile designs from around Barcelona and Toledo that the Imagineers discovered during their research.

However, even Dali himself probably never expected to be surrounded by all the playful Hidden Mickeys that abound in the resort.

Art of Animation

May 2012

The official Disney description for The Art of Animation Resort is "Be surrounded in the artistry, enchantment and magic of Walt Disney and Disney and Pixar movies. Stay at a Disney Resort hotel that invites you to explore the storybook landscapes seen in such classics as *Finding Nemo*, *Cars*, *The Lion King* and *The Little Mermaid*.

"From delightfully themed family suites to wondrously detailed courtyards, Disney's Art of Animation 'draws' you and your family in to become a part of some of your animated favorites."

Basically, the concept was to give guests at the 26th resort at Walt Disney World an opportunity to be immersed in several playful animation environments at an affordable price. In keeping with the bright colors in animated films, the resort itself is a burst of color looking very much like the set of an animated film.

In order to encourage more Disney guests to stay on property rather than in the more budget friendly accommodations in the surrounding area, Disney developed the concept of value resorts that offered some of the same amenities and conveniences as its more expensive resorts but at a more financially accessible price especially for larger groups. Those larger groups often include large groups of cheerleaders, dance teams, Pop Warner football teams and other school groups on a limited budget.

Starting in 1994, three All Star (Sports, Movies, Music) value resorts all designed by the Miami company Arquitectonica were opened. These value resorts featured a food court rather than a sit down restaurant but did include pools (although no towels provided like at the deluxe resorts and no water slides) and free bus transportation to other areas of the property.

All Value hotel rooms at Disney (not counting the family suites at All Star Music and Art of Animation that are 565 square feet) are approximately the same size at roughly a meager 260 square feet when the national average for such a hotel room is 330 square feet.

These resorts were such a success that Disney planned two new value resorts to be called Pop Century celebrating each decade of the 20th Century just as the new Millennium was about to begin. One of the resorts called the Legendary Years would be devoted to celebrating

America from the 1900 – 1940s decades while the other that would be called Classic Years and would showcase the decades 1950- 1990s.

Each half-century resort was to consist of 2,880 rooms in ten buildings each equaling the combined rooms at the three All-Star Resorts.

Construction work took place on both halves of the resort from 1999 through 2001. A bridge originally named the Generation Gap Bridge was constructed across Hourglass Lake to connect both parts of Pop Century and make them accessible to each other.

However, the terrorism attack on September 11, 2001 resulted in a significant drop in tourism as well as a drastic effect on the economy in general so Disney stopped work on the entire resort with even some partial closures at its existing resorts because of lack of demand.

When work finally resumed on Pop Century the economy was only barely rebounding slowly and there was no need for all 5,760 rooms yet, which meant only The Classic Years was initially completed and opened in 2003. The complete and partial shells of The Legendary Years buildings sat untouched even though there were some decorative details in place such as the year markers.

The immediate success of the Classic Years section prompted Disney to announce that the Legendary Years section would be finished and opened in 2007.

However, work never resumed on that section for a variety of reasons and the buildings remained as a type of "ghost hotel" as it was referred to by Disney cast members and guests. The shells were complete with doors in place and more.

In October 2005, the All Star Family Suites were opened on a test basis at All Star Music resort and were hugely successful when they were opened for reservations in February 2006. Strong sales resulted in it being announced in April 2006 that the Legendary Years resort would be completed as an all-suites resorts.

The plan was to convert the existing structures but it was not until January 2010 that Disney announced the resort would be re-themed into Disney's Art of Animation Resort with construction beginning that summer.

The already completed shells meant that Legendary Hall (the main building that was to house the front desk, food court and merchandise shop) and the 1940s building would be changed into Animation Hall and The Little Mermaid section.

Since the Little Mermaid guest buildings had been completed with standard rooms and exterior hallway, they would remain so. The structures of the remaining buildings were incomplete, and so they were completed with interior hallways and configured as family suites.

The phrase "The Art of Animation" has a long Disney heritage.

When Walt Disney was producing the animated feature film *Sleeping Beauty (1959)*, he realized that a great way to publicize the "high art" approach of the film as well as address all the letters that flooded into the studio from young artists interested in animation would be to put together three similar exhibits showcasing the history of animation as well as how animation was done.

He used elements from the film itself to explain the actual animation process. The traveling exhibit was entitled "The Art of Animation: A Walt Disney Retrospective."

One exhibit was showcased in Tomorrowland at Disneyland from May 28, 1960 to September 5, 1966. There were two other traveling versions of the exhibit that toured the United States beginning in 1958 and then one was sent to be shown in Europe and the other to Japan in 1960 to once again promote the release of *Sleeping Beauty* in those countries.

The Japanese exhibit was originally displayed at seventeen department stores throughout Japan, a common practice since Japanese department stores often sponsored fine art exhibits. When the exhibit finished its tour, it was moved to the National Museum of Modern Art in Tokyo.

In addition, Walt had writer Bob Thomas put together a book entitled *The Art of Animation* to explain the history and process of animation.

A dust-jacketed version was released by Simon and Schuster in 1958 and later, an edition without a dust jacket, but with a black cover decorated with brightly colored film strips with the Disney characters instead, was released by Golden Press. This later edition is the one most commonly found in collections since it remained in print for several years.

In 1991, Thomas updated the book still entitled *The Art of Animation* for Hyperion Press but all of that valuable information about *Sleeping Beauty* was pretty much completely thrown out and what remained about early animation was cut back to less than half the book. The other half of the book was devoted to the making of *Beauty and the Beast*.

In 1997, Thomas updated the book again still retaining *The Art of Animation* title for Hyperion Press but this time added a new chapter on some recent Disney animated features, eliminated most of the pages on the making of *Beauty and the Beast* and replaced them so that half the book was now dedicated to the making of *Hercules*.

Disney's Art of Animation Resort is devoted to showcasing four animated feature film favorites in a larger-than-life format, creating distinct decorative environments.

Research showed that modern families were more familiar and emotionally connected with films released during the previous twenty-five years especially those produced by Pixar rather than the original classic Disney Studio ones created by Walt Disney. In addition, selection was made of films prominently represented in the parks by attractions, shows, merchandise sales and more.

The four sections include the following:

Finding Nemo (2003) is a computer animated feature film produced by Pixar about a clownfish father and his friend a female blue tang named Dory sharing adventures to try to find his missing son Nemo. The resort section was the first section of the resort to open on May 31, 2012 along with the Animation Hall building.

The main pool at the resort is the "Big Blue Pool" referencing the name that the undersea creatures call their ocean world. At 11,859 square feet square feet and 310,000 gallons of water, this is the largest resort pool at Walt Disney World. A giant Mr. Ray, whose wingspan is 27 feet, looks over the area, as does a gigantic Crush the turtle, which also includes a colorful reef and the East Australian Current.

Underwater speakers allow guests to hear conversations from characters from the movie as well as musical selections. There's a stereo effect with the sound moving so that the creatures seem to swim past you. The Big Blue Pool is fairly shallow being 4'8" at its deepest. There's real living foliage around the pool which was selected to give the impression of underwater plants like seaweed.

The pool rules are printed on an oversized pair of swimming goggles that appear to be the same ones lost when Nemo was captured since they carry the identification: "P. Sherman 42 Wallaby Way, Sydney, NSW".

Cars (2006) is a computer animated feature film produced by Pixar about the lives of anthropomorphic vehicles in the struggling desert town of Radiator Springs along Route 66. The resort section opened on June 18, 2012.

The Cars section is painted to resemble the desert backdrop of the fictional town of Radiator Springs. The full-sized automotive residents of the small town like Sally, Mater, Doc, Luigi and Guido as well as Lightning McQueen greet guests as they walk down the freshly black-topped road to the rooms situated in a building representing the Cozy Cone Motel from the movie.

Of course, there are the beloved Hidden Mickeys in all four sections of the resort including the section devoted to Cars that has a Hidden Mickey made out of tires and hubcaps on the edges of the carpet. However the Cars section also has "Hidden Cars" in the cloud formations at the top of the buildings.

On the full-sized cars are details that are often unnoticed by guests. Like NASCAR cars, McQueen has a bunch of ads on his cars featuring parodies of human products including Gasprin and Leak Less Adult Drip Pans.

Fillmore is covered in bumper stickers with clever takes on being pro-recycling and the environmentally friendly like "Pardon my back fire I eat veggie fuels". Although Pixar is known for its 3D computer animation, Fillmore has a sticker that proclaims, "Save 2D Animation".

Fillmore also has a registration like-sticker that mentions "Luxo." Luxo is the official mascot of Pixar and is that little lamp you see jumping across the screen at the start of every Pixar film. Fillmore's license plate (51237) is the birthday of George Carlin, the comedian who voiced the character. Carlin passed away in 2008, two years after the first Cars film.

Mater's plate is A-113 and this is a reference that can be seen in some form in all Pixar films (in fact, it is the license number for all the cars in the animated feature). It refers to classroom A113 at the California Institute of the Arts where many students included John Lasseter and other future Pixar artists had classes.

Luigi's plate strangely has the numbers 44.5-10.8 that seems to be a joke about the metric system used in his home of Italy. However, it may be a bit clever than that obvious assumption since it is also the GPS coordinates for a Ferrari manufacturing plant in Maranello, Italy.

While Flo's SHO GIRL vanity plate may not seem all that clever, the Motorama 1957 above it is. The 1957 refers to John Lasseter's birth year, and the Motorama refers to a wild and crazy car show that takes place every two years on the campus of Pixar.

There is also the Cozy Cone Pool with oversized orange traffic cones as cabanas. Cozy Cone Pool is a kid-friendly 74,740-gallon watering hole.

The Lion King (1994) is a Disney animated feature film about a young lion in Africa who must succeed his father as king and battle the tyranny of a usurper who has devastated the Pride Lands of Africa. The resort section opened on August 10, 2012.

The exterior of the buildings depicts an African Savannah, with an elephant graveyard play area displaying a huge elephant skeleton as well as figures of Scar the villain lion and a couple of hungry hyenas protecting the site. This cave-like area is built on a long-lasting soft surface made from recycled sneakers.

A giant-sized Mufasa overlooks the scene from Pride Rock while character scupltures from the movie like Timon and Pumbaa frolic in the surrounding jungle.

The Little Mermaid (1989) is a Disney animated feature film about a young mermaid who falls in love with a human prince and her challenges to live happily ever after. The resort section opened on September 15, 2012, as the fourth and final section of the resort.

The outside area is filled with the treasures that Ariel has rescued from the human world like the statue of Prince Eric and a huge bent fork. In addition, there are 600 cutout objects on resort balconies to help create the feeling of being under the sea.

The Flippin' Fins Pool holds 103,642 gallons of water and features the "Under the Sea Orchestra" conducted by Sebastian the crab.

The outside of each four-story rectangular building at the resort is covered in characters, backgrounds and icons from the respective films. There are more three-dimensional figures than at any other Disney resort and offer multiple photo opportunities like the thirty-five foot tall sculpture of King Triton done by Joni Van Buren from the film *The Little Mermaid*. In total, there are approximately 2,500 figures at the entire resort.

"These themes have both compelling storylines and vivid visuals which will come together to create a truly memorable, immersive resort experience," said Eric Jacobson, Senior Vice President of Walt Disney Imagineering.

"With more multi-generational families vacationing together, guests are looking for places where they can play together and stay together. This resort was designed with the needs of families in mind, as we continue the Disney tradition of providing a great guest experience for every taste and budget."

The total size of the property is 87 acres including 37 of those acres devoted to landscaping and irrigation that covers the equivalent of the size of twenty football fields.

There are over 529,000 square feet of ceramic tiles on the project, enough to cover a standard two-lane road four miles long. There's enough metal railing to wrap around the Amway Center in Orlando eight times.

The project used 23,000 gallons of paint and there are over 2,300 parking spaces. The resort has 227,000 lineal feet of carpet, which if laid out, could stretch from downtown Orlando to the Kennedy Space Center.

The Animation Hall is the check-in center for the resort and includes a self-service business center (a first at a Value resort), arcade, merchandise store and food court. The interior is meant to suggest how animation evolves from simple pencil sketches of a character to the finished full color version.

The examples on the wall opposite the check-in desk progress are enlarged from the actual original rough concept art of the characters from the four films represented at the resort to the final full-colored version, cleverly leading guests in the process to the Ink and Paint Shop and the Landscape of Flavors food court as well as the door leading outside to the various sections. The background music is a loop of music from the four films.

The end of the hall features the "storyboard chandelier" designed by the former head of Pixar animation, John Lasseter. The glass plates are examples of storyboard panels and one of the drawings featuring Lightning McQueen was drawn and signed by Lasseter. When the resort opened, it was the only drawing that was signed in the hallway.

Today there are additional signed drawings. Jerome Ranft, a character sculptor for Pixar signed a drawing of Mater tractor tipping. Pixar artist Josh Cooley autographed the drawing of Lightning McQueen chasing down Chick Hicks and The King.

In that drawing McQueen is numbered "57" instead of the number "95" he was in the film. Originally McQueen was going to be "57", a reference to Lasseter's year of birth but it was eventually changed to "95", the year *Toy Story* debuted.

When the resort first opened to reinforce the overall theme, those people working in the check-in area were not referred to as "cast members" but "concept artists".

The back wall represents a color script used by animation artists to help determine the overall color palette for each scene to establish the proper mood.

The Ink and Paint Shop's wall fixtures are shaped like giant paint jars, arranged by color. Traditionally, specially mixed paint was once used to color the individual cels of an animated film. Today, the coloring is done digitally by computer.

Besides the usual items found in a shop at the WDW resorts, this entire shop is lined with art supplies up on the shelves and the walls. Paint brushes, colored pencils, and paper all represent the tools animation artists use in order to create a feature film.

Landscape of Flavors is the six hundred seat food court with an extensive variety of ever-changing offerings, divided into four sections to reference each of the four animated features represented at the resort and features artwork of the environments of those films on the wall, painted ceiling light fixtures and more.

For instance, the ceiling fixture in the Lion King section simulates looking up through a jungle canopy while The Little Mermaid section has a painting of the grotto holding some of Ariel's treasures that she has gathered.

The flooring is made from all recyclable materials. Guests dine with real silverware on melamine, reusable dishware instead of paper and plastic.

Every night in the Lion King courtyard there's a Disney movie scheduled showing on a large outdoor inflatable screen.

The interior of the rooms reflects the film designated for each section. Each room matches its movie from the bedding to the shower curtains to the shape of the light fixtures and chairs.

The *Finding Nemo* rooms have coral-shaped chairs and ceiling lights that look like bubbles. The bathroom is designed like the sunken ship scene in the movie, right down to the porthole that serves as a mirror and Bruce the shark on the shower curtain.

Pulling down the Murphy bed reveals an image of Marlin and Nemo sleeping in their anemone home. Artwork depicting the East Australian current runs down the Nemo carpet.

Lion King rooms showcase Zazu performing on the headboards and Pumbaa and Timon decorating the shower curtain.

Cars rooms capture a motel (motor hotel) "feel" where tool chests serve as drawers and storage spaces, while a map of Radiator Springs adorns the top of the coffee table.

Disney's Pop Century Resort and Disney's Art of Animation Resort share a Disney Skyliner station that themes in with both resorts. Upon departing the gondola station, Skyliner passengers will ascend over Hourglass Lake and enjoy a panoramic view of both these two colorful resorts.

Value Resorts: All-Star / Pop Century

Walt Disney World introduced its All-Star resorts as a value-level resort experience that was less expensive than the moderate and deluxe priced accommodations already available at other Walt Disney World resort hotels, to compete with nearby bargain non-WDW hotels around the perimeter of the property.

Even though these value resorts are less expensive than other Disney-owned options, they still feature a number of Disney amenities and advantages including proximity to the theme parks.

The Walt Disney Company asked architects Bernardo Fort Brescia and Laurinda Hope Spear of the Miami based architectural firm Arquitectonica to design a classic American "kitchy" motel resort for Disneyland Paris.

They were working on a concept of a 1950s coast-to-coast roadside trip from the alligators and palm trees of Florida to teepees and giant cowboy boots in the western United States.

That project never evolved but as Fort-Brescia recalled it led to the design of the All Star resorts, "It was there that we started evolving the notion, asking the question of why a theme would have to refer to an actual place. We began to explore the idea of themed architecture without place references but idea references instead.

"What if we remove ourselves from architectural themes and go more into the theme as an idea, not as a place or a time? Look at popular entertainment, at sports, music and movies.

"What if we make those the themes and turn them into popular architecture? After all, it's a very American phenomenon. So we presented it as Pop Art and it worked."

To create a value resort, the motel units with outdoor hallways were all identical, cast from the exact same mold so the thing that makes it a Disney resort is the addition of the railings, parapets, stairwells and vertical supports for the balconies decorated with gigantic, iconic images like surfboards, Coca-Cola cans and more.

"It comes from the same American culture as roadside architecture," said Fort-Brescia. "You drive down the roads and there's a big jack rabbit, a big hat or a big cup of coffee."

The first WDW value resort was All Star Sports resort that opened April 29, 1994 and was divided into five sections devoted to competitive sports: Touchdown (football), Center Court (tennis), Home Run Hotel (baseball), Surfs Up (surfing) and Hoops Hotel (basketball).

Surf's Up! buildings opened first on April 29, 1994 followed by Hoops Hotel (May 13, 1994), Touchdown (June 26, 1994), Home Run Hotel (July 22, 1994), and Center Court (August 11, 1994).

That design, by Arquitectonica with the Disney Development Company, was the model for the two subsequent All-Star resorts (Movies and Music) that also featured outsized icons highlighted by neon and fiber optics to bring the themes to life.

Arquitectonica referred to it as "taking icons of popular culture and sports and blowing them up as larger-than-life architectural accents."

When the resort opened, Don Robinson, general manager of the All Star Resorts, said, "The theming, architecture and landscaping all work together to make this a 'fan'- tastic setting."

The 55-foot-tall gold star in front of Stadium Hall weighs over 55,000 pounds. The 46-foot-tall silver star by Surfboard Bay weighs 33,000 pounds.

At the Hoops Hotel court, there are five Washingtonian Palms "playing" a team of five Sabal Palms. The palms are arranged as if the game is about to "tip off". Forty five foot tall megaphones house the stairwells and giant whistles mark the buildings' entrances.

The whistles measure 60 feet long and 20 feet high. The pea inside the whistle is approximately nine feet in diameter. Pennants from college teams (Blue Devils, Tigers, Boilermakers, Gators) and over 70 giant basketballs roughly five feet in diameter line the railings.

At Surf's Up, it would take six surf dudes standing on each other's shoulders to carry one of the oversized 38 foot tall surfboards to the beach. Approximately 950 colorful Red Snapper and Dolphin fish appear to be swimming along a "wavy" balcony. The 38 feet high shark fins that mark the buildings' main entrances would belong to a 300 foot long Great White Shark.

At Center Court, it would take 9,474,609 regulation-sized tennis balls to fill one of the ball cans that decorate the stairwells. Those balls placed end to end would stretch from WDW to Key West. The tennis racquets that line the railing are approximately 51 feet tall. The "tennis" balls attached to the balconies at Center Court are almost five feet in diameter.

At Touchdown, a football player would have to be more than 200 feet tall to be able to wear one of these giant football helmets. The football field is even decorated with giant Xs and Os, while poles and numbers on the buildings show the 40 yard line, 30 yard line, and so on.

At the Home Run Hotel, a 40-foot tall White Ash tree would be needed to make a baseball bat the size of the ones located on the railings. It would take more than 20 million 12-ounce cans of Coke to fill just one of the large Coke cup containers.

All Star Music was the second resort hotel in the All Star Complex and is an homage to the classic musical genres: Broadway show tunes, calypso, country, jazz and rock'n'roll. It was the first Disney Value Resort with family suites. Calypso was the first building to open on November 22, 1994, and Broadway was the last to open on February 17, 1995.

It has a swimming pool shaped like a guitar and another pool that looks like a piano, complete with black-and-white tile steps that look like a keyboard. The Broadway section is paved to look like a New York City street complete with yellow Checker cab sitting at the curb. The Rock'n'Roll section has a giant jukeboxes and guitars. Country Music section has large banjos and cowboy boots.

All Star Movies is the third and final resort hotel in the All Star Complex of value resorts and features buildings themed to Disney movies with massive icons as well.

The Mighty Ducks and 101 Dalmatians sections opened January 15, 1999, Fantasia (based on both the original movie and its 2000 sequel) and Herbie: The Love Bug section opened in March, and the final section, Toy Story, opened in April 1999.

The Disney Character icons at the resort were all created at Walt Disney Imagineering's Tujunga facility in North Hollywood, California.

"The Dalmatians (Pongo and Perdita) are tall but thin. With Buzz Lightyear (forty-seven feet high and weighing thirty thousand pounds) you've got spindly legs topped by a Winnebago. You could literally have an apartment in his chest cavity," said technical director for show production John Nelson.

"It is one of the biggest sculpted pieces Tujunga has ever done. Painting him in terms of time and materials was equivalent to painting fifteen cars."

Pongo is forty feet tall and Perdita is thirty-five feet and their ninety-nine spotted puppies decorate the railings. There is a total of four miles of handrails on the buildings at the resort. Impressions of paw prints and dog bones are embedded in the cement walkways.

The building also features six 36 foot high fire hydrants to offer relief for the dogs.

Woody from *Toy Story* is only twenty-five feet high but the brim of his cowboy hat measures eighteen feet in diameter. There is a total of 142 Green Army Men with an average height of eight feet tall standing guard on two building rooftops and in the six Buckets O'Soldiers.

Eric Merz who supervised the structural engineering for the icons was especially fond of the thirty-six foot tall brooms from *Fantasia* that carried buckets. He recalled, "As far as taking an inanimate object like that, combining th engineering and making it come alive...Well, when the brooms and buckets got to the field and were all assembled, everyone took a breath and said, 'wow'!"

The Fantasia section also contains elements from the sequel film *Fantasia 2000* that wouldn't be released until a year after the section opened so special permission was required of Roy E. Disney who among other titles was then chairman of Feature Animation and the producer of the film.

"It's been a great lot of fun to watch these characters (from the sequel) get replicated in the size they are," said Mr. Disney. "The ballerina is such a pretty little thing in the movie – just a six-inch high doll. It's fantastic to see her blown up to this giant size!"

Besides the ballerina, characters from that film included a jack-in-the-box and several toy soldiers.

The Mighty Ducks section features giant hockey sticks, goalie nets and duck-shaped hockey masks. Goalie nets 31 feet high surround the stairwells.

The gigantic front and rear Herbie sculptures (because Herbie can split in two) on the Herbie section buildings are approximately five times the normal size of a VW Beetle. Each car weighs seven tons with tires that are nine feet in diameter. At night, they illuminate.

A normal-sized Herbie was displayed on a racetrack-themed courtyard. It was later relocated to the Disney MGM Studios backlot tour because people kept climbing on it at the resort making it a safety issue.

The two buildings devoted to Herbie are themed to a racing motif with oversized tools like a wrench, a screwdriver and wheel stating "Winner's Circle". The oversized movie clap board says the production is "Bananas" probably referencing the movie *Herbie Goes Bananas* (1980).

Imagineer John Hench designed several of the icons working with director of sculpting Valerie Edwards in producing the maquettes used for the final figures.

Hench commented, "We use startling icons, beautifully finished in gutsy colors. People smile when they see them. It's one of the magic elements of Disney Parks – engaging optimism."

While the character icons were created at Tujunga, an additional sixty or so larger and smaller ones were fabricated by outside contractors in Kansas City, Pittsburgh, Providence R.I., New Orleans, Los Angeles and even Orlando.

"There is no one in the country that has the capacity to build all of these," stated construction manager Rob Brown.

Due to wetlands careful preservation and incorporation of the environment was a major objective in the overall planning process. The various buildings and associated parking fields were arranged to maintain a natural landscape buffer to the wetlands while maximizing parking efficiency and minimizing distances for guests.

The two pools are the hockey-rink-themed pool in The Mighty Ducks area, and the Fantasia pool where Sorcerer Mickey directs a liquid symphony.

In 2018, the resort underwent extensive room refurbishment.

Pop Century

December 2003

"Disney's Pop Century Resort showcases the impact that popular culture has had on our society, so it's fitting that we're first opening the 1950s through the 1990s areas of this hotel," said WDW President Al Weiss in December 2003, "because those were the years when the term 'pop culture' really grew to become a part of the American lexicon."

The original mission statement for the resort was "We make service fun, and we relive decades of memories with Guests of every generation. Disney's Pop Century Resort – remember when."

For Pop Century, Arquitectonica expanded on its All Star resort design with what they referred to as "supergraphics" meaning huge words and phrases from the appropriate decade above the parapets to blend with the other icons.

The firm worked with in-house designers at Walt Disney Imagineering to create these icons that are designed to break up the linear lines of the architecture.

Just like the All Star resorts, Pop Century's motel units with outdoor hallways were all identical, cast from the exact same mold so the thing that makes it a Disney resort is the addition of the railings, parapets, stairwells and vertical supports for the balconies decorated with gigantic, iconic images

Large shadowboxes in the check-in lobby were filled with original and authentic pop-culture artifacts for each decade including some Disney memorabilia.

A shadow box is an enclosed square or rectangular display case with a glass cover containing a variety of different objects usually centered on a specific theme. These decorative cases with memorabilia began as a military tradition for someone retiring and filled with badges, pin, flags and more from their service.

The lobby at Pop Century: Classic Years has a wall across from the front desk known as Memory Lane filled with shadow boxes showcasing roughly 750 items commemorating the different decades of the resort.

Jayne Alcorn, Show Production Designer for Walt Disney Imagineering worked with her team for six months to bid in online auctions and comb flea markets, antique shops, yard sales and vintage clothing stores as far north as Massachusetts and as far west as California to obtain items that would help set the resort's nostalgic tone.

Alcorn said when the resort opened, "We searched for what America was playing with, what it was wearing and eating, what the popular TV shows and movies were, what inventions came out and what families did for vacation. We think Guests will just come in and reminisce on their own. Who could not be moved by all these memories?"

Al Weiss added, "Because of the popularity of our other value-category resorts – Disney's All-Star Resorts – and the exciting atmosphere created by things like the pop culture icons, shadow boxes and incredible theming, we believe this will be a great addition to our resort inventory."

A 1970s shadow box is dedicated to Walt Disney World with a copies of *LOOK* and *LIFE* magazine devoted to the opening of WDW, a page from the *Orlando Sentinel* of the opening of WDW, the official guidebook, *The Story of Walt Disney World Commemmorative Edition*, a Mickey Mouse back scratch souvenir, a lunch box, ticket book and more. Nearby is a framed photo from the 1976 Magic Kingdom Bicentennial Parade.

Memorabilia from Disneyland and the Mickey Mouse Club television show are showcased in the 1950s shadowbox.

General Manager Dave Vermeulen said, "We believe that people are going to have fun talking about the things they had forgotten they remembered. Each time we see people at the shadowboxes in Classic Hall, they say, 'Wow! I had forgotten about this' or 'I used to have some of these'. We find that people enjoy talking about their memories and I think the theme makes it very easy and conducive for that.

"The background music in Classic Hall and around the pools is going to be themed to the different decades. In Everything Pop shopping and dining, we've been able to program the background music so that, at a couple of times during the day, all the Cast Members are going to pause momentarily and do the twist or another dance. We're trying to just make it fun in everything we do."

Like at the All Star Resorts, there are gigantic icons. "One of the many different learnings we got from the All Star Resorts," said Vermeulen, "related to the fabrication, maintenance and cleaning of the icons."

Nine giant bowling pins stand in the resort's 1950s area. The tenth pin is the bowling pin-shaped pool.

Roughly 125,000 gallons of paint was used to create the bright colors and tie-dyed hues on the buildings' interior and exterior walls.

Service and equipment buildings were disguised across the resort. For instance, the laundry building looks like a bowling shoe storage bin and an equipment building resembles a stack of computer floppy disks.

In the 1960s area, giant "thumbprints" are visible on the ears of the elephant supposedly made of Play-Doh and peeking out of the towering canister.

"Peace of Pizza" delivery trucks at the resort resemble old Volkswagen vans complete with roof-mounted surfboards.

The Fast Forward Arcade was specifically designed to feature both classic video games like Pac-Man and Space Invaders as well as new favorites.

The Disney pin trader location was designed to look like a 1950s camper.

The resort's Rubik's Cube icons reach a peak of 41 feet above the ground. By comparison, a Rubik's Cube puzzle toy is four inches tall. At night the giant Rubik's Cubes illuminate the area.

The resort's 8-track tapes are more than 35 feet tall with tape that is more than one-foot in width. A real 8-track tape is five and one-quarter inches tall with a tape that is only one-quarter inch wide.

The table soccer players are more than twelve feet tall and the "toy" ball is more than two-and-one half feet in diameter.

The giant Big Wheel icon has a recommended weight for a child no more than 877 pounds according to the sticker on the towering riding toy.

The 1970s courtyard pays tribute to the age of disco, with a motion-based disco light mounted in the middle of the courtyard. This color-changing light sends streams of light across a '70s inspired outdoor "dance floor".

DVC Resorts: Kidani Village / Riviera

Several DVC locations are discussed elsewhere in this book. Here are two more. The DVC program began in 1991 with the opening of its first resort now known as Old Key West. It proved so popular that four years later other DVC resorts began to open. Disney Vacation Club resorts represent more than 10% of Walt Disney World's total rooms.

DVC is the timeshare arm of The Walt Disney Company and is operated by subsidiary Disney Vacation Development. The Walt Disney Company got into this business because it identified a need to develop larger on-property accommodation options which met the demand for longer-stay visitors.

Disney research including surveys of theme park visitors showed that many guests did not want to leave the Disney property and wanted to remain on-site, but they stayed off-site because of the additional space provided by resorts not located on Disney property.

Members access their club resorts by purchasing into a points system—receiving an annual allotment of vacation points that can be used in a variety of ways for different types of accommodation.

Kidani Village

2009

In 2009, Kidani Village opened near Disney's Animal Kingdom as a DVC resort. Disney describes the resort as "immerse yourself in the wonders of the wild, surrounded by colorful creatures ... Delight in African-inspired details while you relax in accommodations that capture the adventurous atmosphere of the wild. Feel at home in this village alive with the spirit of the savanna."

Kidani is the Swahili word for "necklace" and was chosen because of the resort's distinctive shape. It was designed as an African necklace with vacation villas forming the beads, walkways creating the knots in between, and the lobby representing the ornament or jewel at its center.

The lobby and the villas extend outwards and resemble the curlicue shape of a water buffalo's horns.

With the opening of the resort, Disney's Animal Kingdom Lodge was renamed Jambo House and the two resorts are now collectively know as Disney's Animal Kingdom Lodge.

Kidani Village offers it own unique savanna view of giraffes, elands, impalas, greater kudus, wildebeests, marabou storks, flamingos, waterbucks and more. There are two savannas each with a different variety of animals: Sunset and Pembe and guests are given a Wildlife Spotting Guide.

It has its own lobby and registration area as well as Samawati Springs pool, Uwanja (meaning "play area") Camp water-play area, Survival of the Fittest fitness center, a table service restaurant Sanaa ("African inspired cuisine with an Indian touch") and Johari Treasures merchandise shop.

According to Tim Wazecha, senior development manager WDI Resorts, the Imagineers came up with a back story for Samawati Springs, "Here we have a watering hole and an animal observation camp from before the hotel was built and it's now abandoned. Because it's been abandoned, the water tower is falling apart and sprouting leak which acts as part of our interactive water-feature area.

"We also have a windsock area. In order to keep the animals away from the food, we started to hang buckets off of the windsock area. Because it's elevated, as it rains, the buckets spill out to get our Guests wet."

Kidani Village was designed with three themes: Fabric, Proverbs, and Art from various African cultures. The art does not refer to just paintings hanging on the wall but hand-carved masks, tribal symbols, sculptures and statuary in alcoves and on recessed shelves specifically designed for them.

The proverbs hold special significance due to their importance in African life. One of the most notable that is inscribed at the resort's main entrance comes from the Asante people of Ghana: "Proverbs are like butterflies. Some are caught. Some fly away."

Referencing this proverb's philosophy a bronze-cast butterfly can be found next to each proverb located at the resort.

The "fabric" theme is very prominent in the lobby. The major patterns used throughout Kidani Village are from the fabrics of the kente cloths of Ghana and the kuba cloths of the Congo.

"Beyond the obvious natural beauty of Kidani Village, the story and attention to detail created by Walt Disney Imagineers is truly amazing," said Kim Marinaccio was general manager of Disney's Animal Kingdom Lodge and Villas. "The themes of art, fabric and proverbs play an important part in telling the story of the African people and Kidani Village."

Kidani Village was designed by architect Peter Dominick Jr., who designed the original Disney Animal Kingdom Lodge resort and it is clear that the style is much the same. The towering ceiling, rich dark wood and grand windows are similar, but the artwork and smaller room size imparts a cozier feel.

Cultural representatives from Africa are the Lobby Greeters, Savanna Guides and Restaurant Greeters to share information about life in their country and their personal journey to WDW. They also share African folk tales each night at the Arusha Rock firepit.

However, in addition to authentic African culture, images of Simba, Rafiki, Timon, Pumbaa and others from Disney's animated classic *The Lion King* appear throughout the resort especially in the rooms.

Other proverbs posted throughout the resort include: "Truth keeps the hands cleaner than soap" (Nigera), "Life is like a ballet performance danced only once" (Mali) and "You must judge a person by the works of their hands" (Africa).

"Friendship doubles joy and halves grief." (Egypt), "It is the pot that boils but the dish gets the credit." (Cameroon) "If you haven't been to two marketplaces you don't know which is the best value." (Burkina Faso) "Smooth seas do not make skillful sailors." (Ethiopia) "If everyone thought alike no goods would ever be sold." (Libya)

"He who does not know the road holds back the one who does." (Kenya) "If you get rich, be in a dark corner when you jump for joy." (Zulu) "Wealth is bits of roasted meat. The great thing is one's kith and kin." (Zimbabwe) "Mother is gold, a father is a mirror." (Nigeria) "When you follow in the path of your father, you learn to walk like him." (Ghana) "It takes a whole village to raise a child." (Nigeria)

"One who goes back to his home does not consider the night too dark. He knows his way." (Uganda) "Though the lion and the antelope happen to live in the same forest, the antelope still has time to grow up."(Ghana) "The road doesn't tell the traveler what lies ahead." (Tanzania) "He who learns, teaches." (Ethiopia) "Sticks in a bundle are unbreakable." (Tanzania)

"When you are sick you promise a goat, but when you are well again, you make due with chicken." (Nigeria) "Life is a shadow and a mist; it passed quickly and is no more." (Madagascar) "One falsehood spoils a thousand truths." (Ghana) "Truth keeps the hands cleaner than soap." (Nigeria)

"It's a bad child who does not take advice." (Asante) "No one tests the depth of a river with both feet." (Asante) "Sickness and disasters come and go like rain, but health is like the sun that illuminates the entire village." (Africa)

Riviera

December 2019

The Riviera resort is the 15th Disney Vacation Club resort and the first stand-alone DVC resort to be built in over eight years.

It was based on a little documented European trip that Walt Disney, his brother Roy and their wives took in 1935 that took them through England, France, Germany and Italy.

During that trip, Walt brought back with him hundreds of books including children's books with illustrations of little people, bees, and small insects that he hoped would inspire the artists at his Burbank Studio. Those nearly 700 books from that trip became the foundation of the Disney Studio library that began that same year under the supervision of Helen Ludwig Hennesy.

That is the reason for the resort having the relaxing study called the Voyageurs' Lounge with its shelves filled with books, all foreign editions from the 1930s including several Disney storybooks.

A display case features an original Charlotte Clark stuffed Mickey Mouse doll from that time period and a similar one is shown in photos of Walt and his wife Lillian from the trip. Near the doll is a hat representing the fedora that Walt often wore, including on this trip, and a photo next to it shows him wearing such a hat.

In the hallway leading to the lounge are black-and-white photos on the wall from Walt's holiday. Many of these photos do not appear in any book like Walt Disney on June 13, 1935 playing with penguins at the London Zoo in a photo by Edward G Malindine for the *Daily Herald*.

Another set of such photos decorate the wall in Primo Piatto (Italian for "first plate") the principal quick-service venue on the first floor near the two pools. While I have spent time standing and studying these pictures in both locations, I have noticed that Disney guests generally ignore them or even question their significance.

The resort only prominently features French and Italian influences to reference the Rivera rather than Walt's travels to other countries during his trip but still provides an opportunity to showcase the European influences on Disney heritage.

Inspired by the cliffside restaurants of the Riviera, Topolino's Terrace is a reference to Mickey Mouse's name in Italian, Topolino or "little mouse". In keeping with the emphasis on European art, for the character breakfast at this location the costumed performers are attired as Mickey the artist, Minnie the poet, Donald the sculptor, and Daisy the dancer.

The Italian Rivera also inspired the black-and-white painting "The Seaside Nap" featuring Mickey and Pluto lounging on their balcony overlooking the sea that is located under the television in the one bedroom villa.

The theme seems less Walt's visit to the Rivera in the 1930s but just an overall "European Disney" concept that extends to modern times including foreign movie posters of Disney animated films on the walls in the first floor hallway near the formal lawn.

Yet there are odd lapses. A framed picture of Lady and the Tramp eating spaghetti is meant to suggest Italy even though the story is wholly American.

While the story theme is not as immersive or consistent as some other Disney resort hotels like Disney's Boardwalk Inn and Villas, the concentration on the Disney connections to Europe is still appealing.

"The approach was to take the inspiration of a classical resort of a grand era along the European coast in a uniquely Disney experience. We do that by creating a level of casual elegance as part of the experience," said Imagineer Dean Huspen.

"While the color palette itself is classical, the pops of colors on the awning and shutters and the area development and even the way we incorporate little discoveries in design features into the ornamental metal work and the railings became that approach."

According to Imagineer Missy Renard, "The inspiration came from the renowned art heritage of the Riviera region itself where there was a prolific amount of work that came from the late 19th century and 20th century masters. What we've done is taken our Disney characters and icons and work them into these series of paintings and different kinds of art that reflect the subject, brush strokes and technique of what the artists were studying."

The goal was to capture a European style and sensibility of art with a Disney twist. In addition, there is a variety of Riviera-themed artwork around the resort that doesn't have anything at all to do with Disney. The luxury vinyl plank flooring is laid in a herringbone pattern to reference ancient Rome's roadways that were a similar pattern to improve stability and durability.

As Disney has stated, "During the early-20th-century, artists along the Riviera were exploring ways to make still life objects come to life on a flat canvas. Artists would first break the objects into individual shapes and forms then accentuate each object with strong outlines."

Inspired by the cubist style of art, Disney artists painted the enchanted objects from *Beauty and the Beast* (1991) – Cogsworth, Lumiere, Chip and Mrs. Potts – as they appear to come to life on a canvas entitled "Still Life With Teapot".

The dramatic hues of sunset inspired Disney artists in painting Rapunzel and Pascal as they watch the glowing lanterns illuminate the evening sky, creating a delightful pattern of shape and color in the painting called "Girl With Lanterns".

The S'il Vous Play interactive children's water play area draws inspiration from the grand public fountains seen throughout Europe with its patina and limestone-inspired design.

Another inspiration for it was the "Dance of the Hours" segment from the animated feature *Fantasia*. The area celebrates music, art, dance and storytelling by featuring whimsical animals from the film frolicking and playing in the water.

An elephant filling a dump bucket with his trunk, hippos and ostriches dancing and playing, as well as hippos splashing water into decorative bowls and basins are meant to bring a smile to guests' faces.

A dedicated Disney Skyline station leads to an archway with two mosaic murals made from one million hand-cut tiles. One mural is the lantern scene from Tangled and the other shows pixie dust circling the Tower of London and arching over to the Neverland Lagoon where the golden Jolly Roger pirate ship takes flight. Both reference flight to tie-in with the Skyliner and both feature European stories.

Artwork referencing Peter Pan is scattered throughout the resort including in the one bedroom villas with a painting inspired by Mary Blair's concept art for that 1953 animated film with the Darling children flying out of their bedroom window and in the hallways a painting of Mrs. Darling reading to her children and Nana the dog.

In the deluxe studio by the bed, there is an homage to a vintage French poster with Mademoiselle Minnie and for sharp-eyed guests in another painting guests can see the red Lightning McQueen racing along a bridge over the sea.

Of course, there are many Hidden Mickeys as well. The hallway carpeting is in gold, blue, and white to evoke a European elegance and hidden in the filigree pattern is the head of Minnie Mouse.

Rich colors, elegant metallics and metals, and playful artwork and décor once again show the care and skill of including artistic influences into a Disney resort hotel.

Other WDW Resort Hotels

Here are short glimpses of three more WDW resort hotels each with its unique theme and personality.

Every WDW resort hotel features one large feature pool usually designed for the entire family and is generally more elaborate with a small water-based playground area nearby for younger children.

Many of the resorts also offer an additional "quiet" or "leisure" pool or pools that are usually frequented by adults who just want to relax. All the Moderate and Deluxe resorts have water slides but the Value resorts do not.

Pool hopping (or the act of visiting pools at hotels you aren't staying in) is, for the most part, not allowed at Walt Disney World. Guests staying at a Disney resort hotel are only able to visit the pools at their hotel with some exceptions for Disney Vacation Club members.

WDI senior development manager for resorts Tim Warzecha said, "Even our pool areas have their own separate identity and storyline that reinforces the overall story of the hotel. Imagineers are storytellers and the most critical part of our job is coming up with the story and reinforcing it throughout all the details."

Imagineers work with various departments and outside contractors to add a variety of elements including colors, textures and lighting solutions. Careful consideration is placed on providing access for all Guests that resulted in things like dual handrails for pool stairs and aquatic wheelchairs to assist with Guest mobility needs.

WDW manager of Worldwide Safety and Accessibility Bob Minnick said that guests especially appreciate the pools having a sloped entry which allows them to walk straight into the pool.

Sometimes known as "zero entry", it means that entering the pool is like at a beach that gently and gradually slopes into the water, becoming deeper with each step. This provides easier access for children, the elderly, and those with mobility issues.

The pools are cleaned daily as needed. Guests are very interested in what the pools look like since it is not just the icing on the cake for the vacation experience but is considered an important reviving getaway after time in the parks.

Disney's Caribbean Beach

October 1988

Disney's Caribbean Beach Resort opened October 1, 1988, as the first Disney moderate resort hotel. When the resort opened it was the fifth largest hotel complex in the United States. It was designed by Fugleberg Koch Architects of Winter Park, Florida.

In keeping with the Caribbean theme, the resort is split into five island-themed "villages": Aruba, Martinique, Barbados, Trinidad and Jamaica. These two story buildings blend tranquil pastel walls and white-wood railings. They feature vividly colored metal roofs.

The five villages surround the 45 acre lake called Barefoot Bay that includes a mile-long promenade filled with walking/running trails and small white sandy beaches.

In the center of the man-made lake is Caribbean Cay, an island with a playground, picnic area, and lots of lush foliage. Caribbean Cay is connected to the promenade on each side by a footbridge.

Cay (pronounced "key") refers to a small, low-elevation, sandy island on the surface of a coral reef and comes from the Spanish word "cayo." It is a popular term for islands in the Caribbean area. Key West was originally called "Cayo Hueso".

"We're building a fun experience, a vacation," said Wing Chao, vice president of the Disney Development Company when the resort opened. "A hotel is an extension of the guest experience. When they leave the Magic Kingdom they can continue their fantasy at their accommodation. We want the theming to be so pervasive that guests feel like they're walking onto a movie set."

That movie set was meant to reflect the brightly colored and laid back atmosphere of the Caribbean with references to its history as a haven for pirates. That includes a pirate-themed pool area with cannons that shoot water. A pirate-ship-themed playground sits in the middle of a kids' pool.

Older kids can climb a spiral staircase to the top of a turret for an 82-foot trip down the larger slide and through the fortress wall.

In January 2009, Disney refurbished many rooms in the Trinidad South village with a pirate theme that included nautical details and pirate ship-shaped beds. Unique touches in the room included the dresser resembling crates and the mini-fridge fitting inside a barrel.

Until 1997, guests could purchase jewelry called "Plata del" that was handcrafted from 370 year old silver coins salvaged from a Spanish galleon that sank off the cost of Florida in 1622.

Each piece of jewelry was struck directly from "Pieces of Eight" recovered from the shipwreck site and came with a certificate of authenticity.

The Custom House that served as the resort's reception building, where guests check in and check out, featured architectural elements like verandahs, handrails, canopies and tile floors that were typical to government buildings of the Caribbean islands.

In 2018, a major refurbishment project resulted in Old Port Royale now acting as "the port of entry" for the resort, where guests can access check-in, concierge services and other resort amenities

The Old Port Royale pool is themed after the Spanish fortress Fuentes del Morro. Port Royale that is also the setting for both the movie and the Magic Kingdom theme park attraction Pirates of the Caribbean.

Yacht and Beach Club

November 1990

Because the Yacht and Beach Club are right next to each other and share so many amenities including a convention space and Stormalong Bay, among other things, it becomes easy to think of them as just one large resort.

The differences are subtle from the Beach Club's light blue exterior compared to the Yacht Club's light grey façade but they feel like a cohesive whole. A nautical theme abounds at Yacht Club, decorated with scale models of boats and subtle compass designs throughout.

The Beach Club is themed after a New England seaside cottage. Overall the two resorts feel dedicated to showcasing comfort and "elegance" rather than a more immersive story experience.

Architect Robert Stern said, "The Yacht Club is shingle style, kind of a button-down blue blazer look while the Beach Club is more stick style, less formidable." Both hotels imbue the same era and overall idea.

Both hotels use a high-compression fiberboard called Werzalit to simulate the traditional beaded clapboard siding of shore hotels in the East.

Initially the hotels because of their nearness to the International Gateway entrance to World Showcase were going to be themed to countries represented in Epcot. Among other ideas, a French hotel and a Bavarian hotel were considered and rejected.

The designers struggled to come up with the same authentic detailed look that Imagineers had contributed to the individual pavilions. The goal was to create something classy, trendy but nostalgic.

New York architect Robert A. M. Stern saw the struggles that were taking place. His design philosophy was "Interpretation rather than innovation", meaning that his designs reflect his affection for the past reinterpreted in his own vision.

CEO Michael Eisner called Stern a "Super Imagineer" and the two developed a strong friendship. Eisner's vacation home in Aspen was designed by Stern.

Stern served on The Walt Disney Company Board of Directors from 1992 to 2003 and has designed many buildings for Walt Disney World including the Casting Center, the Boardwalk Resort, and the urban design work for the city of Celebration.

"You have to remember that Disney is a dream world rooted in a dream view of life and architectural history," stated Stern.

Newport Bay Club in Disneyland Paris is drawn from Stern's original designs for the Yacht and Beach Resorts that was to be one huge hotel over a mile in length, the same distance as walking from the Mexico Pavilion to the Canada Pavilion on the promenade of the World Showcase.

Quite literally one end of the Yacht and Beach complex has a door that opens right near the Dolphin resort while walking the corridors and breezeways to the other end where a door opens near Epcot itself.

It was decided that one huge hotel so close to the massive Swan and Dolphin resorts would be too overwhelming at the time. So Stern redesigned his concept into one continuous structure with two related themes: New England club and mid-Atlantic shore. That is why there are evergreens rather than palm trees to landscape the areas.

The Yacht and Beach Club Resorts were meant to invoke the more genteel turn- of-the-century civility and charm.

The Yacht Club is more formal, nautical and reminiscent of the rustic yet elegant, shingle-covered Victorian seaside resorts that were built toward the end of the last century in New England towns such as Newport, Marblehead, Cape Cod and Bar Harbor. It was meant to be more "upper crust", sophisticated and sedate so gray colors were used.

Shingle Style homes were never the more humble dwellings of the local fishermen. They were meant to be vacation "cottages" for the very wealthy. And, as the new look became popular, Shingle Style homes popped up in fashionable neighborhoods that were far from the seashore. Eventually, the style fell out of favor in the early 1900s but experienced a revival in the second half of the 20th century.

The Beach Club is more informal and airy in expression. It is modeled on the many Stick Style cottages and resorts that could be found in mid-Atlantic towns like Cape May, New Jersey. Stern used blue and white to capture what he called the "sand between your toes" feeling.

Stick Style buildings are noted for a number of unique features all united by the use of "sticks" or basically, flat board banding and other applied ornamentation in geometric patterns that adorn the exterior clapboard wall surface.

Stormalong Bay is a three acre water mini-park encompassing 750,000 gallons of water and featuring waterfalls, a lazy circular river, pulsating water jets, one of the highest Disney resort waterslides disguised as a clipper ship shipwreck caused by a storm along the bay and an elevated tanning deck. However, perhaps the most unique aspect of the pool area is the sandy bottom.

A large amount of non-resort guests were taking advantage of the area so in 1997, a white fence with only three entrances was built to surround the pool with cast members checking IDs of people wanting to use it.

The lighthouse at the end of the dock is meant to be reminiscent of a lighthouse in Cape May originally built in 1859. It not only provides a directional beacon but also lends an air of timeless authenticity.

Grand Floridian Resort & Spa

July 1988

Newspaper advetisements in the summer of 1988 proclaimed: "Journey back to the turn-of-the century...to another time and another place. The Grand Floridian Beach Resort. An oasis of elegance that's the first of its kind since the golden age of pleasure travel.

"Bright white towers and gabled roofs echo the Victorian architectural influence that has come to symbolize Florida's carefree winters and balmy summer nights."

Disney held a special press event June 23-26, 1988 that brought in 1,400 members of the media to celebrate the latest additions to Walt Disney World including Mickey's Birthdayland, the Norway pavilion's Maelstrom attraction, Mickey's 60th birthday and new production at Disney MGM Studios.

In addition, it was the official dedication of the Grand Floridian Resort that opened July 1, 1988. CEO Michael Eisner and actor Burt Reynolds cut the ceremonial ribbon stretched between two palm trees to open the resort.

An aquatic ballet was performed in the 275,000 gallon pool. Singers and dancers performed a medley of turn-of-the-century tunes. Everyone was in formal dress to dance in the atrium to the music of The Palm Beach Society Orchestra.

Burt was honored by Disney as a "grand" Floridian at a gala dinner that night because of his many connections to the state. He was actually on WDW property to tape a segment of the game show that he co-produced *Win, Lose or Draw* being filmed at Disney MGM Studios.

The Grand Floridian was inspired by the Victorian era beach resorts built along Florida's east coast during the late 19th century and early

20th century when wealthy and famous people from the north would travel by train to warmer climes.

The exterior is influenced by the iconic Hotel del Coronado in Coronado, California, with red gabled roofs and white walls. However, design elements were also taken from the Mount Washington Resort in Bretton Woods, New Hampshire, the Grand Hotel on Mackinac Island, Michigan, as well as the Belleview-Biltmore Hotel in Bellair, Florida.

The Belleview Hotel, as it was initially known, was constructed by railroad tycoon Henry B. Plant in 1897 as a resort destination to boost tourist travel on his railroad line serving the west coast of Florida, which he had acquired in 1893. The hotel closed in 2009 and was demolished in 2015.

Mizner's Lounge's name comes from Addison Mizner, an architect who specialized in "Gatsby-esque" mansions in Palm Beach and Boca Raton.

The architecture of the Grand Floridian is a collage of American, English, French and Caribbean. Rather than a historically accurate Victorian color theme that would have been too dark and somber for this playful seaside resort, the Imagineers selected soft greens, blues and peaches.

Of particular interest, 1900 Park Fare restaurant features Big Bertha, an antique fairground band organ built in Paris, France by Gavoli & Co in the late 1800s, installed in the wall fifteen feet above the guests. It plays music utilizing simultaneously the instruments of pipes, drums, castanets, bells, cymbals, and xylophone played originally by paper piano-roll "books".

It was named "Big Bertha" because of the female band leader mounted on the front of the instrument.

The organ was used from 1909 to 1955 in Ramona Park, an amusement park in Grand Rapids, Michigan known as the "Amusement Mecca of Western Michigan." The park was demolished in 1955 and the three antique band organs used for the merry-go-round went into storage in Alabama for many years where they were discovered in 1963 and restored.

The Grand Floridian Resort and Spa is a showcase of amazing details from the Chinese-style aviary in the lobby that was crafted in Spain to the vintage Victorian piano in the lobby obtained from an estate in Georgia to the entrance of Victoria & Albert's that features on the walls eleven original maps of Florida dated from 1775 up to the period of railroad tycoon Henry M. Flagler's railway lines in the late 1880s.

In December 2004, CEO Michael Eisner told the cast at a town hall meeting at Disney's Coronado Springs Resort, "I've met people who were here during the hurricane (Charley), had guests who have written me and said they'd like to make a reservation at Disney's Grand

Floridian Resort & Spa during the next hurricane. They were never treated so well and never had such a good time."

In August 2017, Walt Disney World installed a memorial sculpture of a lighthouse in a little alcove near the Big Pine Key building near the beach to honor Lane Graves.

Lane Thomas Graves was the two year-old boy who was snatched by an alligator on June 14, 2016 at about nine o'clock in the evening at the Seven Seas Lagoon. His body was found after a sixteen hour search on June 15 by divers.

Graves was with his family from Elkhorn, Nebraska. His parents are Matt and Melissa Graves and at the time they were also accompanied by their four year old daughter.

The Orange County Sheriff's Office recovered the body of the boy, intact and about fifteen yards from where he was taken and about six feet underwater. A medical examiner determined that Lane had a traumatic neck injury and drowned and it was ruled an accident.

Lane's death marked the first alligator attack on the park's property since a predator bit the legs of an eight-year-old boy, Paul Santamaria, who survived, at Disney's Fort Wilderness campground in 1986. Lane's death was the first alligator fatality in WDW's 45 year old history.

Alligators have been prominently seen on WDW property since its opening in 1971. During the search for Lane, investigators pulled and killed six gators from the area but were not able to fully determine if they had captured the culprit. Officials estimated the responsible gator to be between four and seven feet long and two of the gators were at least seven feet.

The Florida Fish and Wildlife Conservation Commission, which generally responds to nuisance gator reports, gives Disney full autonomy in handling the problem and isn't often involved.

The family was relaxing on the shore in a play area when Lane bent over to scoop wet sand into his small plastic bucket in order to build a sandcastle on the beach. The area had signs posted against swimming in the lake, but they didn't warn of the lurking gators.

Lane's father, who was standing nearby heard a splash and turned to see the alligator grab Lane's head and jumped into the water, pulling on the gator's snout in an unsuccessful attempt to free his son from its grip. Seconds later, the gator pulled Lane underwater and both disappeared into the Seven Seas Lagoon. The father was injured and treated.

After the attack, Disney built wide boulder walls and fences along the Seven Seas Lagoon beach in an effort to keep alligators away from the shore. They also put up signs warning of alligators and snakes and instituted training for cast members.

The statue of a lighthouse is a symbol of the Lane Thomas Foundation — a charitable fund created by the boy's parents after his death that helps financially support families with children who need organ transplants.

The gold and blue statue, marked with two stars, was been placed near where the tragedy occurred. A plaque at the bottom reads: "Presented to the Lane Graves Foundation. A beacon of hope. A light of love."

In a statement issued by Lane's parents they said: "We find comfort that so many people continue to remember our sweet boy, Lane, and we believe the lighthouse stands as a beacon of hope and support for families in the depths of despair."

George A. Kalogridis, the president of Walt Disney World Resort, stated, "To provide continued awareness of the foundation and its mission, we commissioned an original sculpture of the lighthouse the foundation uses as a symbol of love and hope, to be installed on our property."

The memorial is both a lovely and tragic reminder of the life and death of Lane Graves.

Appendix A: WDW Hotels Never Built

Ever since Walt Disney World opened, the Walt Disney Company has announced the building of additional resort hotels. Some of these announcements included detailed concept artwork and even elaborate models.

Listed here are all the proposed hotels that were almost built but for a variety of reasons were delayed and cancelled. Some concepts were incorporated into other WDW resort hotels that were eventually built.

Cosmopolitan Hotel

The word "cosmopolitan" refers to having an international perspective. In a vernacular sense, the word refers to places where people of various ethnic, cultural and/or religious backgrounds live nearby and interact with each other.

While it was probably a "placeholder" name, it was the name chosen by Walt Disney for the hotel in his original version of Epcot. A totally climate-controlled city center, built around the 30-story cosmopolitan hotel and convention center was the centerpiece of his hub. The area would be pedestrian-centric and contain an international shopping district that would later inspire elements in Epcot's World Showcase.

The *Walt Disney's Epcot '66* film describes it: "Among its major features will be a cosmopolitan hotel and convention center, towering 30 or more stories, shopping areas, where stores and whole streets recreate the character and adventure of places round the world, theaters for dramatic and musical production, restaurants and a variety of nightlife attractions, and a wide range of office buildings, some containing services required by EPCOT's residents, but most of them designed especially to suit the local needs of major corporations.

"This towering hotel is the visual center of EPCOT, the shining jewel at the center of the city. It will offer tourists and vacationers not only the most modern guest rooms and convention facilities, but also a seven-acre recreation deck, located high above the pedestrian and shopping areas of the city.

"But, hidden from view, directly beneath the hotel is another kind of vital center, EPCOT's Transportation Lobby. Although, out of sight to hotel guests, this transportation terminal will play a key role in the city of tomorrow's ability to meet the needs of both visitor and resident.

"Two separate, but interconnecting transit systems will move people into and out of EPCOT in speed, safety, and comfort through this central terminal. Both are electrically powered—the high speed monorail, for rapid transit over longer distances, and a concept new to the American city for shorter travel distances, the WEDWAY PeopleMover."

In the Disneyland Carousel of Progess attraction, in the final scene, right behind mother and father, the huge picture window offered a glimpse of the towering Cosmopolitan Hotel in the background.

After the final scene, guests could board a speed ramp escalator to go to the second floor to see a huge model of "Progress City." In 1967, the Walt Disney Company was still debating about pursuing Walt's dream, so the city was not referred to as "EPCOT." Since General Electric's slogan was "Progress is Our Most Important Product" the name "Progress City" was chosen, as GE would have been a major participant in the planned community in Florida and was sponsoring the Carousel of Progress attraction.

Built one-eighth of an inch to a foot, it was 6,900 square feet. It was 115 feet wide, and 60 feet deep. It had 2,500 moving vehicles (monorails, peoplemovers, moving sidewalks, electric trains), 20,000 trees, 4,500 structures (Walt insisted the interior of the buildings be finished, furnished and lit), 1,400 working street lights and it all came alive as the audiences moved from one side of the room to the other on a three-tiered audience viewing area. Of course, at the very top center was a towering model of the cosmopolitan hotel.

Proposed Magic Kingdom Hotels

In 1967, the Disney Company created a full-color map to indicate the resort hotels that would surround the Magic Kingdom theme park.

That map showed a Cape Cod Village, a South Seas glass skyscraper in the shape of a pyramid, Yesterday Hotel (to be located on Magic Kingdom's Main Street), Frontier Village, Spanish Colonial Hotel, Oriental Motel, the Dutch hotel, and the African Hotel. These were placeholder names to suggest the types of hotels that would be eventually approved.

By 1969, these possible resorts had been narrowed down to the Disney Persian Palace, U.S.A. Disney (that would become briefly Tempo Bay Resort and finally the Contemporary Resort), Far East Disney, Venice Disney and Disney South Pacific (that would become the Polynesian). Frontier Village was renamed Diamond D (for Disney) Dude Ranch on its way to becoming Fort Wilderness Resort and Campground.

YESTERDAY HOTEL

In place of Disneyland's famed Opera House, the Magic Kingdom had what is now called the Town Square Theater.

When the Magic Kingdom opened in 1971, that beautiful building was officially the elegant Main Street Hotel that housed the Gulf Hospitality Center. The legendary Dorothea Redmond had created concept art for the possibility of building an actual upscale Victorian hotel on Main Street that would allow guests to walk directly into the park.

The hotel would not only have encompassed the actual building as it is today but expanded into the backstage area that became a cast member parking lot.

Some of those design elements for an actual hotel still remain including the individual balconies on the upper floor windows and the broad front porch with rocking chairs.

Since the Walt Disney Company had never operated a hotel before and the development of plans for an elaborate series of nearby themed hotels beginning with the Contemporary and the Polynesian had become overwhelming, the idea of an in-park hotel was postponed for a later time.

According to the original storyline, the hotel was located next to the Train Station so that people would have a place to stay while they waited for their train connection or visiting the city.

When the Magic Kingdom opened in 1971, this beautiful building was the unofficial central location for all of Walt Disney property, where guests could make reservations for resort rooms, dinner shows, golfing and other recreational activities.

The large, polished wooden counter was primarily staffed by friendly and attractive young women who extolled the virtues of Gulf Oil, of course, and handed out maps and brochures that assisted guests with driving routes, places to visit in Central Florida and selecting hotels or motels at which to stay on their trip.

In addition to the service stations located on the property for both guests and employees, Gulf Oil had exclusive rights for oil products used on the property as it did at Disneyland.

"Etched glass doors, potted palms, comfortable velvet settees and antique chairs set the mood for relaxation and comfort," claimed the 1972 "Gulf Personal Tourguide (sic) to Walt Disney World," describing the Hospitality Center. These items like the interior counter suggested a turn-of-the-century hotel lobby.

It was a full-sized building rather than utilizing forced perspective because it was necessary to block the guests' view of the Contemporary resort, which would have conflicted with the theme of Main Street. The

Contemporary was still clearly visible in Tomorrowland because it had a vaguely timeless futuristic look that didn't detract from the "world of the immediate future" theme.

The Hospitality House officially closed March 1990 and became Disneyana Collectibles. It became the Town Square Exposition Hall in 1998 and closed in 2011. It was then re-themed as the Town Square Theater that opened in April 2011.

THE ASIAN

The Asian resort hotel was scheduled to open by 1973. Land had been cleared and prepared where Disney's Grand Floridian Resort and Spa stands today. A square plot of land prominently jutted out into the Seven Seas Lagoon and the nearby road had been dubbed "Asian Way".

According to Disney publicity, "The Asian hotel will be strongly Thai in its motif. A theme restaurant and lounge at the top of its 160-foot tower building will provide an enchanting setting for nighttime dancing and stage show entertainment. Each of its 600 rooms, including 50 elegant suites in royal Thai decor, will look out on the lagoon or a central recreation area."

The Asian's imminent completion was heralded on the official recorded monorail spiel and WDW literature like the Stockholders' Annual Report. There were also plans to have large meeting rooms under the guest area of the resort for conventions.

The Asian had gotten to the point that an approved sample interior for the rooms was completed and elaborate Oriental gardens had been designed by landscaper Bill Evans.

Guest rooms would have been arranged in a square around the perimeter with two-thirds of the guest rooms having beautiful garden or lake views. The remainder of the rooms would have been in the tower building providing a view into the central recreation area that would have featured a themed pool.

THE VENETIAN

Located between the Contemporary Resort and the Ticket and Transportation Center near the water bridge on the Seven Seas Lagoon, the Venetian would have resembled the current Italian pavilion at the World Showcase at Epcot in terms of architecture and style.

According to Disney publicity, "At the Venetian resort, an enclosed small boat harbor and intricate system of waterways will recreate the old world charm of the famed Italian 'City of Canals'. Shopping will be a unique experience as guests travel by gondola along 'streets of water' and under ornate bridges linking various sections of the resort.

"The style is reminiscent of St. Mark's Square, complete with a 120-foot campanile that will toll the time. The entire lobby will be glass-topped, creating a brilliant, sunlit atrium effect indoors."

THE PERSIAN

Located to the north and slightly east of the Contemporary Resort on Bay Lake, the Persian would have been laid out in a circular pattern with a large central building featuring a 24-foot blue dome. Smaller blue domes would have highlighted the white columns and buildings.

According to Disney publicity, "Stepping right out of The Arabian Nights is the Persian resort, which will reign like an exotic far-Eastern palace on the Northwest shore of the lake. Jewel-like mosques and columns will rise above landscaped courtyards, while terraced sundecks offer sculpted swimming pools and 'old Persian' dining facilities. Guest will practically be able to sail to their own rooms through a sheltered marina."

After a stop at the Contemporary, the monorail would have journeyed to the Persian. From there, instead of going directly to the Ticket and Transportation Center, the monorail would take a short detour through nearby Tomorrowland, just like the monorail at Disneyland, to offer guests a glimpse of the highway in the sky of the future.

CYPRESS POINT LODGE

The land in the area near the Fort Wilderness Resort & Campground had been cleared of trees by 1971 although some claim that this was originally meant for additional campground.

The 1973 WDW souvenir guide states that an unnamed "Lodge" was planned to be built in this location for guests. A rough replica of the resort was featured in the model in the post show area of Magic Kingdom's The Walt Disney Story attraction.

In the early 1980s, it was given the name Cypress Point Lodge but because of cost overruns in the building of Epcot Center, the resort was cancelled. Later Wilderness Lodge was built in the same location.

With the development of Epcot Center, the need for more hotel rooms on property to accommodate the hoped for influx of visitors became apparent and so plans were announced for more resorts.

Disney executive Dick Nunis was quoted in the May 1982 issue of the cast newspaper *Eyes and Ears*: "We also have in design three hotels. The Mediterranean will be located between TTC and the Contemporary. The Cypress Point Lodge will be west of River Country and be themed as a western hotel. It'll include log cabins along Bay Lake."

The third hotel would have been the Grand Floridian since preparation for the area had already been done years earlier. All three hotels were announced in 1980.

The November 4, 1982 issue of *Walt Disney World Eyes & Ears* provided the following description of the rustic, moderate resort:

"Cypress Point Lodge will be a medium-sized hotel facility, located on the south shore of Bay Lake near our Fort Wilderness Campground Resort. Encompassing 550 rooms and 50 log cabins on the beach, Cypress Point Lodge will offer a romantic notion of a turn-of-the-century hunting lodge secluded in a deep forest.

"Neither the trees nor the buildings dominate the entire area; but blend together in a natural harmony. One can almost hear the crackling fireplace and feel the large wooden beams offer a haven of security and comfort.

"Cypress Point Lodge will also include: two restaurants, a pool, extensive beach, and lake dock. Guests will commute in and out of Cypress Point Lodge by watercraft."

One of the advantages of building the hotel was it was not on the monorail loop and so would not disrupt its operation or the Magic Kingdom.

Obviously the location and theme echoed the Wilderness Lodge Resort that would be built in 1994 but with several key differences including several separate waterfront cabins that would have made the area feel more like a villa.

However, cost overruns for the building of Epcot Center resulted in Cypress Point Lodge being cancelled and it is no longer mentioned in any documentation starting in 1983.

With the arrival of new CEO Michael Eisner in 1984, he chose to develop both the Grand Floridian and a lodge themed resort but with much different approaches.

GRANDE VENEZIA RESORT

Disney's Grande Venezia Resort would have been located where the the previously announced Venetian resort would have been built. This resort was designed by Walt Disney Imagineering in conjunction with architectural firm Wimberly, Allison, Tong & Goo, the same firm that helped design the Grand Floridian.

The hotel was to rival the Grand Floridian to be the most luxurious of all the resorts. Concept blueprints called for intricately-designed buildings with terra cotta roofs, canals with functioning gondolas, lighted fountains, a masquerade- themed pool, a conference center, and a wedding chapel.

THE MEDITERRANEAN RESORT

The same site was also considered for a planned Greek-themed complex in the late 1990s. Known as Disney's Mediterranean Resort, the hotel would have been themed to a Greek fishing village built on the banks of the Seven Seas Lagoon and was also planned to rival the Grand Floridian in luxury and price.

In 1991, Disney described it to travel agents as "minutes from the Magic Kingdom and yet world's away, the Mediterranean Resort will become the fourth Disney hotel to be located on the monorail system. The deluxe property, which is scheduled for completion in 1992 will recreate all the luxury and style of the 'jet set' hot spots throughout the Greek Islands.

"With contributions from renowned southwest U.S. architect Antoine Predock, the opulent village will feature elegant, vaulted arches, quiet courtyards, sparkling pools and powder-white beaches as well as 45,000 square feet of meeting space."

Allegedly the hotel wasn't built due to poor ground samples and the swampy nature of the ground at the site, which would have made the Mediterranean too expensive to build for Disney's liking.

NEW ORLEANS HOTEL

In the early 1980s, Disney executive Dick Nunis pushed for an expansion of the Shopping Village at Lake Buena Vista (better known as Disney Springs today) by creating a moderately priced themed resort to resemble New Orleans.

The Empress Lilly restaurant would have been a steamboat that had docked to unload its cargo at this riverfront town of New Orleans where the guest rooms would have been "hidden" in buildings resembling a cotton mill or a boatwrights shop. The rooms would be on the upper floors with the bottom floor reserved for shops and restaurants.

Guests loved that the Village was a quiet alternative to the Magic Kingdom and did not require an admission fee. It also became a popular location for local residents as well.

Nunis told cast members in a May 1982 issue of *Eyes &Ears* cast newspaper that "From the Empress Lilly, we're going into a New Orleans street, and you'll walk right into a beautiful New Orleans hotel".

The hotel would have six hundred rooms with the same French Quarter theme as New Orleans Square at Disneyland. A name for the hotel was never officially confirmed.

An illustrated marketing packet was produced by the Walt Disney Company in September 1981 (and later revised in April 1982) for the project, that detailed what was called "Lake Buena Vista New Orleans Square".

The lushly landscaped area, making use of already existing Florida flora, would have included approximately 120,000 square feet of restaurants, entertainment venues and merchandise shops. The area would have been themed in an old New Orleans motif and would have rippled out from Royale Circle.

One of the restaurants was tentatively titled "Garden Restaurant" with one façade facing the Empress Lilly, looking like a Southern mansion, and a different façade facing the Lagoon.

Like at Disneyland, there would have been a Café Orleans with Cajun and Creole inspired cuisine in a casual setting.

The entertainment venues would have included a Preservation Hall Jazz Lounge. Jazz artists had already been performing periodically at the Village Restaurant to so much popularity that a cover charge had to be instituted. A more raucous time was had at the full bar in the Baton Rouge Lounge of the Empress Lilly that featured Dixieland Jazz.

An intriguing mystery was that one of the exterior designs for a building in the brochure was very reminiscent of the exterior of the Pirates of the Caribbean attraction at Disneyland even though the attraction was already in existence at the Magic Kingdom.

A New Orleans themed resort, named Port Orleans, did appear on Walt Disney World property on May 17, 1991, thanks to Fugleberg Koch Architects of Winter Park, Florida in collaboration with the Disney Development Company.

It was themed to the French Quarter of New Orleans around the mid-1800s and was situated by the Sassagoula River, a man-made Disney waterway named after the Native American word for the Mississippi River.

It was characteristic of the New Orleans French Quarter with balconies, wrought iron railings, cobblestone streets, and courtyards but with Disney touches like jazz playing alligators leading guests to the pool area.

On March 1, 2001, the resort officially merged with Dixie Landings and became Port Orleans: French Quarter with Dixie Landings becoming Port Orleans: Riverside.

DISNEY MGM FILM NOIR HOTEL

Before the decision to build the Twilight Zone Tower of Terror at Disney MGM Studios was made, several other proposals were under consideration including a hotel attraction inspired by the novel *The Shining* featuring the various characters that appeared in several other of author Stephen King's novels in different rooms.

Another suggestion was a partial walking tour narrated by Vincent Price (who had recorded the original Disneyland Paris Phantom Manor narration) about a group of movie stars who had been staying at the hotel but mysteriously disappeared.

Throughout the tour, guests would discover clues and when they finally entered the elevator what had happened to those missing people became very clear but it was too late to get out.

CEO Michael Eisner suggested expanding the idea by making the hotel an actual in-park Disney resort themed to a 1939 "film noir" movie murder mystery. It would revolve around the hotel manager who had gone crazy and would have included period costumed staff interacting with guests much like the eventual Tower of Terror.

At night, there would be screams and activity taking place in the hallways and lobby as well as clues for the guests to uncover. It was even suggested having resort guests brought directly from the airport in a 1939 vehicle with the shades drawn to immerse them in the time period.

Eventually it was felt it would be too expensive, too complicated and too disruptive to the guest experience and later evolved into the Twilight Zone Hollywood Tower of Terror.

ALPINE RESORT

Blizzard Beach was originally going to be connected to a Disney resort. Some Disney fans know that Imagineer Eric Jacobson had a collection of snow globes in his office and that they inspired the idea of a water park with a winter theme. However, there is more to that story as well.

Located where the Coronado Springs Resort site now stands, Disney's Alpine Resort would have overlooked the melting snows of Blizzard Beach. The Alpine Resort would have been a moderately priced hotel and as one of the perks for staying there, guests would have been able to ride a chair lift over the street to the water park.

One of the reasons, the idea of a hotel connected to a water park was eventually rejected according to Imagineer Kathy Mangum was "the water parks need to be rehabbed just about every year, which means draining them and sandblasting the bottom. We didn't want the guests overlooking an empty water park. It would ruin the story".

In addition, Disney Legal was concerned about the liability of the proposed ski lift.

WILDERNESS JUNCTION

In 1976, Edward Prizer, editor of *Orlando-Land* magazine, had lunch with Dick Nunis, who at the time was executive vice president of both Disneyland and Walt Disney World.

At that moment in time, Nunis was preparing after the short interview to put on a pair of boots and stake out a bunch of new campsites at Fort Wilderness Resort and Campgrounds.

Nunis mentioned that one of the reasons that River Country was a favorite of his was that Walt Disney himself came up with the idea long ago, based on an old swimming hole when he went as a kid. He planned to put it in Disneyland but there wasn't room and the idea gathered dust until they brought it out for Walt Disney World.

Nunis said there were plans to add a stockade and a replica of a frontier town to the Fort Wilderness Resort and campground.

"We're going to have lots of fun things there," he told Prizer. "I've always wanted to do a fun place called Sadie Mae's Palace. Another thing we'll have in the old town will be Granny Kincaid's Farm where kids can pet animals and jump in the hay. That's another of Walt's ideas that we never developed.

"Fort Wilderness has room for 350 to 400 more campsites. Then we'll go somewhere else and build another campground. More bike paths are going to be added. We have a mile of trails around the campground. We'll add more to connect with the Contemporary, the Polynesian and the Magic Kingdom. We'll be building paths for five years and we will have ten miles of them."

In 1992, the Disney Company announced a new addition to the Fort Wilderness area that was strongly supported by Nunis called at the time Buffalo Junction (and later referred to as Wilderness Junction).

The plans were to build an upscale 600-room moderately-priced resort between Disney's Fort Wilderness Resort and Campground and the Wilderness Lodge in the style of Disneyland Paris' Cheyenne Hotel complex that resembles a movie back lot for a Western movie. "Experience the yee-ha atmosphere of a Wild West frontier town. YEE-HA COW BOY! Put your boots on, hang on to your hat and get on your horse!"

It would have been themed to the Old West of Dodge City. One of the main attractions would have been a version of Disneyland Paris' *Buffalo Bill Wild West Show* prompting the name Buffalo Junction originally. A large frontier rodeo-type structure was going to be built at the outskirts of town near Vista Boulevard, where there would have been a ton of parking available for those guests who just wanted to spend a few hours of shopping, eating or seeing the show.

The bottom level of the buildings would have shops and restaurants, while the upper levels would have rooms for guests. All three resorts would have been connected with a new operating version of the Fort Wilderness Railroad. There would have been a stop at Pioneer Hall/ Crockett's Tavern, another at the southwest corner of Wilderness

Lodge and a big station with support facilities right in the center of Fort Wilderness Junction.

The story would begin at Fort Wilderness, representing the original frontier period of the United States. Wilderness Junction would showcase the expansion out to the Wild West, and, finally, the story would end at Wilderness Lodge, where Americans now live in harmony with their environment. Americans had finally realized the importance of conserving its natural resources by developing National Parks.

In response to a national economic recession in 1992, Fort Wilderness Junction and several other "Disney Decade" projects were postponed indefinitely especially with the success of DVC properties which is where the company started concentrating its attention and resources.

In October 2018 it was announced the creation of a DVC resort *Reflections: A Disney Lakeside Lodge* on that site. Nine bungalows are planned for the present Clementine Beach and the demolition of Mickey's Backyard BBQ in the area originally meant for Fort Wilderness Junction. Described to DVC members as "refined nature" and construction of "steel, glass and wood," the resort appears modern and minimalist.

Appendix B: Entertainment Architecture

The Walt Disney Company is known for its unique vocabulary and for coining new terms that become common usage, like "Audio-Animatronics". In the 1990s, the term "architheming" appeared in Disney literature.

By the turn of the current century, it completely disappeared and had been replaced by the term "entertainment architecture" that had been coined by then Disney CEO Michael Eisner.

Eisner stated, "In creating our new buildings, we have gone for quality and excitement. We have hired some of the world's most prominent architects and have given them the opportunity to fully flex their imaginations and contribute to the creation of a landscape that can't be found anywhere else on the planet.

"In our architecture, Disney continues to produce the kind of groundbreaking entertainment that keeps the Disney name magical to people around the world. Our architecture is part of the show."

That was part of the introduction written by Eisner to the limited edition 20-page full-color booklet, "Architheming at the Walt Disney World Resort," published in 1992 by Walt Disney World Seminar Productions (part of Disney University) to be given to guests taking a seminar on Disney architecture.

The cover of the book was a double door that opened to the text and photos inside. The doors had the humanistic doorknob character from the Disney animated feature *Alice in Wonderland*, or more precisely, a photo of the physical re-creation of that animated doorknob that was on the front doors of the Walt Disney World Casting Center.

Walt Disney World Seminar Productions included "Wonders of Walt Disney World" programs for young people and "Disney Learning Adventures" for adults (including special classes for management and educational professionals, as well).

The WDW Seminar Productions were absorbed into the Disney Institute shortly after it opened in 1996. The youth programs were renamed Y.E.S. (Youth Education Services) and the adult programs were renamed D.A.D. (Disney Adult Discoveries).

The Disney term "architheming" was coined by Disney University instructors Ken Cannon and Kaye Bundey to explain how WDW combined the basics of architecture with the concept of story theming. The term never really took hold with the general public or the Walt Disney Company and is not used today, but was prominent on Walt Disney Company literature of the 1990s.

When I worked as an instructor for Disney Adult Discoveries in the late 1990s, two of the tours that I instructed were inspired by that original "architheming" class and were titled "Disney by Design" and "Disney's Amazing Architecture".

Both tours were designed to expose guests to the creative use of architecture to tell stories both inside and outside the Walt Disney World theme parks.

There was some initial classroom instruction, but, primarily, the classes consisted of taking guests out in van to various locations to describe the architecture of places like the Casting Center, Team Disney, Reedy Creek Fire Station on Buena Vista Drive, Disney's Wilderness Lodge, the Italy pavilion in Epcot's World Showcase, and more. The classes were incredibly popular.

When Eisner came on board in 1984, he became a well-known patron of architects.

"You can have bad architecture that costs just as much as good architecture," he remarked at the time. "Most hotel companies are driven by operations, so you have these hotels that were built in the '70s that function beautifully but are as ugly as the day is long. It costs the same to do well as badly. It's exactly the same price if you build 1,200 ugly rooms."

Eisner saw hotel architecture as an opportunity to redefine the Walt Disney Company as the need for new resorts to accommodate guests at Walt Disney World became apparent.

"Look, we are an entertainment company," Eisner said. "We're Disney. We've got to have the biggest, the best, the most tasteful. Impact is what great architecture is all about."

However, the newly formed Disney Development Company supposedly monitored all the well-known architects they engaged fairly closely so they did not exceed the agreed upon "competitive budget." Eisner's preference for architecture was what he called "strength with lightness" that meant a sound design but with a whimsical touch.

In the May 1992 issue of the architectural magazine, *Interiors*, a lengthy article, written by Jean Gorman, it was stated that "the [Disney] craze for big-name architects began partly as a practical response to increasing the company's profit-making potential and partly as a conscious effort to develop and refine its image outside the parks...

"Driven by Eisner's enthusiastic fascination for architecture, the Disney Development Company looked beyond the in-house team of Imagineers toward outside architects who could appeal to a sophisticated consumer.

"Eisner maintains that being a name-brand architect is not the only criterion for consideration. The willingness and ability to design projects that are compatible with Disney's entertainment philosophy also plays into the selection process."

An article in the July 29, 1991 issue of *Time* magazine stated:

"Disney has a reputation among architects (as among filmmakers) for tightfistedness and micro-management. On each (architectural) project, Eisner is brought in five times to review the plans, approving masonry textures, paint colors and light fixtures.

"One reason the chairman says he meddles more in the design of a hotel than he does, for instance, in the production of *The Marrying Man* (a troubled 1991 Disney live-action feature film) is that 'movies go away, but buildings stand as monuments to your bad taste'.

"Plus he thinks he's good at inspiring architects. 'I know how to make creative people see that something is not as good as they can do. Or I tell architects Don't give up. Don't accommodate.' Eisner thinks big and will not take 'no' for an answer... He doesn't know exactly what he wants, but he wants it to be amazing, and he wants it badly."

At least one architect, James Stirling, declined an invitation to participate in designing a Disney structure. French architect Jean Nouvel proposed a resort hotel for Disneyland Paris based on a Rationalist theme, while architect Peter Eisenman suggested an underground hotel for that theme park.

While those projects never went beyond the initial discussion stage, some projects greenlit by Eisner also did not develop further, like Antoine Predock's Mediterranean Resort, a theme hotel inspired by the Greek Islands that was planned to open in 1992 at Walt Disney World around the Seven Seas Lagoon.

Instead, Predock designed the Hotel Santa Fe for Disneyland Paris that opened in 1992, with a Pueblo Revival architecture style to represent the American Southwest.

Wing T. Chao, who was the senior vice president for master planning, architecture and design with Disney Development Company in the 1980s and 1990s, had a master's degree in architecture from Harvard University. He credited Eisner with Disney's patronage of architects.

"It's because of his (Eisner's) personal love of art and architecture, and his leadership. He personally gets involved with our architects at every design meeting," Chao told the *Orlando Sentinel* newspaper in July 11, 1990.

Eisner's mentor in architecture was Victor Ganz, a vice president of New York's Whitney Museum of American art, who Eisner said "literally took me by the hand and helped me understand and appreciate art. I wanted to use the architects who were on the cutting edges, the young and new breed."

It was Ganz who recommended Michael Graves to Eisner, as well as some other architects.

Chao told reporters that Eisner was just continuing the vision established by Walt Disney. "Walt wanted to give his guests the same quality of experience in their hotels that they get in the parks," Chao said.

Chao kept a file of information on roughly 700 architectural firms, from which he culled likely candidates when a new project arose.

To support this architectural agenda, in 1997, Disney Adult Discoveries produced a limited-edition full color 60-page booklet titled *Walt Disney World Architecture* to distribute in the "Disney by Design" tour.

Once again, Michael Eisner wrote the introduction:

"Fun. Magic. Dreams. It's who we are. Our guests come here to be amused, startled and delighted, and there is no reason that unique experience should stop once they leave the magic of our Theme Parks. That's why we've sought out some of the best architects in the world to help us expand our vision to resorts and buildings beyond the Theme Parks. We are making a daring new statement in architecture. One of impact and imagination...a big 'Wow!'

"The three-dimensional dreams you'll see and read about here are intended to take you on their own unique emotional journeys where something unexpected and surprising turns up around every corner. Each tells a story and each story is a new adventure you're invited to share. So, please come in and join us on a new flight of fantasy."

The cover had an image of Mickey's sideways face composed of architectural elements like real bricks, the inside rings of a tree, a decorative window and similar objects.

Every entry was two pages. One page had a big color photograph and a paragraph about the architect, while the facing page had a description of the structure. The entries concentrated on the buildings outside of the theme parks, primarily the WDW resorts.

Clyde Brady, a partner with Hunton, Brady, Pryor, Maso of Orlando, told the *Orlando Sentinel* that the immediate effect of Disney entertainment architecture was that "we're seeing people coming to us, looking for theme architecture. Everything's got to have a theme or a certain character."

Chao stated that Disney entertainment architecture fell into three design categories: "modern," as in Isozaki's "abstract" Team Disney building; "derivative," either of a style or period, as in Stern's Yacht and Beach Club resorts; and "fanciful," as in Graves' Dolphin and Swan.

"Some projects overlap categories," he reminded reporters.

After the Dolphin dedication, Eisner was asked if he thought his approach to entertainment architecture would result in better architecture outside of Disney property.

"The answer is 'yes,' " Eisner said, "It can't hurt that we're helping push architecture forward."

Before the Disney Institute opened, Eisner addressed the staff and he said that he felt his two greatest legacies to the Walt Disney Company would be culinary (better quality food offerings in a Disney theme park than merely the standard hot dogs and hamburgers) and architecture (that entertainment architecture could work outside of a theme park).

Appendix C: WDW Resort Property

It is not just the WDW Resort Hotels themselves but the details in the surrounding area that complete the experience. These details are so seamless that most guests never pay attention.

ENTRANCE GATEWAYS

The concept for Walt Disney World was that guests would unexpectedly discover the vacation destination so there was only minimal signage along the highways to build anticipation. The Ticket and Transportation Center was across a large body of water so that when guests finally arrived at the Magic Kingdom, they couldn't see the parking lot or any other references to the real world.

Surrounding the Magic Kingdom were "infinity roads" that twisted and turned seemingly forever without any evidence of fencing, signage or trimmed landscaping that would encourage drivers to turn around and go in the other direction.

By the time Michael Ovitz was hired as president in 1995 to take the role previously held by Frank Wells, the attendance had grown so large that this intriguing conceit was no longer effective. When Ovitz and his wife visited the Walt Disney World property, Judy Ovitz complained that she couldn't tell where Disney property began.

Michael Ovitz approached CEO Michael Eisner with the complaint and as a gesture to show his willingness to work with the new president authorized the building of three gateways on the perimeter of Walt Disney World property.

Groundbreaking ceremonies were in April 1996 for three colorful gateways that would define when guests had arrived on WDW property. One gateway was planned for World Drive, another for Epcot Drive and the final one at the beginning of Hotel Plaza Boulevard.

Ovitz had suggested that they be decorated by huge iconic smiling figures of Mickey and Minnie because the primary audience was families with children.

Disney artist Don "Ducky" Williams told me: "Yes, that is my artwork of Mickey and Minnie but I didn't do it specifically for those entranceways. I did a lot of work of the Disney characters in poses that could be used on material and it was in the Disney Design Group files. Imagineering just took it which they often did and never told me and used it. That was not a problem. It was part of my job to do things like that."

The images of Donald and Goofy were done by Disney Design Group artist Darren Hunt.

The entranceways were officially completed in September of that year and were similar but with slight variations. Each gateway was thirty feet high with sixteen foot high characters and a purposely bright color palette of red, yellow, purple and green to match already existing property signage.

Arches with colorful flags adorned the World Drive and Epcot Drive entrances but no arch on the one at Hotel Plaza Boulevard.

According to Hal McIntyre, vice president of WDI Planning and Infrastructure in 1996, the goal of the collaboration between Imagineering (that designed the gateways) and Walt Disney World was to "create a first class, high quality image that marks the resort's boundaries. The gateways' message is simple: You have arrived at Walt Disney World!"

McIntyre pointed out that the idea of a prominent gateway to the property had continually been brought up over the years beginning as far back as 1988. At that time, gateways had been designed and were ready to move forward when for undisclosed reasons they were shelved at the next to last minute sometime in 1990.

Senior show designer Michale Warzocha emphasized that the gateways were meant to represent WDI's "tribute to the WDW Resort front door". He acknowledged the contribution and support of Ovitz to finally getting these gateways done.

Ovitz was let go in January 1997 after being vocal about his frustration with his interactions with Eisner and the vague definition of his authority.

WALT DISNEY WORLD PURPLE SIGNS

In many ways, Walt Disney World has always been a seamless experience to the point that for years cast members joked that guests left their brains in their cars when they visited.

WDW works very hard at making things as seamless as possible and a lot of thought, effort and planning goes into making certain decisions.

Why are WDW traffic signs purple and not the typical green and white that are seen on the roadways leading into the popular vacation destination?

The road signs scattered around WDW are the work of Sussman/Prejza & Co, a Los Angeles design firm that was hired in 1989 to tackle the design for the wayfinding and traffic signs of Walt Disney World and EuroDisney (now Disneyland Paris).

Walt Disney World encompasses an area larger than the city of San Francisco and at this point in time all visitors arrive by highway or freeway until perhaps an expansion of the Sun Rail.

Sussman/Prejza's task was to develop a vehicular signing system that would be unique in spirit, clean, easy to follow, and capable of being expanded as the area continued to grow.

The theme park was divided into several major districts. A hierarchy of signs was established to first lead visitors toward a specific district, and once there, toward a distinct destination. The 1,000 sign system includes large freeway signs, major and minor road directionals, regulatory signs, gateways, and bus graphics.

The firm up until that point was best known for its work on the design and signage for the 1984 Olympics in Los Angeles, which featured similarly bold color palettes as the ones chosen for WDW. It was how they attracted the attention of the Walt Disney Company in the first place with so many Disney executives and Imagineers living in Los Angeles.

As for the colors on WDW traffic signs, according to designer Deborah Sussman, the firm drew inspiration from the big cheese himself, Mickey Mouse. The black, red, and yellow colors used on the signs were chosen to mimic the color palette of Mickey Mouse.

The signs were further fleshed out with complimentary colors which are colors that lie on the opposite side of the color wheel. Red's complementary color is green, and yellow's complementary color? Purple.

Using those complementary colors makes the signs easier to read and, of course, a sign that was prominently black would be difficult to read at night. A traffic sign that was primarily yellow would be difficult to see clearly during the day and one that was largely red would detract from warning signs that were red.

Different colored flags were put out around the property to survey guests to see which color they best remembered. Apparently the purple and red flags had a higher instance of being clearly recalled and that helped confirm the final color choices.

In addition, purple helps define when a guest is actually on WDW property because it is a different color than the typical road signs. As usual, no detail is too small to be considered when it comes to defining Disney.

Why is Disney able to control the color of road signs?

Disney has their own governing jurisdiction called the Reedy Creek Improvement District. The district is responsible for overseeing the public services of the property, including the fire department, EMS, water treatment, electric and roadways and bridges.

With that authority, it was no problem to decide to make the road signs purple. Guests give little thought today about the different color other than thinking, "I am on WDW property". Like so many other things, it is just another thing that is accepted and not questioned.

LAKE BUENA VISTA MONORAIL

When Walt Disney World opened in 1971, the newest version of the monorail system was instantly popular with guests not just as an attraction as it was at Disneyland but as a viable form of transportation.

A monorail system had always been in Walt Disney's original plans for the Florida Project and even after his passing the Walt Disney Company intended to expand the operating system.

A few years after opening, the Imagineers seriously discussed expanding the monorail system to the Lake Buena Vista Shopping Village (now Disney Springs) and had done some preliminary work including setting some foundations for pylons.

Disney Legend Tom Nabbe stated, "Yes, but it wasn't just the monorail; there was going to be a PeopleMover going up and down what is now Hotel Plaza Boulevard. I was in meetings and one of the concerns was how to justify the cost in the 'off hours' when there would be little usage.

"I suggested that they redesign the cars so that they were more modular and then could be used to also deliver product as well as people. Of course, they weren't interested in listening to me."

Imagineer Tom K. Morris added, "That Peoplemover plan that Nabbe told you about was part of the 'Satellite Community' idea in the early 70's that would have eventually linked up with Epcot (the real community).

"World Showcase was originally going to be the next satellite community after LBV. As the idea for Epcot morphed into a showplace, they still had plans to link it to LBV by PeopleMover until the idea for satellite communities went away. There is a booklet they published on the idea, and I've seen that booklet online but can't remember where. Wing Chao was in the middle of all this back in the day."

Morris is right that Disney's plans included expanding the Village to over three hundred percent of its initial size and create a community. However, it was so remote when it was first built in 1975 that in the ticket books sold at Magic Kingdom, there was a ticket that was good for a complimentary round trip bus transport to the Village to get guests to visit it.

There would have been a transportation hub roughly where the Team Disney building exists today and that is where the monorail station would have been. That would also have been the location of the main PeopleMover station so guests could have taken that transportation method to hook up with the monorail and then go to the parks and the resorts near the parks.

Plans at Disney constantly change although this particular plan was still in serious discussion up to 1982. However, the cost overruns connected to the building of Epcot Center as well as the uncertainly of the Walt Disney Company's future at the time with the threats of hostile takeovers that eventually led to the installation of Michael Eisner and Frank Wells pretty much doomed this whole idea.

ELECTRICAL WATER PAGEANT

Today, the Electrical Water Pageant entertains Disney's Polynesian Village Resort, Disney's Grand Floridian Resort & Spa, Disney's Wilderness Lodge, Disney's Fort Wilderness Resort and Campground and Disney's Contemporary Resort.

It was so immediately popular that it inspired the creation of the Main Street Electrical Parade at Disneyland.

When Walt Disney World opened in 1971, the Seven Seas Lagoon was dark and forbidding at night. As a backdrop for the South Seas Luau to lighten things up, the Electrical Water Pageant was created as a temporary solution.

It premiered "officially" at a nighttime press event luau on the shore of the Polynesian Village Resort on Sunday, October 24th as part of the three day weekend dedication festivities of Walt Disney World although there had been many previous soft-opening voyages to test it and work out any bugs.

It was a reasonably simple and inexpensive option. Several floating barges were pulled across the lagoon by a boat. On each barge was a flat, framed, twenty-five foot tall, wire screen decorated with Christmas tree lights powered by a noisy generator that couldn't be heard out on the water in the distance.

A sea serpent, a whale, jumping dolphins, seahorses and even King Neptune frolicked on the man-made body of water.

Weather permitting, it is performed every night. The pageant barges are stored in the canal behind the Production Center building at Magic Kingdom located behind Splash Mountain. The canal can be seen clearly from the monorail.

The pageant includes two "strings" of seven barges each. Each string extends approximately 456 feet in length. The two together are barely one hundred feet shorter than the length of an aircraft carrier.

Each of the 14 barges features a twenty-five foot high, thirty-six foot long wire screen decorated with lights.

Five people are required to operate the fleet: two pilots, two co-pilots and one safety-boat operator. The job of the safety-boat operator is to handle any problems once the barges are underway as well as assisting in pushing the barges around corners since the turning radius is literally a quarter of a mile unassisted.

The crew reports to the Production Center at 8:30pm each night where they don headsets, radios and appropriate clothing in case of cold or foul weather. They head out to the barges roughly ten minutes later.

A pilot sits in a booth on the first barge and the co-pilot sits in a booth on the last barge of the string. Both are connected with the audio headsets

They untie the barges and take off to head for their first show at Disney's Polynesian Village Resort at approximately nine o'clock.

The loop continues with shows roughly fifteen minutes apart at Disney's Grand Floridian Resort & Spa, Disney's Wilderness Lodge, Disney's Fort Wilderness Resort and Campground, Disney's Contemporary Resort and finally outside the entrance of the Magic Kingdom park.

The barges arrive just a few moments before each show primarily because of the wind. They can not simply sit in one spot because the screens act as sails so any wind can play havoc even though the pilots try to form a sort of rainbow arc. Basically, there are just platforms on pontoons so are more fragile than most guests suspect.

The show begins immediately everyone is in position. The first string will signal the second string by light, letting them know that the show is ready to go. The co-pilot on barge 14, the last barge on the second string, has master audio control.

He flips a switch and it pumps music through a transmitter from his string to the first string's receiver so everything is in sync.

The co-pilots on each string flip switches to activate the lights on each screen when he or she hears the music cues.

The Paul Beaver version of Gershon Kingsley & Jean Jeaque Perrey's *Baroque Hoedown,* created specially for the Electrical Water Pageant, was used from 1971 until 1977.

The very same soundtrack was later used by Disneyland's original Main Street Electrical Parade from 1972 until 1974 when it was re-recorded and updated by Don Dorsey.

The Electrical Water Pageant that guests see today consists of much the same floats in the same formation dating back to 1977. The only difference is in 1996 a new musical score was created for both the opening and closing of the Electrical Water Pageant as well as each creature depicted in the pageant.

Going over the water bridge between Seven Seas Lagoon and Bay Lake is "like dragging a garden hose through your house without touching anything" said coordinator David Kaumeier who operated the show for three decades.

"We can hear guests hooting and clapping 100 yards away and we get a great satisfaction from that. We're the only crew that does this type of work in the world."

CROSSROADS

It has been announced that all occupants of the Crossroads shopping center will be evicted by August 2021. The location served the hotel guests on Hotel Plaza Boulevard as well as Disney Resort Hotel guests and Disney cast members.

If something is not physically in the theme parks or the resorts, it can be invisible to millions of Disney guests. I have had Disney friends who have absolutely refused to go there to eat because it is "not Disney".

Actually for over a decade, this shopping and dining area was a Disney owned location. It was designed by Hunton, Brady, Pryor, Maso of Orlando, who were also responsible for construction drawings and construction administration for the Isozaki Team Disney building across from Downtown Disney.

The Crossroads shopping center at Lake Buena Vista where State Road 535 intersects with Hotel Plaza Boulevard was developed by the Disney Company in late 1988 and then later sold off to GE Capital Realty Group in 2001.

The 155,000-square-foot plaza's more than 20 tenants include multiple restaurants, like Red Lobster, Pirate's Cove mini-golf (almost hidden in the back of the complex), and the region's last Gooding's supermarket.

When the complex opened in February 1989, the McDonalds had a colorful interior decorated with authentic Disney memorabilia, ranging from comic books to toys to lithographs and more. It was like a mini-museum.

Unfortunately, these items were displayed without any protection to light, heat and humidity and by the time the location was updated, those items had faded and deteriorated and were discarded.

Jungle Jim's was a popular family restaurant filled with unusual, amusing items, including a helicopter prop from the movie *M*A*S*H* (1970), amidst the jungle décor.

Unfortunately, by 2006, the quality of service and food had dropped drastically and the restaurant had become a hangout on Monday nights for young gang members from Kissimmee.

It escalated that same year with a stabbing of a young man named Cory Swift by John Feliciano over gang colors. The restaurant closed shortly thereafter and remained vacant for a long while. It was just an example of how the tone of the area had changed since its opening.

While originally, there were a handful of small gift shops, including some selling Disney souvenirs, today the complex is predominantly restaurant oriented and includes Buffalo Wild Wings, Quizno's, Fuddruckers, Flippers Pizza, Dakshin Indian Cuisine, Tom and Chee, T.G.I Fridays, Sweet Tomatoes, Chevy's Mexican Restaurant, McDonald's, Uno Pizzeria & Grill, Taco Bell, Red Lobster, Noodles & Company, Moe's, Johnnies Hideaway, and Perkins.

The location provided quick and inexpensive meals for WDW cast members on their way to and from work, as well as a nice variety of choices. It also provided a nearby 24 hour grocery, Goodings, within walking distance for vacationers staying in nearby hotels. Of course, some of the higher prices reflected the fact that they were the "only game in town" for some tourists.

In January 2017, it was announced that the entire area would be demolished to make way for a reconfiguration of the area to improve the flow of traffic that often gets congested.

Traffic gets clogged on the I-4 as people try to exit onto 535. Studies show only about 20 percent of this traffic is headed toward the Disney property. Primarily, commuter traffic heading up 535 to the new residential developments north of Disney and south toward Kissimmee and Poinciana are causing much of the problem.

The project was set to begin sometime between 2018 and 2020. The interchange is not part of the I-4 expansion already underway, but would be part of the next phase. However, the coronavirus pandemic delayed work.

Disney and Reedy Creek met several times with Florida Department of Transportation officials to discuss the project and associated I-4 improvements since 2014 and several different plans were proposed.

In January 2017, Tom Biggs, of Walt Disney Imagineering, met with transportation planners to discuss changes and was reported pleased with the proposal.

The project's current design includes a feature that will take some traffic on a loop ramp that connects with Hotel Plaza Boulevard, the road leading into Disney. That ramp, an exit and drainage ponds would go on the Crossroads land.

Ultimately the area provides a service of affordable restaurants near WDW property that Disney doesn't want.

Retail consultant David Marks, president of Marketplace Advisors, said some restaurants might be able to find another nearby place to relocate, even though it would be more expensive for them, but the plaza's shutdown could also generate more business for Disney Springs.

About the Author

Jim Korkis is an internationally respected Disney historian who has written hundreds of articles and thirty books about all things Disney over the last forty years. Jim grew up in Glendale, California where starting at the young age of fifteen, he was able to meet and interview some of Walt's original team of animators and Imagineers.

In 1995, he relocated to Orlando, Florida where he worked for Walt Disney World in a variety of capacities including Entertainment, Animation, Disney Institute, Disney University, College and International Programs, Disney Cruise Line, Disney Design Group, Disney Vacation Club, Disney Learning Center, Yellow Shoes Marketing and more.

During that time, he was often tasked with researching and sharing the history of Walt Disney World with cast members and operating participants through presentations and articles. He has written seven other books just about Walt Disney World.

His original research on Disney history has been used often by the Walt Disney Company as well as other organizations including the Disney Family Museum.

While he enjoys staying in a hotel room, he never feels completely comfortable not being surrounded by all his stuff as well as the fear that others have complete access to the room. However, he loves not having to clean up after himself and finding a mint on his pillow every evening.

Several websites feature Jim's articles about Disney history:

- MousePlanet.com
- AllEars.net
- Yesterland.com
- CartoonResearch.com
- YourFirstVisit.net

In addition, Jim is a frequent guest on multiple podcasts as well as a consultant and keynote speaker to various businesses, schools and groups.

Jim is not currently an employee of the Disney Company.

To read more stories by Jim Korkis about Disney history, check out his other books, all available from ThemeParkPress.com.

- *Kungaloosh! (2021)*
- *Secret Stories of Extinct Walt Disney World (2020)*
- *Hidden Treasures of the Disney Cruise Line (2020)*
- *The Vault of Walt, Volume 9, Halloween Edition (2020)*
- *The Vault of Walt, Volume 8, Outer Space Edition (2019)*
- *Disney Never Lands (2019)*
- *Secret Stories of Extinct Disneyland (2019)*
- *The Unofficial Walt Disney World 1971 Companion (2019)*
- *The Vault of Walt: Volume 7, Christmas Edition* (2018)
- *Secret Stories of Mickey Mouse* (2018)
- *More Secret Stories of Disneyland* (2018)
- *Extra Secret Stories of Walt Disney World* (2018)
- *Call Me Walt* (2017)
- *Walt's Words* (2017)
- *Other Secret Stories of Walt Disney World* (2017)
- *Secret Stories of Disneyland* (2017)
- *The Vault of Walt: Volume 6* (2017)
- *Gremlin Trouble* (2017)
- *Donald Duck's Daddy* (2017)
- *More Secret Stories of Walt Disney World* (2016)
- *The Vault of Walt: Volume 5* (2016)
- *The Unofficial Disneyland 1955 Companion* (2016)
- *How to Be a Disney Historian* (2016)
- *Secret Stories of Walt Disney World* (2015)
- *The Vault of Walt: Volume 4* (2015)
- *Everything I Know I Learned from Disney Animated Features* (2015)
- *The Vault of Walt: Volume 3* (2014)
- *Animation Anecdotes* (2014)
- *Who's the Leader of the Club? Walt Disney's Leadership Lessons* (2014)
- *The Book of Mouse* (2013)
- *The Vault of Walt: Volume 2* (2013)
- *Who's Afraid of the Song of the South?* (2012)
- *The Revised Vault of Walt* (2012)

About Theme Park Press

Theme Park Press publishes books primarily about the Disney company, its history, culture, films, animation, and theme parks, as well as theme parks in general.

Our authors include noted historians, animators, Imagineers, and experts in the theme park industry.

We also publish many books by first-time authors, with topics ranging from fiction to theme park guides.

And we're always looking for new talent. If you'd like to write for us, or if you're interested in the many other titles in our catalog, please visit:

www.ThemeParkPress.com

Theme Park Press Newsletter

Subscribe to our free email newsletter and enjoy:

- Free book downloads and giveaways
- Access to excerpts from our many books
- Announcements of forthcoming releases
- Exclusive additional content and chapters
- And more good stuff available nowhere else

To subscribe, visit www.ThemeParkPress.com, or send email to newsletter@themeparkpress.com.

Read more about these books
and our many other titles at:

www.ThemeParkPress.com

Printed in Great Britain
by Amazon

17839316R00122